WILLS AND THE ADMINISTRATION OF ESTATES

The University of Law

WILLS AND THE ADMINISTRATION OF ESTATES
FIFTH EDITION

Jacqueline Kempton

This edition published 2025 by
The University of Law
2 Bunhill Row
London EC1Y 8HQ

British Library Cataloguing in Publication Data

A catalogue record for this book is available from the British Library.

ISBN 978 1 80502 260 2

Preface

This book is part of a series of Study Manuals that have been specially designed to support the reader to achieve the SQE1 Assessment Specification in relation to Functioning Legal Knowledge. Each Study Manual aims to provide the reader with a solid knowledge and understanding of fundamental legal principles and rules, including how those principles and rules might be applied in practice.

This Study Manual covers the Solicitors Regulation Authority's syllabus for the SQE1 assessment for Wills and the Administration of Estates in a concise and tightly focused manner. The Manual provides a clear statement of relevant legal rules and a well-defined road map through examinable law and practice. The Manual aims to bring the law and practice to life through the use of example scenarios based on realistic client-based problems and allows the reader to test their knowledge and understanding through single best answer questions that have been modelled on the SRA's sample assessment questions.

For those readers who are students at the University of Law, the Study Manual is used alongside other learning resources and the University's assessment bank to best prepare students not only for the SQE1 assessments, but also for a future life in professional legal practice.

We hope that you find the Study Manual supportive of your preparation for SQE1 and we wish you every success.

The legal principles and rules contained within this Manual are stated as at 1 May 2025.

Acknowledgements

The author would like to thank Gill Williams for her contribution to previous editions of this Manual and Professor Lesley King for her invaluable assistance.

Contents

Table of Cases

Table of Statutes

1 Validity of Wills and How Property Passes on Death

SQE1 syllabus

This chapter will enable you to achieve the SQE1 assessment specification in relation to functioning legal knowledge concerned with wills and the administration of estates.

- Validity of wills and codicils:
  - Testamentary capacity
  - Duress and undue influence
  - Formal requirements
- Property passing outside the estate:
  - Joint property
  - Life policies
  - Pension scheme benefits
  - Trust property

Note that for SQE1, candidates are not usually required to recall specific case names or cite statutory or regulatory authorities. However, in this chapter, the test for testamentary capacity known as the *Banks v Goodfellow* test and s 9 Wills Act 1837 may be referred to in the SQE1 assessment as such. Otherwise, references to cases, statutory and regulatory authorities are provided for illustrative purposes only.

Learning outcomes

By the end of this chapter you will be able to apply relevant core legal principles and rules appropriately and effectively, at the level of a competent newly qualified solicitor in practice, to realistic client-based and ethical problems and situations in the following areas:

- the requirements for a valid will;
- professional conduct issues arising out of the preparation of wills;
- how property passes on a person's death; and
- challenging the validity of a deceased person's will.

1.1 Introduction

Wills are seen as one of the most important documents a person can draw up in their lifetime; many people will consult a solicitor to ensure that they get proper advice and create a valid will.

When a person dies, one of the most pressing questions is who will inherit their property? The first question people usually ask is whether or not there is a will. However, many valuable assets pass independently of the terms of the will; therefore, the first question should be: do any assets pass outside the will? After the solicitor has ascertained which assets pass independently, the next step is to consider whether the deceased left a will and, if so, whether it is valid.

Any assets which do not pass independently or under a valid will fall to be distributed according to the intestacy rules. The intestacy rules are contained in the Administration of Estates Act 1925 and they are dealt with in **Chapter 4**. While they provide a valuable 'fall-back position', they cannot reflect the different wishes of individual testators and are often seen as the reason why everyone should make a will.

This chapter looks at:

- property passing outside the will and intestacy rules;
- wills terminology;
- the requirements for a valid will;
- capacity;
- intention; and
- formalities of execution.

1.2 Property passing outside the will and intestacy rules

A number of different kinds of property pass independently of the terms of any will or the intestacy rules.

1.2.1 Joint property

Where property is held by more than one person as beneficial joint tenants, on the death of one joint tenant their interest passes by survivorship to the surviving joint tenant(s).

Example

George makes a will leaving all his estate to a charity. He and his brother Harry have a joint bank account and own a house as beneficial joint tenants in equity. On George's death, his interests in the house and the bank account pass automatically to Harry, not to the charity under the terms of George's will.

The doctrine of survivorship does not apply to land held as tenants in common. The share of a tenant in common passes on their death under their will (or under the intestacy rules).

1.2.2 Insurance policies

Where a person takes out a simple policy of life assurance, the benefit of that policy belongs to them. On the person's death, the policy matures and the insurance company will pay the proceeds to the deceased's personal representatives (the people who administer an estate after the deceased's death); they will distribute the money according to the terms of any will or the intestacy rules.

However, a person may take out a life assurance policy and write it in trust for the benefit of specified individuals. Alternatively, a policy may be transferred to, or assigned to named beneficiaries. This may occur when the policy is first taken out or at a later date.

Once the policy has been written in trust or given away, the benefit of the policy does not belong to the policy holder. On the policy holder's death, the policy matures and the insurance company will pay the proceeds to the named beneficiaries (or to trustees for them) regardless of the terms of the deceased's will or the intestacy rules.

1.2.3 Pension benefits

Many pension schemes provide for the payment of benefits if an employee dies 'in service'. Commonly, a lump sum calculated on the basis of an employee's salary at the time of their death is paid by the trustees of the pension fund to members of the family or dependants chosen at the trustees' discretion. Such discretionary schemes usually allow employees to leave a letter of wishes for the trustees indicating which people they would like to benefit. The letter of wishes is not binding on the pension fund trustees, but they will normally comply with its terms.

Such pension benefits do not belong to the employee during their lifetime and pass on death independently of the terms of any will and of the intestacy rules.

A few pension schemes provide that the lump sum must be paid to the employee's personal representatives (PRs). The PRs must then distribute the money according to the terms of the employee's will or the intestacy rules.

1.2.4 Trust property

The deceased may have had an equitable interest as a beneficiary of a trust. Many equitable interests come to an end on the beneficiary's death, eg life interests. In these situations, the trust property will devolve according to the terms of the trust and not the deceased life tenant's will.

Example

Susan created a trust of company shares for her husband for life, remainder to her children. The husband dies leaving his estate to charity. On the husband's death, the company shares held in the trust will pass to Susan's children under the terms of the trust. They will not devolve under her husband's will to the charity.

1.2.5 Analysis of beneficial entitlements on death

After a person's death, the family may consult a solicitor to advise on who inherits the deceased's estate. The solicitor will deal with the deceased's assets in the following order:

(a) Property passing outside the will

(b) Property passing under the will

(c) Any property not disposed of in (a) and (b) passing on intestacy.

Example

Ada has died. She left the following assets:

Asset	£
House (owned as beneficial joint tenants with husband) Value of Ada's interest	500,000
Holiday cottage (owned as tenants in common with Ada's brother) Value of Ada's share	250,000
Shares in various quoted companies	200,000
Cash in accounts in Ada's sole name	50,000
Life Assurance Policy assigned to Ada's daughter 12 years ago.	70,000
Collection of paintings	30,000

Ada had no debts, and her valid will left her paintings to her daughter but contained no other gifts.

How will Ada's estate be distributed?

Passing outside the will

House. Ada's share passes by survivorship to Ada's husband	500,000
Life Assurance Policy proceeds pass to Ada's daughter	70,000

Passing under the will

Collection of paintings passes to Ada's daughter	30,000

***Passing on intestacy** (see Chapter 4)*

Holiday cottage (owned as tenants in common with Ada's brother) Value of Ada's share	250,000
Shares in various quoted companies	200,000
Cash in accounts in sole name	50,000

1.3 Wills terminology

Below is an example of a will. Typically wills contain more clauses, but a number of provisions have been omitted here in the interests of providing a simple example.

This is the Last Will and Testament of me Finlay Brand of The Old Vicarage, Church Lane, Cambridge which I make this 12th day of April 2021

1. I revoke all former wills, codicils and testamentary dispositions.
2. I wish my body to be cremated.
3. I appoint George Marston of 3 Station Road, Cambridge to be my executor.
4. I give the gold watch which I inherited from my father to my nephew James Brand.
5. I give £10,000 to the charity Cancer UK.
6. I give The Old Vicarage to Alison Peters.
7. I give all the rest of my property after deducting debts and legacies to my sister Megan Wilson.

Signed by Finlay Brand) *Finlay Brand*

in our joint presence and then by us in his)

Hannah James	*G. James*
Hannah James	George James
2 Varsity Common	2 Varsity Common
Cambridge	Cambridge
Accountant	Nurse

A person making a will is called a testator (or testatrix if female).

The will follows the usual structure and contains some common clauses.

(a) Revocation clause

Clause 1 revokes prior wills. It is important to include such a clause to make it clear that earlier wills are of no effect (see **3.2.1**).

(b) Direction as to disposal of the body

Some testators wish to include directions concerning how their body is to be disposed of, for example cremation, woodland burial or donation for medical research. Finlay has included a direction at clause 2. Such directions have no legal effect and the testator should ensure that their close family and friends are aware of their wishes.

(c) Appointment of executors

In Clause 3, Finlay appoints George Marston as his executor (or personal representative). An executor (or executrix for a woman) is the person who deals with the testator's affairs after their death. Their task is to collect in all the testator's assets, pay the deceased's debts and any inheritance tax and then distribute the remaining assets to whoever is entitled under the will. The ability to choose executors to deal with the estate is one of the reasons for making a will. After Finlay dies, the executor will make an application to His Majesty's Courts and Tribunals Service Probate (HMCTS) for a grant of probate which confirms that the will is valid and that the executor has authority to act (see **Chapter 8**). The grant will not be issued if there is any doubt as to the validity of the will.

(d) Gifts

In the remainder of his will Finlay leaves gifts of his property. Clauses 4–5 are 'legacies', which is the term for gifts of personalty. Strictly speaking, Clause 6 is a 'devise' (a gift of realty). However, the term 'legacy' is often used to cover realty and personalty. Gifts in a will can be further classified as specific, general, demonstrative, pecuniary or residuary.

- *Specific gift*

  This is a gift of a specific item or items which the testator owns, which is distinguished in the will from the rest of the testator's assets. Clause 4 in Finlay's will is an example of the specific legacy and clause 6 is an example of a specific devise.

- *General gift*

  This is a gift of an item or items corresponding to a description. If the testator does not own the item(s) at death, the executors must obtain the item(s) using funds obtained from the estate. An example would be 'I give 100 shares in X plc to my son'. If the testator does not own 100 such shares at his death, then they must be purchased. General legacies are rare unless they consist of gifts of money.

- *Demonstrative gift*

  This is a gift that is general in nature but is directed to be paid from a specific fund, for example, 'I give £500 to X to be paid from my Nationwide savings account'. If the account exists at the date of the death and contains £500 or more, the legacy is paid from the account and is classified as specific. If there is no account (or if it contains less than £500), the legacy is paid, in whole (or in part), from the rest of the estate and to that extent is classified as general.

- *Pecuniary gift*

  This is a gift of money. This gift will usually be general, but could be demonstrative, or possibly even specific, for example, 'I give the £100 held in the safe in the study'. Clause 5 in Finlay's will is an example of a general pecuniary legacy.

- *Residuary gift*

  In Clause 7, Finlay leaves 'the rest' of his money and property to Megan. This is called 'the residue'. A residuary gift comprises all the money and property left after the testator's debts, the expenses of dealing with the estate and the other gifts made under the will have all been paid. It is a sweeping-up provision but is usually the most substantial gift in the will.

1.4 The requirements for a valid will

In order to create a valid will, a testator must have the necessary capacity and intention, and must observe the formalities for execution of wills laid down in the Wills Act 1837. All three requirements must be met; a failure to meet any one requirement invalidates the will. These requirements will be considered in turn:

- capacity in **1.5**;
- intention in **1.6**; and
- formalities in **1.7**.

1.5 Capacity

1.5.1 The test

In order to make a valid will, an individual must be aged 18 or over (with certain limited exceptions) and must have the requisite mental capacity. This testamentary capacity was defined in *Banks v Goodfellow* (1870) LR 5 QB 549 as 'soundness of mind, memory and understanding'. Testators must understand:

(a) the nature of their act and its broad effects (the fact that they are making a will which will have effect on their death);

(b) the extent of their property (although not necessarily recollecting every individual item); and

(c) the moral claims they ought to consider (even if they decide to reject such claims and dispose of their property to other beneficiaries).

In addition, the testator must not be suffering from any insane delusion which affects the disposition of property.

The general rule is that testators must have capacity at the time they execute their wills. An exception to this rule was established in *Parker v Felgate* (1883) 8 PD 171 – a will can be valid if the testator has capacity when they give instructions for the will even if they lose capacity by the time the will is executed. The will is valid if the instructions were given to a solicitor, who prepared the will in accordance with the instructions, and at the time the testator executes the will, they appreciate that they are signing a will prepared in accordance with their previous instructions.

The Mental Capacity Act (MCA) 2005 introduced a statutory test to determine whether a person has capacity to take a decision. There was some uncertainty as to whether the Act applied to capacity to make a will but case law suggests that it does not, and the *Banks v Goodfellow* test still applies to wills (*Scammell v Farmer* [2008] EWHC 1100 (Ch), *James v James* [2018] EWHC 43 (Ch), *Clitheroe v Bond* [2021] EWHC 1102 (Ch)). The relevance of the two tests was revisited more recently in *Baker v Hewston* [2023] EWHC 1145 (Ch). *Banks v Goodfellow* was reaffirmed as the test applicable in the context of testamentary capacity, although HHJ Tindall went on to say that the two tests are broadly consistent and that the statutory test could therefore provide a useful 'cross-check'.

It should be borne in mind that if a testator is mentally incapable of making a valid will, a 'statutory will' may be made on their behalf under the MCA. The Court of Protection empowers an authorised person to execute the will and then gives effect to the will by affixing the court seal. The Court of Protection will require full details of the deceased, their family, property and previous wills and will approve a draft will only if it is in the testator's best interests.

1.5.2 The 'golden rule'

If the testator lacks capacity, the will is void. A solicitor preparing a will for a testator whose mental state is in doubt (possibly due to age or ill health) should follow the 'golden rule' suggested in *Kenward v Adams* (1975) The Times, 28 November. The solicitor should ask a medical practitioner to provide a written report confirming that the testator has testamentary capacity and also ask the doctor to witness the will. The solicitor should record their own view of the testator's capacity in a file note. The written evidence should be kept on the file in case someone challenges the validity of the will after the testator's death.

1.5.3 The burden of proof

1.5.3.1 The general rule

The general rule is that it is for the person who is asserting that a will is valid to prove it. However, it would place a huge burden on executors if they were always required to provide evidence of the testator's mental state at the time of making the will. The question of whether the will is valid arises after the testator's death when the executors apply for a grant of probate. This could be many years after the testator executed their will and it is likely to be difficult to gather evidence of the testator's mental state when the will was made. Fortunately, executors are usually able to rely on a presumption.

1.5.3.2 Presumption of capacity

Despite the general rule, in the vast majority of cases, executors do not have to prove capacity because there is a presumption that the testator satisfied the mental capacity test. The presumption applies if the will is rational on its face and the testator showed no evidence of mental confusion before making the will. In the event that someone wishes to challenge the validity of the will on the ground that the testator lacked capacity, the burden shifts to the challenger to prove lack of capacity.

The courts are less likely to find that the testator lacked capacity if a rational will was prepared by an experienced, independent solicitor who met the testator and explained the will to them. Equally, a report or witnessing by a medical practitioner in accordance with the 'golden rule' will make it very difficult to challenge the will on the ground that the testator lacked capacity.

Example

Mary died recently. Her will gave her substantial estate to charity and appointed her solicitor, Simon, to be her executor. Mary's estranged son, Wesley, claims that the will is invalid because she lacked mental capacity.

Is Wesley likely to succeed?

Wesley is alleging that Mary lacked capacity presumably on the ground that she did not understand the moral claims to which she would be expected to give effect, contrary to the third limb of Banks v Goodfellow. His claim is tenuous. The will is valid if Mary was aware of Wesley's claim but decided not to give him anything in her will.

If the will is rational and there was no evidence of mental confusion before the testatrix executed the will, there is a presumption that the testatrix had capacity. The will appears to be rational because Mary and her son were estranged and therefore, it is understandable that Mary might not want to leave him her estate. The burden of proof would be on Wesley to produce evidence that Mary lacked capacity when she executed her will. This would be a difficult burden to discharge, especially if the will was drawn up by the solicitor who met the testatrix and explained the will to her.

1.6 Intention

1.6.1 Meaning of intention

When the will is signed, the testator must have both general and specific intention. This means that the testator must intend to make a will (as opposed to any other sort of document), and must also intend to make the particular will now being executed (ie the testator must know and approve its contents).

The testator must know and approve the contents of the will at the time when the will is executed. However, the exception in *Parker v Felgate* (**1.5.1** above) applies.

1.6.2 The burden of proof

1.6.2.1 The general rule

Again, the general rule is that it is for the person asserting that a will is valid to prove it. However, usually, it is not necessary to prove intention because a presumption of knowledge and approval arises.

1.6.2.2 Presumption of knowledge and approval

A testator who has capacity and has read and executed the will is presumed to have the requisite knowledge and approval. However, this presumption does not apply in the situations listed below.

- **Testator blind/illiterate/not signing personally**

  The presumption that the testator knew and approved the contents of their will does not apply if the testator was blind or illiterate, or another person signed the will on the testator's behalf (eg because the testator had an injured hand).

  In these cases, HMCTS will require evidence to prove knowledge and approval before they will issue a grant of probate. It is usual in such cases to include a statement at the end of the will stating that the will was read over to the testator, or read by the testator who knew and approved the contents.

- **Suspicious circumstances**

  Similarly, the presumption of knowledge and approval does not apply if there are suspicious circumstances surrounding the drafting and/or execution of the will (eg the will has been prepared by someone who is to be a major beneficiary under its terms or who is a close relative of a major beneficiary).

  In such cases, because the presumption does not apply, the executor or person putting forward the will must remove the suspicion by proving that the testator did actually know and approve the will's contents.

Wintle v Nye [1959] 1 All ER 552

Nye, a solicitor, prepared a will for an elderly testatrix which gave him the bulk of her large estate. She was of 'limited intelligence', unversed in business and relied for advice on Nye who had been the family's solicitor for years. The will was complicated, she did not get independent advice, the solicitor retained the original will and did not give her a copy.

After she died, her cousin, Colonel Wintle, challenged the validity of the will. The House of Lords held that the suspicious circumstances of the beneficiary preparing the will meant that there was no presumption of knowledge and approval. The burden of proof was on the solicitor, Nye, to prove that the testatrix knew and approved the contents of the will. In the circumstances of the case this was a very heavy burden to discharge. At this point, Nye threw in the towel and declared that he no longer wanted to defend the validity of the will.

Gill v Woodall [2010] EWCA Civ 1430

The Court of Appeal found that the presumption did not apply where the beneficiary played no part in the preparation of the will. Mrs Gill, a Yorkshire farmer, who was on excellent terms with her daughter and grandson, left everything to the RSPCA after leading her daughter to believe that she would inherit everything. Mrs Gill had gone with her husband to see a solicitor in order that they would both make wills. She suffered from a severe anxiety disorder and agoraphobia, the result of which was that she would have experienced panic when at the solicitor's office. There was no evidence that she had read the will or had it explained to her, which meant that the Court of Appeal held that the circumstances of the case were so unusual that the presumption did not apply. The burden of proof lay with the RSPCA to establish that Mrs Gill had known and approved the contents of her will but they failed to discharge this burden. The will was declared void and Mrs Gill's daughter inherited under the intestacy rules.

A solicitor should not accept instructions from a third party to draw up a will for a testator (see **5.11**). They should interview the testator in the absence of the third party to ensure that any will drafted reflects the testator's wishes.

1.6.3 Force, fear, fraud, undue influence and mistake

Where a testator with capacity appears to have known and approved the contents of the will, any person who wishes to challenge the will (or any part of it) must prove one or more of the following to prevent some or all of the will from being admitted to probate:

- **Force or fear** (through actual or threatened injury), or
- **Fraud** (eg after being misled by some pretence), or
- **Undue influence** (where the testator's freedom of choice was overcome by intolerable pressure, but without convincing their judgement). Undue influence in the context of wills means coercion or duress. Persuasion stopping short of coercion is not undue influence.

  You will note that it is necessary to *prove* undue influence in relation to a will. This makes it very difficult for a person to challenge a will on this basis. They will need to collect evidence from family, friends and carers. It is such a serious allegation that a claimant who fails to substantiate their claim will be penalised in costs.

Example

Arthur died recently at the age of 90. His will, made last year, left his substantial estate to Yvonne, a care worker, who visited him every week in the last two years of his life. Yvonne wrote out the will at Arthur's request. Arthur signed it in accordance with s 9 Wills Act 1837.

Bella, Arthur's niece and closest relative, claims that the will is invalid due to lack of knowledge and approval.

Is the claim likely to succeed?

There is a presumption of knowledge and approval if the testator had capacity and executed the will. However, the presumption does not apply here because there are suspicious circumstances; the beneficiary, Yvonne, wrote out the will for the testator. The burden of proof that Arthur knew and approved the contents of the will lies with Yvonne.

If Yvonne manages to produce evidence of Arthur's intention, then Bella will need to contend that Yvonne exerted undue influence. Undue influence is coercion as opposed to persuasion. The court would demand strong evidence of undue influence due to the seriousness of the allegation. If the claim is made on insufficient evidence, Bella will be penalised in costs.

- **Mistake**

  The presumption of knowledge and approval does not apply if all or part of the will was included by mistake. Any words included without the knowledge and approval of the testator will be omitted from probate. In this respect, it is important to distinguish between actual mistake (ie absence of knowledge and approval) and misunderstanding as to the true legal meaning of words used in the will. In the latter case mistaken words will not be omitted.

1.7 Formalities of execution

1.7.1 Section 9 Wills Act 1837

Section 9 of the Wills Act 1837 provides:

No will shall be valid unless–

(a) it is in writing, and signed by the testator, or by some other person in his presence and by his direction; and

(b) it appears that the testator intended by his signature to give effect to the will; and

(c) the signature is made or acknowledged by the testator in the presence of two or more witnesses present at the same time; and

(d) each witness either–

 (i) attests and signs the will; or

 (ii) acknowledges his signature,

 in the presence of the testator (but not necessarily in the presence of any other witness), but no form of attestation shall be necessary.

The various requirements are explained below.

- The will must be in writing.

There are no restrictions on the materials or type of wording, so it could be typed or handwritten, in Braille or shorthand. The will does not have to be written on paper. For example, a will written on an eggshell has been admitted to probate. An electronic will held only on a computer probably would not be considered 'writing'. Although the possibility of permitting electronic/paperless wills is part of the Law Commission's consultation on Wills, many argue that the purpose of s 9 is to prevent fraud and it would be too easy for a third party to change an electronic will fraudulently.

- The will must be signed.

The testator should sign the will. Generally speaking, any kind of signature is acceptable provided the testator intends the signature to represent their name. For example, *In the Estate of Cook* [1960] 1 All ER 689 a will signed 'Your loving mother' was held to be valid because the signature was sufficient to identify the testator and she intended the words to represent her name. Also, crosses and thumbprints have been accepted.

Section 9 allows another person to sign the will on the testator's behalf in the testator's presence and at their direction. This is useful if the testator is too weak to sign the will or if they have injured their hand. The testator must give the person a positive and discernible direction (verbal or non-verbal) that they want the person to sign on their behalf.

- The testator must have intended to give effect to the will by his signature.

It is not enough for the will simply to bear a signature. It must appear that the testator intended that his signature would cause the will to take effect.

Example

A testator does not sign the actual will but places it in an envelope on which he writes 'The last will and testament of Kenneth Brown'. It is doubtful whether the name on the envelope would be regarded as a signature which the testator intended would give effect to his will.

- The signature must be witnessed.

There are two stages to the process. First, the testator's signature must be made or acknowledged in the presence of two witnesses. The two witnesses must be present at the same time. The reason for this stringent requirement is to provide protection against fraud or coercion. The second stage is for the witnesses to sign the will in the presence of the testator (but not necessarily in the presence of each other).

'Presence' requires mental and physical presence. To be mentally present, the witnesses must be aware that the testator is signing a document. They do not have to know that it is a will. To be physically present, they must see or be able to see the testator signing; there has to be an unobstructed line of sight between the witness and the testator.

Acknowledging signatures is an alternative if the witnesses were not present at the signing stage. Acknowledgement means that the person confirms that the signature is theirs.

Examples

A testator signs in front of one witness. Clearly this is not valid. A second person enters the room. The testator can acknowledge their signature in front of the second witness. Both witnesses then sign the will in the testator's presence. This is a valid execution.

A testator signs the will in front of two witnesses. Witness 1 signs in the testator's presence. The testator leaves the room to answer the telephone and Witness 2 signs before the testator returns. The will is validly executed if Witness 2 acknowledges their signature to the testator.

There are no formal requirements relating to the capacity of witnesses, although they must be capable of understanding the significance of being the witness to a signature. If either of the witnesses is a beneficiary under the will or is the spouse or civil partner of a beneficiary, the will remains valid but the gift to the witness or to the witness's spouse/civil partner fails (s 15 Wills Act 1837; see **2.7.2**).

- Remote witnessing.

In the light of the period of social isolation required by the Covid-19 pandemic, in 2020, the Ministry of Justice put legislation in place to allow remote witnessing for a limited period. The statutory instrument provided that for wills made between 28 September 2020 and 31 January 2024, s 9 of the Wills Act 1837 was amended so that 'presence' included presence by means of videoconference or other visual transmission.

The procedure for remote witnessing was far from straightforward. In cases of doubt about a will executed under these provisions, reference should be made to the government guidance issued at the time.

1.7.2 Privileged wills

There is one exception to the rule that wills must comply with the requirements of s 9. A will made on actual military service or by a mariner or seaman at sea may be in any form, including a mere oral statement (s 11 Wills Act 1837). The only requirement is that the 'testator' intends to dispose of his property after his death. For example, in a 1981 case, a soldier on active service in Northern Ireland during the 'troubles' said 'if I don't make it, make sure Anne gets all my stuff'. He died the following day. His oral statement was held to be a valid will passing all his property to his fiancée, Anne.

1.7.3 The burden of proof

1.7.3.1 The general rule

Again, the general rule is that it is for the person who is asserting a will is valid to prove it. However, in most cases, no proof is necessary because there is a presumption of due execution.

1.7.3.2 The presumption of due execution

The presumption arises if the will includes a clause which recites that the s 9 formalities were observed, such as, 'Signed by the testatrix in our joint presence and then by us in hers'. Such a clause is called an attestation clause. The presumption means that anyone challenging the validity of the will on the ground that it was not validly executed has the burden of proving this was the case.

If the will does not contain an attestation clause, HMCTS will require an affidavit of due execution (or witness statement verified by a statement of truth) from a witness or any other person who was present during the execution, or, failing that, an affidavit of handwriting evidence to identify the testator's signature, or they will refer the case to a judge (all of which involve time and expense).

1.7.4 Solicitors' duties

It is important for solicitors preparing wills to give clear instructions to their clients explaining how to sign and witness the will, and warning that beneficiaries and those married to or in a civil partnership with beneficiaries should not be witnesses. It is preferable for the clients to execute at the solicitors' office where execution can be supervised.

If the testator executes the will at home, the solicitor should ask them to return the will so that the solicitor can check that s 9 appears to have been complied with and that the witnesses are not beneficiaries or their spouses or civil partners.

Failure to carry out these duties may lead to liability in negligence. It has been held that solicitors preparing wills owe a duty of care to the prospective beneficiaries.

Humbleston v Martin Tolhurst Partnership [2004] EWHC 151 (Ch)

The will (giving the estate to the testator's cohabitee) was not executed at the solicitor's office. The witnesses signed the will but the testator did not. The will was brought back to the solicitor's office by the cohabitee. The secretary who received the will told the cohabitee that it was 'in order'. The absence of the testator's signature rendered the will invalid and the cohabitee received nothing. It was held that the firm had been negligent and had to pay damages to the cohabitee equivalent to the amount she should have received under the will.

Summary

- To make a valid will, the testator must have capacity and intention (usually at the time they sign the will) and must execute the will in accordance with s 9 Wills Act 1837.
- A solicitor drafting a will owes a duty to the prospective beneficiaries as well as to the testator to ensure that the will is valid. The solicitor should take steps to prevent problems arising after the testator's death (eg by including an attestation clause in the will; by following the 'golden rule' in appropriate cases).

- To decide what happens to a person's property when they die, approach the assets in the following order:
  - Do any assets pass independently of the will or intestacy rules?
  - Is there a *valid* will which disposes of the remaining property?
  - If there is no valid will or it does not dispose of all the deceased's property, apply the intestacy rules.
- A solicitor instructed by executors to obtain a grant should consider whether they can rely on the presumptions of capacity, knowledge and approval and due execution of the will. If not, they will have to produce evidence in order to obtain a grant of probate (see **8.6.2(b)**).
- A person challenging the validity of a will must establish lack of capacity or intention or non-compliance with s 9 Wills Act 1837. It is important to consider the presumptions to establish where the burden of proof lies.

Sample questions

Question 1

A woman died last week. In her valid will, she left her entire estate to a registered charity. She owned a half share in her house as a beneficial tenant in common with her husband. The proceeds of her life policy are payable to her estate. She also owned some shares in quoted companies, money in a bank account and she held a life interest in a trust created by her father's will.

What will the charity receive?

A The half share in the house, the proceeds of the life policy, the shares, bank account and the trust fund.

B Only the half share in the house, the proceeds of the life policy, the shares and the bank account.

C Only the proceeds of the life policy, the shares and the bank account.

D Only the half share in the house, the shares and the bank account.

E Only the shares, the bank account and the trust fund.

Answer

Option B is correct. A beneficial share in a tenancy in common passes under the deceased tenant in common's will (contrast a beneficial joint tenancy). The life policy proceeds are part of the estate passing under the will because they were not written in trust or assigned to another. The shares and bank account were in the woman's sole name and they pass under her will.

Option A is wrong. The trust fund is not part of the estate passing under the will. It will pass according to the terms of the father's will trust.

Option C is wrong because it omits the share in the house which will pass under the will to the charity.

Option D is wrong because it omits the proceeds of the life policy which will pass under the will to the charity.

Option E is wrong because it omits the proceeds of the life policy which will pass under the will to the charity and wrongly includes the trust fund which passes outside the will.

Question 2

A man died last week. His will, made six months ago, left his substantial estate to his niece. A solicitor drafted the man's will on the niece's instructions and the niece was present when the man executed the will at the solicitor's office. The man's daughter wants to know if she can challenge the validity of the will. The daughter says that the man was lucid and that various relatives have reported that the niece put pressure on him to make the will in her favour.

Which of the following best describes whether the daughter can challenge the validity of the man's will?

A The daughter has no grounds to challenge the validity of the man's will.

B The daughter could challenge the validity of the man's will on the ground that he lacked testamentary capacity.

C The daughter could challenge the validity of the man's will on the ground that he did not know and approve the contents.

D The daughter could challenge the validity of the man's will but she would have to rebut the presumption of knowledge and approval.

E The daughter could challenge the validity of the man's will because there is a presumption of undue influence.

Answer

Option C is correct. The facts suggest that the niece pressurised the man into making the will which casts doubt on his knowledge and approval.

Option A is therefore wrong.

Option B is wrong. The facts state that the man was lucid and therefore possessed mental capacity.

Option D is wrong. The presumption of knowledge and approval would not apply here due to the suspicious circumstances (the beneficiary brought about the preparation and execution of the will).

Option E is wrong. There is no presumption of undue influence as regards wills. The person alleging undue influence has to prove it.

Question 3

A testatrix signed her will with two witnesses present. The two witnesses signed at different times. Each signed in the presence of the testatrix but not in the presence of the other witness. The will contains an attestation clause.

The executor was present throughout the execution process. The testatrix has now died.

Will the executor be able to obtain a grant of probate of the will?

A Yes, because the executor can rely on the presumption of due execution.

B No, because the witnesses did not sign at the same time.

C Yes, because the executor will prove that the formalities have been complied with by providing an affidavit of due execution.

D No, because the executor did not act as a witness.

E No, because the witnesses did not acknowledge their signatures to each other.

Answer

Option A is correct. The will was validly executed in accordance with s 9 Wills Act 1837. The testator signed in the presence of two witnesses as required and they each signed in the testator's presence. The witnesses do not have to sign in each other's presence. The attestation clause raises a presumption that the will was validly executed.

Option B is therefore wrong.

Option C is wrong. Although on the facts the executor could provide an affidavit of due execution, none is required due to the presumption of due execution raised by the attestation clause. Affidavits are required only if there is no such presumption.

Option D is wrong. The will was properly executed as explained above. There is no need for an executor to act as a witness in addition or substitution.

Option E is wrong because the original execution was valid. There was no need for the witnesses to acknowledge their signatures to each other.

2 Wills: Establishing Entitlement

SQE1 syllabus

This chapter will enable you to achieve the SQE1 assessment specification in relation to functioning legal knowledge concerned with wills and the administration of estates.

- The validity of a will and interpretation of the contents of a will. The distribution of testate, intestate and partially intestate estates.
- The interpretation of wills.
- Effect of different types of gifts.
- Failure of gifts.

Note that for SQE1, candidates are not usually required to recall specific case names or cite statutory or regulatory authorities. However, in this chapter, the substitutional provision in s 33 Wills Act 1837 may be referred to in the SQE1 assessment. Otherwise, references to cases, statutory and regulatory provisions are for illustrative purposes.

Learning outcomes

By the end of this chapter you will be able to apply relevant core legal principles and rules appropriately and effectively, at the level of a competent newly qualified solicitor in practice, to realistic client-based and ethical problems and situations in the following areas:

- applying the rules of interpretation;
- the circumstances in which a will can be rectified;
- the reasons for the failure of gifts in a will; and
- establishing the entitlement of beneficiaries in a will.

2.1 Introduction

This chapter looks at establishing entitlement under the terms of a will (sometimes referred to as construing the will). When a testator dies, the people dealing with the estate must decide (usually with the help of a solicitor) the effect of the will in the light of the circumstances at the date of the testator's death. In order to determine the effect of the various gifts in the will they will need to consider the actual wording used in the will, what property the testator owned, who the people named or described in the will are and whether they have survived the testator.

The people dealing with the estate are called executors, if they were appointed by the will, and administrators, if there was no appointment in the will. There are statutory rules as to who is able to act as an administrator (see **Chapter 8**). Both executors and administrators may be referred to generically as 'personal representatives'.

This chapter looks at:

- basic presumptions;
- establishing the testator's intentions;
- rectification;
- property passing under the will;
- identifying the beneficiaries; and
- failure of gifts.

2.2 Basic presumptions

The first step in establishing entitlement in a testate estate is to carefully study the wording of the will itself. In many instances this will be a straightforward process. A will should be drawn up so as to properly and accurately reflect the testator's intentions. When drawing up a will getting the wording right is essential. It is not possible, even for a court, to change or rewrite a will to reflect others' opinions as to what the testator wanted or the court's best guess as to what the testator would have wanted had they thought about it. However, not all wills are drafted perfectly: practitioners can make mistakes; many wills are homemade. If the meaning of the will is not clear cut it is necessary to interpret, or ask a court to interpret, the wording of the will.

When interpreting a will, the task is to discern the testator's intentions through the language of the will itself. In trying to establish those intentions the court applies two basic presumptions:

(a) Non-technical words bear their ordinary meaning

It is possible for some words to have several different meanings and then the court has to try to determine the meaning the testator intended given the context of the will as a whole – eg 'money' can mean notes and coins, but it can also mean everything an individual owns.

(b) Technical words are given their technical meaning

For example, in *Re Cook* [1948] 1 All ER 231 the testatrix made a gift of 'all my personal estate ...' The court gave the word 'personal' its technical meaning of personalty as opposed to realty.

These presumptions may be rebutted if from the will (and any admissible extrinsic evidence) it is clear that the testator was using the word in a different sense. The testator can use words in their own way provided it is clear from the will that that is what the testator intended. The court cannot, however, invent different meanings.

2.3 Establishing the testator's intention

In recent years the courts have moved away from a strict application of rigid rules to a more natural approach to the interpretation of wills. Nevertheless, the court's function remains the same, ie to determine the intention of the testator as expressed in the will when read as a whole. The court needs to establish what the words used by the testator mean in this particular case - ie what are the testator's expressed intentions. The court will focus on the ordinary meaning of the words but will also take account of context and common sense.

The court interprets the will by looking at the words in the will itself. The basic rule is that the court is not prepared to consider other evidence in order to try to establish what the testator intended. If the meaning remains unclear the gift will fail for uncertainty (see **2.7.1**).

There are, however, some limited circumstances in which the court will look at external or extrinsic evidence in order to ascertain the testator's intentions. The admission of extrinsic evidence is governed by s 21 Administration of Justice Act 1982:

(1) This section applies to a will:

  (a) in so far as any part of it is meaningless;

  (b) in so far as the language used in any part of it is ambiguous on the face of it;

  (c) in so far as evidence, other than evidence of the testator's intention, shows that the language used in any part of it is ambiguous in the light of surrounding circumstances.

(2) In so far as this section applies to a will extrinsic evidence, including evidence of the testator's intention, may be admitted to assist in its interpretation.

Section 21 therefore permits extrinsic evidence (including evidence of declarations made by the deceased) to be admitted to interpret the will insofar as any part of the will is meaningless or the language used is ambiguous or evidence (other than evidence of the testator's intention) shows that the language is ambiguous in the light of the surrounding circumstances.

Thorn v Dickens [1906] WN 54

This case is an example of the language of a will being ambiguous in the light of the surrounding circumstances (the case was decided under the old common law principle on which s 21 is based).

The will left 'all to mother'. On the face of it there is no ambiguity - the estate goes to the testator's mother. However, the words did not fit the surrounding circumstances because the testator's mother was already dead when the testator made his will and the testator was well aware of the fact that his mother was dead. Extrinsic evidence was permitted which showed that the testator was in the habit of referring to his wife as 'mother'. This was only allowed because there was no one fitting the description of 'mother' when the will was made.

Section 21 involves a two-step process. The case must come within one of the three options in s 21(1). Only then will the court look at extrinsic evidence, including evidence of the testator's intention. In any event the extrinsic evidence is only an aid to interpretation, it cannot be used to rewrite the will.

2.4 Rectification

The aim of interpreting a will is to discern the testator's intention as revealed by the wording of the will. The court has no power to rewrite the will so that it accords with the opinion of others, even the court, as to what the testator could or should have intended. The court has no power to write a different will for the testator. The court does, however, have a very limited power to correct, or rectify a will. This arises where the testator's intentions are clear, but the wording of the will does not carry them into effect.

This narrow power is found in s 20 Administration of Justice Act 1982:

> If a court is satisfied that a will is so expressed that it fails to carry out the testator's intentions, in consequence—
>
> (a) of a clerical error; or
>
> (b) of a failure to understand his instructions,
>
> it may order that the will shall be rectified so as to carry out his intentions.

The ability to rectify only arises where the will fails to carry out the testator's intentions and that failure has one of two causes: either in consequence of a clerical error or a failure to understand instructions. The first point to note is that the testator must have had 'intentions', a will cannot be rectified to include something that the testator had never thought about.

'Clerical error' means an error of a clerical nature and would include writing or omitting something by mistake.

Joshi v Mahida [2013] WTLR 859

The will was written by the solicitor at the testator's hospital bedside. The solicitor should have written 'my one half share' but in fact wrote 'one half of my share'. This was held to be a clerical error and the will was rectified accordingly.

An example of a failure to understand instructions is:

Sprackling v Sprackling [2008] EWHC 2696 (Ch)

The testator gave instructions to his solicitor to draw up a will including a gift of a farmhouse and a small parcel of surrounding land to his second wife. The solicitor misunderstood the instructions to mean that the gift was of the entire farm (including agricultural land, business premises, cattle etc). Fortunately, the testator's intentions were clear from the draft will which the testator had written out himself and handed to the solicitor. The will was rectified accordingly.

Section 20 is very narrow. It would not be possible, for example, to rectify a will because the solicitor who wrote the will misunderstood the law or thought that the words chosen achieved the desired outcome, but they did not do so.

If words are included in a will by mistake, the court may allow the will to be admitted to probate with those words omitted. This is an issue of the testator's knowledge and approval point (see **1.6.3**).

2.5 Property passing under the will

Once the meaning of the wording of the will has been established, the personal representatives will need to give effect to them.

Certain types of property pass independently of the will either because they have their own rules of succession (eg property held as beneficial joint tenants), or because the testator did not own them beneficially at death (eg life assurance policies written in trust) (see **1.2**). When the personal representatives have decided what property is capable of passing under the will, they must apply the terms of the will to that property.

So far as the assets which form the subject matter of a gift are concerned, the basic rule is that the assets are determined according to those in existence at the date of death - the will is said to 'speak from the date of death'.

The basic rule is stated in the s 24 Wills Act 1837 which provides:

> Every will shall be construed, with reference to the real estate and personal estate comprised in it, to speak and take effect as if it had been executed immediately before the death of the testator, unless a contrary intention shall appear by the will.

This means that the will is interpreted as if it had been executed immediately before death. A gift of 'all my estate' or 'all the rest of my estate' takes effect to dispose of all property the testator owned when they died, whether or not the testator owned it at the time the will was made.

The will speaks from the date of death unless a contrary intention appears in the will. A contrary intention can be shown by the use of particular words. Examples of words which could show a contrary intention are words which refer to the 'present', ie the time when the testator made the will, provided that the reference is essential to the description: 'the house which I now own.'

If the testator uses the word 'my' when referring to a specific asset (eg 'my' car) it is possible that the court could interpret this as meaning the gift is of the car which the testator owned at the date of the will. However, if the asset concerned is generic in that it is capable of increase or decrease between the date of the will and the date of death, eg 'my collection of cars', then this will be taken to mean the cars in the collection at the date of death.

2.6 Identifying the beneficiaries

Where the beneficiaries are referred to by name, identification is usually just a matter of locating them, establishing whether they survived the testator and, if not, the effect of their prior death on the gift (see **2.7.5**).

However, sometimes beneficiaries are referred to by description.

2.6.1 The general rule

Section 24 Wills Act 1837 (see **2.5**) applies to property, not to people. Generally, references to beneficiaries are construed as to people alive at the time of the will's execution - the will 'speaks from the date of execution'.

If the will contains a gift made, say, to 'Kate's eldest daughter' this is construed as a gift to the person who fulfilled that description when the will was made. If Kate has two daughters, Emily and Jenny, and Emily is the elder of the two, the gift passes to Emily. If Emily predeceases the testator, the gift does not pass to Jenny; although she is now Kate's eldest surviving daughter, she did not fit the description at the time the will was executed.

Again, the rule that so far as people are concerned, the will speaks from the date of execution, is subject to a contrary intention appearing in the will.

2.6.2 Family relationships

Often beneficiaries are unnamed but described by reference to their relationship to the testator. Where the will refers to a class of beneficiaries, for example 'my children' or 'my nephews', it is necessary to determine who fulfils that description.

As a general rule, such gifts are taken to refer to blood relationships. So, a gift to 'my children' will be a gift only to the testator's own children and not to the children of the testator's spouse or civil partner (so-called step-children), or to those of a cohabitant. However, the rule will not apply if the will provides otherwise.

Reading v Reading [2015] EWHC 946 (Ch)

The will included a gift to 'my wife ... and any issue of mine who are alive at the start of or born during the trust period'.

The court was prepared to interpret the word 'issue' as including the testator's step-children. The court found that there was sufficient evidence to demonstrate that the testator had intended his step-children to share a pecuniary legacy with his own children: the will included a substitutional gift of residue to both his own children and his step-children in the event that his second wife predeceased him, and the general wording suggested step-children were intended to share in both cases.

2.6.3 Special rules relating to children

The normal meaning of issue is direct descendants of any generation so, as well as the testator's children, it will include grandchildren, great-grandchildren and so on.

Adopted children are normally treated as children of the adoptive parents, although the will may provide otherwise. An adopted child would be included within the description of 'children' in their adoptive parents' will, but not in the will of their birth parent (although if a child is adopted before their interest in an estate becomes vested, their interest is unaffected by the adoption). Again, this is subject to a contrary intention shown in the will.

In the case of succession to property under modern wills, it is irrelevant whether or not a child's parents are married to each other. So, a gift of 'my estate to my sons in equal shares' would include not only the testator's two sons from his marriage, but also the son born as the result of an extra-marital affair. This is subject to a contrary intention shown in the will.

There are special rules which apply to determine the parentage of children born as a result of assisted reproduction under the Human Fertilisation and Embryology Act 2008 (see **4.10**). In essence a gift, for example, to 'my children' will include any children of whom the testator is a legal parent under the Act.

2.6.4 Gender recognition

Under the Gender Recognition Act 2004 an individual who has obtained a full gender recognition certificate from the Gender Recognition Panel is legally recognised in their acquired gender. Section 15 provides that the fact that a person's gender has become the acquired gender under the Act does not affect the disposal or devolution of property under a will or other instrument made before 4 April 2005. However, it will do so if the will or other instrument is made after that date.

Example

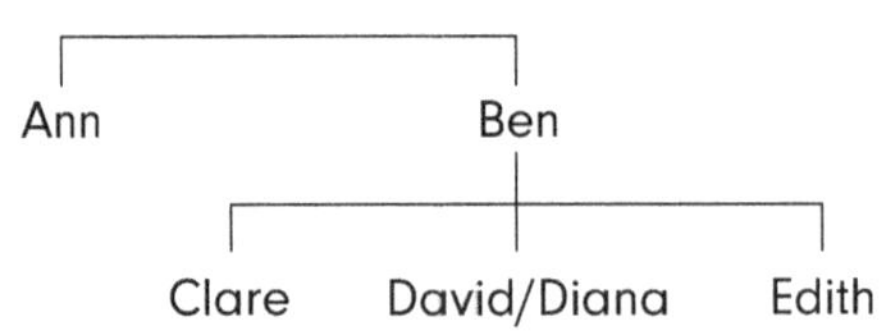

David obtains a full gender recognition certificate as a woman (Diana) in 2021.

Ann dies in 2025 with a will leaving everything to 'my nieces equally'.

If the will is made before 4 April 2005, Diana cannot share in Ann's estate but she can if the will is made on or after that date.

Section 18 of the Act provides that where the disposition or devolution of any property under a will or other instrument (made on or after the appointed day) is different from what it would be but for the fact that a person's gender has become the acquired gender under the Act, an application may be made to the High Court where expectations have been defeated. Where the court is satisfied that it is just to make an order, it has a wide discretion as to the appropriate order to make. For example, it could order payment of a lump sum, transfer or settlement of property.

Trustees and personal representatives are protected under s 17 from: (a) being under any duty to enquire whether a full gender recognition certificate has been issued or revoked before conveying or distributing any property; and (b) being liable to any person by reason of a conveyance or distribution of property made without regard to whether a full gender recognition certificate has been issued to any person or revoked without the trustee or personal representative having been given prior notice. However, the section does not prejudice the right of a person to follow the property, or any property representing it, into the hands of another person who has received it unless that person has purchased it for value in good faith and without notice.

2.6.5 Spouses/civil partners

The terms 'husband/wife' and 'civil partner' are not synonymous. So, a gift to 'John's wife' will fail if John never marries but enters a civil partnership instead.

2.7 Failure of gifts

When determining entitlement under a will, it is necessary to establish whether the gifts made under the will are effective. This is not the same as establishing the validity of the will (see **Chapter 1**). The will itself may be valid, but individual gifts may fail.

A gift made in a will can fail for a variety of reasons. Where a gift fails, the basic effect is that the subject matter falls into the residuary estate and will be taken by the residuary beneficiary; where a gift of residue fails there will be a partial intestacy and the residuary estate will pass under the intestacy rules (see **Chapter 4**).

2.7.1 Uncertainty

If it is not possible from the wording of the will to identify the subject matter of the gift or the recipient, the gift will fail for uncertainty. Obviously, the court will first seek to establish the testator's intentions and consider its powers of rectification (see **2.4**), but if the meaning cannot be discerned the gift fails. The only exception is a gift to charity which does not sufficiently identify the charity. Provided that it is clear that the gift is exclusively for charitable purposes the court can direct which charity is to benefit.

2.7.2 Beneficiary witnesses will

If a beneficiary, or their spouse or civil partner, acts as a witness, the gift to the beneficiary fails (s 15 Wills Act 1837). However, the beneficiary or spouse/civil partner remains a competent witness and so the will is validly executed.

The rationale behind the failure of a gift to a beneficiary is public policy: a witness should be impartial. The witness may be called upon to give evidence as to the manner of execution and it would be wrong for them to have a vested interest in proving the will to be valid. However, a gift will also fail if the will is witnessed by the beneficiary's spouse. 'Spouse' means the person to whom the beneficiary was married at the time that the will was executed. The rationale here is less easy to discern as s 15 does not cater for others closely associated with the testator, so a gift will survive if, for example, the witness was the beneficiary's child or the beneficiary's cohabitant or, indeed, the person the beneficiary subsequently marries.

A gift will not fail if the will is validly executed without the beneficiary's signature (or that of their spouse/civil partner). So, for example, if there are three witnesses to the will, one of whom is a beneficiary, the gift to that beneficiary is effective because the will is still validly executed even if the beneficiary's signature is ignored. Similarly, the gift will not fail if there is a codicil (see **3.4**) which confirms the original will and which is not witnessed by the beneficiary (or spouse/civil partner).

2.7.3 Divorce or dissolution

Where after the date of the will the testator's marriage or civil partnership is dissolved, annulled or declared void, 'any property which, or an interest in which, is devised or bequeathed to the former spouse or civil partner shall pass as if the former spouse or civil partner had died' on the date of the dissolution or annulment of the marriage or civil partnership (ss 18A and 18C Wills Act 1837) (see also **3.2.3**).

Example

Fauzia makes a will in which she leaves all her estate to her husband, Sabiq, with a substitutional provision that, if Sabiq dies before her, the property should pass to her children equally. Fauzia and Sabiq are later divorced but Fauzia does not change her will. She dies, survived by Sabiq and the children. Under s 18A, the gift to Sabiq fails. Even though Sabiq in fact survived Fauzia he is treated as if he died on the day of the divorce. The substitutional gift takes effect and Fauzia's estate passes to the children.

Sections 18A and 18C only apply where a marriage has been dissolved or annulled by the court. If the couple simply live apart, the gift and appointment remain valid.

2.7.4 Ademption

A specific legacy (ie a gift of a particular item or group of items of property) will fail if the testator no longer owns that property at death. The gift is said to be 'adeemed'. Ademption usually occurs because the property has been sold, given away or destroyed during the testator's lifetime.

Example

In her will Ellen gives 'my gold bracelet' to her sister Grace and the rest of her estate to her husband Harry. Ellen no longer owns the bracelet when she dies. Grace receives nothing: her legacy is adeemed. All Ellen's estate passes to Harry under the residuary gift.

Problems may arise where the asset has been retained but has changed its nature since the will was made. For example, where the will includes a specific gift of company shares, the company may have been taken over since the will was made so that the testator's shareholding has been changed into a holding in the new company. In such a case, the question is whether the asset is substantially the same, having changed merely in name or form, or whether it has changed in substance. Only if there has been a change in substance will the gift be adeemed.

Another area of potential difficulty occurs where the testator disposes of the property described in a specific gift but before death acquires a different item of property which answers the same description; for example a gift of 'my car' or 'my piano' where the original car or piano has been replaced since the will was made. It has been held that the presumption in such a case is that the testator intended that the specific gift was to be of the particular asset they owned at the date of the will so that the gift is adeemed. By referring to 'my' car or piano, the testator may be taken to have shown a contrary intention as specified in s 24 Wills Act 1837 (see **2.5**). However, this interpretation may vary according to the circumstances, and the respective values of the original and substituted assets may be taken into account.

If the property given is capable of increase or decrease (eg, 'my shares', 'my jewellery'), the testator will normally be taken to have made a gift of any items satisfying the description at death (see **2.5**).

Example

Thea makes a will leaving 'all my jewellery' to her niece, Nilu. After the date of the will, all her jewellery is stolen. Six months later she receives money from her insurance company and buys new jewellery. Then she dies.

(a) Because Thea has used a phrase which is capable of increase and decrease, she is treated as intending to pass whatever jewellery she has at the date of her death. Nilu will, therefore, take the replacement items.

(b) Had the gift been of 'my pearl necklace', Thea would probably be treated as intending to pass only the necklace she owned at the date of the will. Nilu would not have taken any replacement necklace.

(c) Had Thea died after receiving the insurance money but before buying replacement assets, Nilu would have taken nothing. She has no right to the insurance money under the terms of the gift.

A testator may wish to add to or change a will in a minor way and so may execute a codicil (see **3.4**). A codicil is a supplement to a will which, to be valid, must be executed in the same way as a will. The significance of a codicil in the context of a gift of property is that it republishes the will as at the date of the codicil. Thus, if the testator makes a will in 1990 leaving 'my gold watch' to a legatee, loses the watch in 2000 and replaces it, the gift of the watch in the will is adeemed. If, however, the testator executes a codicil to the will in 2003, the will is read as if it had been executed in 2003 and so the legatee will take the replacement watch.

2.7.5 Lapse

2.7.5.1 Basic rule

A gift in a will fails or 'lapses' if the beneficiary dies before the testator. If a legacy lapses, the property falls into residue, unless the testator has provided for the possibility of lapse by including a substitutional gift. If a gift of residue lapses, the property passes under the intestacy rules (see **Chapter 4**), unless the testator has included a substitutional gift in the will. Where no conditions to the contrary are imposed in the will, a gift vests on the testator's death. This means that provided the beneficiary survives the testator, for however short a time, the gift takes effect. If the beneficiary dies soon after the testator the property passes into the beneficiary's estate.

It is possible to show a contrary intention, for example by wording a gift to make it clear that the property is to pass to whoever is the holder of a position or office at the date of the testator's death.

The general rule is that, as regards people, a will 'speaks from the date of execution' (see **2.6.1**). A gift made to 'the eldest son of X' is taken to mean a gift to the person fulfilling that description at the date the will is made. If that person dies, the gift does not pass to the eldest surviving son. However, if the testator makes a codicil to the will, it republishes the will and the will is treated as made at the date of the republication. Hence, if the eldest son dies between the date of the will and the codicil, the will is construed as referring to the person who is the eldest son at the date of the codicil.

2.7.5.2 Section 184 Law of Property Act 1925

If the deaths of the testator and beneficiary occur very close together, it is vital to establish who died first. The law of succession does not accept the possibility that two people might die at the same instant. If the order of their deaths cannot be proved, s 184 provides that the elder of the two is deemed to have died first. If the testator was older than the beneficiary, the gift takes effect and the property passes as part of the beneficiary's estate.

Scarle v Scarle [2019] EWHC 2224 (Ch)

A husband and wife were found dead at their home. They had both died from hypothermia. The wife was 10 years younger than the husband, but there was some forensic evidence which suggested that she might have died first.

The order of deaths was crucial as the couple held their house as beneficial joint tenants together with £18,000 in a joint bank account. The survivor would take the whole by survivorship. It was a second marriage for both, and each had one daughter from their previous marriages. The dispute was between the daughters.

The court held that the forensic evidence was not sufficient to establish the order of deaths. Therefore, the presumption applied, and the husband was deemed to have died first. The wife's daughter inherited everything.

2.7.5.3 Survivorship clauses

Commonly, gifts in wills are made conditional upon the survival of the beneficiaries for a specific period of time, such as 28 days. These survivorship provisions prevent a gift from taking effect where the beneficiary survives the testator for only a relatively short time or is deemed to have survived by s 184. As with any other contingent gift, if the beneficiary fails to satisfy the contingency, the gift fails.

2.7.5.4 Lapse of gifts to more than one person

A gift by will to two or more people as joint tenants will not lapse unless all the donees die before the testator. If a gift is made 'to A and B jointly' and A dies before the testator, the whole gift passes to B.

If the gift contains words of severance, for example 'everything to A and B in equal shares', this principle does not apply. If A dies before the testator, A's share lapses and B takes only one share. The lapsed share will pass under the intestacy rules unless, as is often the case, the testator included a substitutional gift to take effect if one of the original beneficiaries predeceased.

If the gift is a class gift (eg 'to my nieces and nephews equally if more than one'), there is no lapse unless all the members of the class predecease the testator.

2.7.5.5 Section 33 Wills Act 1837

An exception the doctrine of lapse applies to all gifts by will to the testator's children or remoter issue (ie direct descendants) unless a contrary intention is shown in the will. Its effect is to incorporate an implied substitution provision into such gifts. It provides that where a will contains a gift to the testator's child or remoter descendant and that beneficiary dies before the testator, leaving issue of their own who survive the testator, the gift does not lapse but passes instead to the beneficiary's issue. The issue of a deceased beneficiary take the gift their parent would have taken in equal shares. This is particularly important when establishing entitlement under the will because the substitutional gift does not appear on the face of the will.

Example

Tom's will includes a gift of £40,000 to his daughter, Caroline. Caroline and her daughter Sarah both die before Tom, but Caroline's son, James, and Sarah's children, Emma and Daniel, all survive him. Under s 33, the legacy is saved from lapse. James takes half the gift (£20,000). Sarah would have taken the other half but, as she has predeceased Tom, her half passes to her own children equally. Thus, Emma and Daniel take £10,000 each.

Section 33 does not apply if the will shows a contrary intention. This is usually shown by including an express substitution clause.

2.7.6 Disclaimer

A beneficiary cannot be forced to accept a gift. A beneficiary can disclaim the gift, which will then fall into residue or, in the case of disclaimer of a gift of residue, pass on intestacy (see **7.3**). A beneficiary who disclaims a gift is treated as having predeceased the testator, which will allow the beneficiary's issue to replace them under s 33 Wills Act 1837 (see **2.7.5.5**).

However, a beneficiary who has received a benefit from a gift (eg a payment of income) is taken to have accepted the gift and may no longer disclaim.

2.7.7 Forfeiture

As a matter of public policy, a person should not profit from their own wrongdoing. The long established forfeiture rule provides that an individual should not benefit from the estate of a person they have unlawfully killed or where they have unlawfully aided, abetted, counselled or procured that person's death.

The rule applies to any entitlement whether it arises by survivorship, under the intestacy rules or under the terms of a will. In the case of property which would otherwise have passed by survivorship, the effect of the operation of the forfeiture rule is to sever the joint tenancy.

The rule applies to various forms of unlawful acts including murder, manslaughter, aiding and abetting suicide and causing death by careless driving. However, the rule does not apply where the killer was insane. In most cases the actions of the perpetrator will result in them being convicted of some criminal offence. However, a conviction is not necessarily required for the forfeiture rule to apply. For example, in a 'suicide pact', the perpetrator may also have taken their own life; in *Morris v Morris* (below) the police had concluded that the circumstances were such that the public interest did not require them to pursue a prosecution.

Subject to a contrary intention in the will, a person who forfeits an entitlement is to be treated as having predeceased the testator. This means that if a child of a testator forfeits, their issue can be substituted under s 33 Wills Act 1837 (see **2.7.5.5**).

Example

Terry is murdered by his daughter, Denise. His will leaves everything to Denise who has a son, Sean. Denise forfeits her entitlement under the will, but she will be treated as if she had predeceased Terry, with the result that Terry's estate will pass to Sean.

Save in respect of cases of murder, the Forfeiture Act 1982 allows the court to modify the effect of the forfeiture rule. The court can modify the effect of the rule in any way including granting complete relief. The court must not make an order unless satisfied that the justice of the case demands it having regard to the conduct of the deceased and the applicant, and all the surrounding circumstances. The application for the relief must be made within three months of the date of conviction (if relevant). The time limit is strict, and the court has no discretion to extend the period.

Morris v Morris [2024] EWHC 2554 (Ch)

The testatrix was suffering from a rare and incurable neurological disorder. As her condition worsened, she became determined to seek an assisted death. The testatrix's husband made all the necessary arrangements and travelled with her to the clinic in Switzerland where, with the assistance of the medical staff, she took her own life. The court decided that the husband's actions were such as to bring him within s 2(1) Suicide Act 1961 (aiding and abetting suicide) and consequently his interest under the terms of her will was forfeit (in contrast, other family members whose only actions were to accompany the testatrix to the clinic 'as a comfort' were not subject to the forfeiture rule). The court found that the husband had been motivated by compassion and respect for his wife's wishes; he had even handed himself in to the police on his return from Switzerland. In the circumstances, the court was prepared to modify the effect of the forfeiture rule so that the husband could take his full entitlement under the will.

Summary

- The task when interpreting a will is to establish the testator's intention as expressed in the will when read as a whole.
- The court will only look at extrinsic evidence where the wording is:
  - meaningless
  - ambiguous on the face of it
  - ambiguous in the light of surrounding circumstances
- The court's powers to rectify a will are limited to cases where it fails to carry out the testator's intentions, in consequence of:
  - a clerical error
  - a failure to understand the testator's instructions
- As regards property a will 'speaks from the date of death'.
- As regards people a will 'speaks from the date of execution'.
- A gift in a will can fail in a number of circumstances:
  - Uncertainty
  - Beneficiary witnessed the will
  - Divorce/dissolution
  - Ademption
  - Lapse
  - Disclaimer
  - Forfeiture

Sample questions

Question 1

A woman makes a will in which she appoints her only brother and his son (her nephew) as her executors. She makes gifts of £5,000 to charity, £10,000 to her best friend, and gives the rest of her estate to her brother.

The two persons who witnessed the will are the husband of the best friend and the nephew.

Which of the following best describes the position in relation to the woman's will?

A The will is invalid because the best friend's husband witnessed the will.

B The will is invalid because the nephew witnessed the will.

C The will is valid but the best friend's gift will not take effect because her husband witnessed the will.

D The will is valid but the brother's appointment as executor fails because he is a beneficiary.

E The will is valid but the nephew's appointment as executor fails because he witnessed the will.

Answer

Option C is correct. A gift in a will fails if a beneficiary or their spouse acts as witness (s 15 Wills Act 1837). The best friend is a beneficiary and her husband acted as a witness.

Option A is wrong as a will is not invalidated if a beneficiary or their spouse acts as witness.

Option B is wrong as a will is not invalidated if an executor is a witness.

Option D is wrong as a gift in a will does not fail by virtue of the fact that the beneficiary is also the executor.

Option E is wrong as a witness can be an executor.

Question 2

A woman died recently. Her valid will gave her entire estate (all assets in her sole name) to 'such of my daughters who are living at my death and if more than one in equal shares'. The woman was a widow, and had one daughter as a result of her marriage. This daughter died six months before the woman, leaving a daughter (the granddaughter), now aged 12 years. For the last four years the woman has been living with her boyfriend and his daughter (now aged 16 years). The woman and her boyfriend also have a daughter together, who is now aged two years.

Which of the following best describes entitlement to the woman's estate?

A The boyfriend's daughter and the two-year-old daughter will share the estate.

B The granddaughter will take the whole estate.

C The granddaughter and two-year-old daughter will share the estate, provided that they each attain the age of 18.

D The two-year-old daughter will take the whole estate.

E The granddaughter and two-year-old daughter will share the estate.

Answer

Option E is correct. The gift to 'my daughters' will be interpreted as meaning a gift to only her own daughters (whether legitimate or not), and not that of her boyfriend (option A is therefore wrong). Although the first daughter had predeceased, she had left a child who takes in substitution for her mother (s 33 Wills Act 1837).

Options B and D are wrong in that they wrongly exclude the two-year-old daughter and granddaughter respectively.

Option C is wrong as although the granddaughter and the two-year-old daughter are entitled they do not have to satisfy a condition of reaching the age of 18 years because this was not a stipulation in the will.

Question 3

A husband and wife own their house as beneficial joint tenants. They both make a will in which each left their entire estate to the other. Sometime later, the husband is convicted of the wife's murder.

Which of the following best describes the husband's entitlement to the wife's estate?

A The house passes to the husband by survivorship; the gift in the will is forfeit.

B The husband will receive the whole estate if the court decides to modify the effect of the forfeiture rule in that way.

C The house passes to the husband by survivorship; the gift in the will lapses.

D The husband is not entitled to anything from the estate.

E The house passes to the husband by survivorship; the rest of the estate passes under the intestacy rules.

Answer

Option D is correct. The husband is responsible for the wife's unlawful killing and therefore he cannot benefit from the wife's estate under the forfeiture rule. The forfeiture rule applies to both the wife's interest in the house (the effect is that the joint tenancy is severed so the wife's interest cannot now pass by survivorship) and to the gift in a will. As a result, options A, C and E are wrong.

Option B is wrong because the court is not able to modify the effect of the forfeiture rule as the conviction is for murder.

3 Wills: Revocation, Additions and Alterations

SQE1 syllabus

This chapter will enable you to achieve the SQE1 assessment specification in relation to functioning legal knowledge concerned with wills and the administration of estates.

- The validity of a will and interpretation of the contents of a will. The distribution of testate, intestate and partially intestate estates.
- The planning, management and progression of the administration of an estate.
- Alterations and amendments to wills.
- Methods of revocation.
- Effect of marriage and divorce of a testator.
- Use of codicils.
- Effect of alterations made to wills both before and after execution.

Note that for SQE1, candidates are not usually required to recall specific case names or cite statutory or regulatory authorities. Cases are provided for illustrative purposes only.

Learning outcomes

By the end of this chapter you will be able to apply relevant core legal principles and rules appropriately and effectively, at the level of a competent newly qualified solicitor in practice, to realistic client-based and ethical problems and situations in the following areas:

- the circumstances in which a will can be revoked;
- the nature and effect of a codicil; and
- the effectiveness of alterations to a will.

3.1 Introduction

This chapter looks at the ways in which a will can be changed. It will rarely be the case that a will made by the testator when in their twenties will be suitable to address the circumstances which exist when they die in their nineties. Changes will occur over a lifetime which result in the terms of the will no longer being as appropriate as they once were. Divorce, a death in the family, the birth of a child, a new relationship and an improvement in financial circumstances are all examples of changes which may affect the suitability of a will.

Every testator should keep their will under review and, where circumstances require or where they simply change their mind, take steps to make appropriate and effective changes.

This chapter looks at:

- revocation;
- mutual wills;
- codicils; and
- alterations.

3.2 Revocation

Revocation is the formal act of cancelling or withdrawing a will. The effect of revocation is to nullify the will, either as a whole or in part.

A fundamental characteristic of a will is that it is revocable. In just the same way that an individual is free to leave their property in whatever way they choose, having made that choice in the form of a will, they are equally free to change their mind. The rule is that a testator is free to revoke their will at any time provided that they have capacity to do so. Capacity in this context means the same capacity required to make a will (see **1.5**).

There are three situations in which a will can be revoked:

- by a later will or codicil;
- by destruction; or
- by marriage/forming a civil partnership.

3.2.1 By a later will or codicil

Under s 20 Wills Act 1837 a will may be revoked in whole or in part by a declaration to that effect in a later will or codicil (see **3.4**) (or in a written declaration executed in the same manner as a will (see **1.7**)). No particular wording is required, but a professionally drafted will usually begins with a statement such as 'I hereby revoke all former wills previously made by me'. The inclusion of such a statement in a will is sufficient to revoke previous wills.

If a will does not contain an express revocation clause, it operates to revoke any earlier will or codicil by implication to the extent that the two are inconsistent. This could result in complete revocation of the earlier will if the two are totally inconsistent or there could be just a partial revocation in which case the two wills will need to be read together in order to piece together the testator's intentions.

Example

Five years ago, Sanjay made a will in which he left 'my entire estate to my sister, Gita'. Three years later Sanjay made a will in which he left 'my holiday cottage to my nephew,

Jamie'. The later will does not contain an express revocation clause. Reading the two wills together, the first will remains valid and disposes of Sanjay's estate with the exception of the holiday cottage. The holiday cottage passes to Jamie under the terms of the later will.

Although dating a will is not one of the formal requirements in s 9 Wills Act 1837, it is advisable to date a will so that the chronology can be established for the purposes of revocation.

Exceptionally, the court may construe a testator's intention to revoke an earlier will by an express revocation clause as being conditional upon a particular event (eg the effectiveness of the new will). If that condition is not satisfied, the revocation may be held to be invalid so that the earlier will remains effective. (This is referred to as the doctrine of 'conditional revocation' or the doctrine of 'dependent relative revocation'.)

3.2.2 By destruction

A will may be revoked by 'burning, tearing or otherwise destroying the same by the testator or by some person in his presence and by his direction with the intention of revoking the same' (s 20 Wills Act 1837).

Physical destruction is required: symbolic destruction (eg simply crossing out wording or writing 'revoked' across the will) is not sufficient, although if a vital part (eg the signature) is destroyed, this partial destruction may be held to revoke the entire will. If the part destroyed is less substantial or important, then the partial destruction may revoke only that part which was actually destroyed. The test is whether the remainder of the will is intelligible and can still operate in the absence of the destroyed part.

The act of destruction must be carried out with the intention to revoke. A will destroyed by accident is not revoked. Where a will has been destroyed, but not successfully revoked, the court will look at evidence to establish the contents of the will. The best evidence would be a copy of the original will. However, it may be necessary to look at other evidence, such as oral evidence from those involved in drawing up the will. If the contents can be reconstructed, an order may be obtained allowing its admission to probate as a valid will.

Cheese v Lovejoy (1877) 2 PD 251

Several years after making his will, the testator put a line through various parts of it. He then wrote 'All these are revoked' on the back of the will and kicked it into a pile of waste paper in his sitting room. The will was retrieved by the testator's enthusiastic housekeeper, who put it on the kitchen table where it remained for the next eight years until the testator's death.

The court held that the will was not revoked because on the wording of s 20 there has to be the two elements together – destruction coupled with the intention to revoke. Here the testator clearly intended to revoke the will, but he had not destroyed it. The judge said, 'All the destroying in the world without intention will not revoke a will, nor all the intention in the world without destroying: there must be the two.'

The act of destruction must be carried out by the testator themselves or by someone else in the testator's presence and by their direction. If destruction is to be carried out by someone else, the testator must direct the act of destruction for it to be effective. In *Crewe v Oakley* [2024] EWHC 2847 (Ch), a silent nod from the testatrix was held to be sufficient authority for her solicitor to complete the destruction of the will on her behalf. Destruction carried out by someone else in the testator's absence, say in another room, is ineffective to revoke the will.

Sometimes, the court may apply the doctrine of dependent relative revocation to save a will, on the basis that the testator's intention to revoke their will by destruction was conditional upon some future event (eg upon the later execution of a new will). If that event did not in fact take place, the original will may be valid even though it was destroyed. The contents of the original will may be reconstructed from a copy or draft.

Example

Ranvir, who is estranged from her family, makes a will leaving her estate to her friend, Tina. A few years later, Ranvir destroys the will having decided to make a new will leaving her estate to her friend, Charlene, instead. Ranvir dies before her new will is executed.

If Ranvir destroyed the will primarily with the purpose of excluding Tina from benefitting from her estate, the court will infer that the revocation of the will was absolute. However, if it can be shown that Ranvir wanted to benefit Charlene but would have preferred Tina to take rather than those entitled on intestacy, the court will infer that the revocation was conditional on the execution of a valid will leaving her estate to Charlene. Tina will take the estate as the condition has not been fulfilled.

3.2.3 By marriage or formation of a civil partnership

If the testator marries or forms a civil partnership after executing a will, the will is revoked (ss 18A–18C Wills Act 1837). Revocation is automatic. This is significant as in many cases the testator will be ignorant of the fact that their marriage will have this consequence. This is the only life event which has this consequence; for example, a will is unaffected by equally significant events such as the death of a spouse or the birth of a child.

The rule does not apply where it appears from the will that the testator makes the will prior to and in expectation of a forthcoming marriage or civil partnership with a particular person and that the testator did not intend the will to be revoked (ss 18(3) and 18B(3) Wills Act 1837). Two elements must therefore be satisfied:

- The expectation must be of a forthcoming marriage to a particular person. A will made in a general expectation of marriage is not sufficient.
- The testator must intend that the will is not to be revoked by the marriage.

Both elements must be evident from the will. Essentially this requires the will to recite the fact of the expected marriage with the particular person and a wish that the will is not to be revoked.

A will made in contemplation of marriage which complies with these requirements is effective even if the intended marriage never takes place, unless the will is expressed as being conditional on the marriage taking place. Although a marriage with anyone other than the particular person anticipated revokes the will.

Example

Judi and Helga are engaged to be married. They make wills in expectation of their marriage leaving their respective estates to each other. They then have a row and break off the engagement. Judi dies 10 years later without changing her will. Helga will take Judi's estate.

It is possible for same-sex civil partners to convert their civil partnership into a marriage. Where a civil partnership is converted to a marriage, the conversion will not revoke an existing will of either party nor affect any dispositions in the wills.

The effect of marriage can be contrasted to that of divorce (see also **2.7.3**). If the testator makes a will and is later divorced, or if the civil partnership is dissolved (or the marriage or civil partnership is annulled or declared void), then under ss 18A and 18C Wills Act 1837 the will remains valid but:

(a) provisions of the will appointing the former spouse or civil partner as executor or trustee take effect as if the former spouse or civil partner had died on the date on which the marriage or civil partnership is dissolved or annulled; and

(b) any property, or interest in property, which is devised or bequeathed to the former spouse or civil partner passes as if the former spouse or civil partner had died on that date.

This means that substitutional provisions in the will which are expressed to take effect if the spouse/civil partner predeceases the testator will also take effect if the marriage/civil partnership is dissolved or annulled.

Sections 18A and 18C only apply where a marriage has been dissolved or annulled by the court. If the couple simply live apart, any gift or appointment remains valid.

3.3 Mutual wills

As stated above, provided the testator has capacity, they can revoke their will at any time. This means that even if the testator declares that the will is irrevocable, that declaration will not be binding.

However, it sometimes happens that a testator agrees not to revoke their will or not to revoke a particular gift in the will. Any such agreement cannot detract from the fundamental principle that a will is revocable. Having made the agreement the testator remains free to revoke the will and make a new one. However, if the agreement amounts to a contract and the testator is in breach, this may give rise to a contractual remedy. This may result in the estate paying contractual damages to a disappointed beneficiary.

An extension of the concept of agreements not to revoke is the doctrine of mutual wills. Mutual wills arise where two people make wills in similar terms and agree that whichever of them survives will irrevocably leave their estate in a particular way.

Mutual wills arise in a variety of circumstances, but a typical example would be where a husband and wife both make wills leaving their respective estates to each other with the proviso that whichever of them survives leaves their estate to the wife's daughter from a previous relationship. If, say, the wife is the first to die, then, as a will is revocable, the husband could revoke the mutual will and make a new one in different terms. That would be a valid testamentary act. However, given that the wife fulfilled her side of the bargain, it is clearly unconscionable for the husband now to go back on his promise. If the husband does revoke his will, equity will step in in the form of the doctrine of mutual wills. The effect of the doctrine is to impose a constructive trust over the husband's estate in favour of the wife's daughter as the beneficiary under the original mutual will. The effect of the doctrine is not to invalidate any new will, but the testator's intentions may obviously be frustrated in practice by the imposition of the trust.

The doctrine does not simply arise by virtue of people making wills in similar terms. Married couples often make wills in identical terms (referred to as mirror wills), but that is not sufficient to make them mutual wills. For the doctrine to apply there must have been an agreement. The wills must have been made as the result of a clear agreement between the testators as to the disposal of their estates and part of that agreement is that the survivor will not revoke their will (or, less commonly, that they will leave their estate in a particular way).

The constructive trust arises when the first testator dies without having revoked their will. At that point the first testator has carried out their side of the bargain, so it would be wrong to allow the survivor to renege on their side.

The essence of the agreement giving rise to mutual wills is that the survivor will not revoke their will. But this does not guarantee that the ultimate beneficiary will actually receive their intended benefit. This is because during their lifetime the survivor, as an absolute owner, is free to use their money and property in whatever way they choose. To take an extreme example, the survivor might make a series of disastrous investments and lose all their money with the result that there is nothing to pass on under the terms of the mutual wills. However, the survivor is not permitted to make dispositions during their lifetime with the intention of defeating the agreement in the mutual wills.

Given that a will is always revocable, during their joint lives it is possible for both testators to revoke their mutual wills as a joint decision. However, it may be that during their joint lives one testator unilaterally revokes their will. This is a breach of the agreement and so the other testator's remedy is the contractual one of seeking damages for the loss suffered as a result of the breach. The effect is also to release the other testator from the agreement not to revoke.

3.4 Codicils

Rather than revoking a will, the testator may wish to effect some additions or amendments to the will. This can be achieved through a codicil. A codicil is a document, executed in the same way as a will, which supplements an existing will. A codicil can be used to amend, add to or revoke in part, an existing will. The will and the codicil must therefore be read together in order to ascertain the testator's wishes.

A properly executed codicil has the effect of republishing the existing will. Republication confirms the will and causes the will to take effect as if made at the same time as the codicil, but incorporating any changes made by the codicil. The testator must have intended to republish the will. This can, but does not have to, be evident on the face of the codicil (eg by an express statement). Otherwise the courts are generally willing to infer the required intention from a mere reference to the existing will.

Under s 34 Wills Act 1837 a republished will is deemed to have been made at the time of republication. This can have important consequences for the operation of the will. So, for example, the rule that a will speaks from the date of execution so far as people are concerned (see **2.6**) means that a description of people in a will is taken to refer to those who satisfy the description at the time of republication. If the gift is to Bob's eldest son and the eldest son dies between the date of the will and date of the codicil, the will is construed as referring to the person who is Bob's eldest son at the date of the codicil. Similarly, a gift which is invalid because the beneficiary has acted as a witness (see **2.7.2**) will be saved if the will is republished by a codicil which is not witnessed by the beneficiary.

A codicil can be used to revive a will which has previously been revoked. Section 22 Wills Act 1837 provides that a revoked will can be revived by 'the re-execution thereof, or by a codicil executed in a manner hereinbefore required and showing an intention to revive the same'. The effect of revival is to resurrect the revoked will which then takes effect as if made at the time that it was revived. To have this effect the codicil must in some way evidence the testator's intention to revive the will. This could be an express statement or the inclusion of a disposition which means that the testator could have had no other intention but to revive the will. However, a mere reference to the will does not suffice. Whether the codicil shows the requisite intention is a matter of construction.

From a practical point of view, if the changes are substantial it is usually advisable to make a new will rather than rely on a codicil.

3.5 Alterations

Sometimes where a testator wants to make some changes to their will, rather than go to the lengths of revoking the original or executing a codicil the testator will make the changes on the face of the will itself. This raises the question of whether the will is to be read so as to include the alterations. The key issue is as to when the alterations were made.

If the alterations were made before the will was executed they are valid provided that the testator intended the alterations to form part of the will. However, any alterations are presumed to have been made after the will was executed unless the contrary can be proved. It may be necessary to obtain extrinsic evidence, for example from the witnesses, to evidence that the alterations were already there when the will was executed.

Alterations made after the will was executed will be valid if those alterations were themselves executed like a will (s 21 Wills Act 1837) (see **1.7**). However, the initials of the testator and the witnesses in the margin next to the amendment will suffice. If the alteration is valid then the will must be read to take account of it.

Where an invalid alteration has been made, the original wording of the will stands provided that it can be deciphered. The requirement is that the original wording must be 'apparent'. This means optically apparent. The original wording of the will must be capable of being read on the face of the will by ordinary means. For example, the original wording will be apparent if it can be read using a magnifying glass or by holding the will up to the light. It is not possible to ascertain the wording by extrinsic evidence (eg from the solicitor who drew up the will). Nor is it possible to ascertain the wording by interference with the will (eg applying chemicals) or by producing another document (eg an X-ray of the will).

An exception to the requirement that to be valid an alteration must be executed, occurs when the testator makes an amendment which simply obliterates the original wording. Here there is a revocation of the original wording by destruction, provided that the act of destruction is accompanied by the intention to revoke. The obliteration of, say, the figure in a pecuniary legacy, revokes the original wording even though the alteration is unexecuted, and the result is that the beneficiary receives nothing. The will itself remains valid, but it takes effect without the obliterated words.

In some instances where the testator obliterates the original wording the court may be prepared to apply the conditional revocation rule. This is most likely to apply where the testator obliterates the original wording and, at the same time, adds some substitute wording – ie the court finds that the testator only intended to revoke the original words on condition that the substitute words were effective. The condition has not been satisfied because the substitute words are unexecuted and therefore invalid. The original words have not been revoked and the court will look at any evidence to establish whether those original words can be reconstructed, including any of the methods which cannot be used when considering whether wording is apparent (eg a copy of the original will). This is because the issue is not whether the wording is apparent, but whether it can be ascertained.

Example

Tamal makes a professionally drawn will which leaves '£10,000 to my nephew, Nalin'.

After executing the will, Tamal decides he wants to change the legacy to Nalin:

(a) He draws a thin line through '£10,000' and writes above it '£20,000'.

This is an unexecuted alteration and will have no effect. The original wording is still apparent. The gift remains a gift of £10,000.

(b) He does exactly the same as in (a) but writes his name next to the alteration and gets two people to witness his signature.

This is an executed alteration and takes effect to alter the gift to £20,000.

(c) He draws a thick line through '£10,000' in such a way that the original wording is wholly unreadable.

This is an obliteration and will be treated as revoking the original gift. The gift is treated as a gift of nothing.

(d) He does exactly the same as in (c) but writes '£20,000' above the obliteration.

This is an obliteration and would be treated as revoking the original gift were it not for the fact that Tamal has substituted words. A court is likely to conclude that Tamal's intention to revoke the original gift was conditional on the substitution being able to take effect. As the substitution is not effective, the original gift will take effect (provided it is possible to discover what the original gift was).

Summary

- A testator with testamentary capacity is free to revoke their will at any time.
- There are three methods of revocation:
  - by a later will or codicil
  - by destruction
  - by marriage/formation of a civil partnership.
- A codicil is a document, executed in the same way as a will which can be used to amend, add to or revoke in part, an existing will.
- A codicil republishes the original will.
- Where testators make wills as the result of a clear agreement as to the disposal of their estates and part of that agreement is that the survivor will not revoke their will, the doctrine of mutual wills may apply to impose a trust over the survivor's estate.
- Alterations made before a will was executed are valid provided that the testator intended the alterations to form part of the will.
- Alterations made after a will was executed will be valid if the alterations were executed like a will.
- Where an invalid alteration has been made, the original wording of the will stands provided that it is apparent.
- An alteration which obliterates the original wording revokes the original wording by destruction, provided that the act of destruction is accompanied by the intention to revoke.
- The court may be prepared to apply the conditional revocation rule (dependant relative revocation) where the testator obliterates the original wording and adds some substitute wording.

Sample questions

Question 1

A man wrote out a will as follows:

> 'I make this will in the hope that I will soon be married, so I leave everything to my wife and declare this will to be irrevocable whatever may happen in the future.'

The will is validly executed.

A year later the man met a woman and, after a whirlwind romance, they were married. However, the marriage did not last and the couple are now divorced.

Is the will valid?

A Yes, because it was made in contemplation of marriage.

B Yes, but the gift to the wife fails as a result of the divorce.

C Yes, because the testator declared the will to be irrevocable.

D No, because the will was revoked by the subsequent divorce.

E No, because the will was revoked by marriage.

Answer

Option E is correct. A will is revoked by marriage.

Option A is wrong because in order to be saved from revocation the will must be made in contemplation of marriage to a particular person. A general expectation or hope of marriage is not sufficient.

Option B is wrong because, although the option sets out the usual effect of divorce on a gift in a will, on the facts this will had already been revoked.

Option C is wrong because a general declaration that a will is irrevocable is of no effect.

Option D is wrong because divorce does not revoke a will.

Question 2

A testator made a valid will two years ago leaving everything to his son and appointing him as his executor. Last month the testator had an argument with his son and decided that he would disinherit him. Following the argument, the testator asked his neighbour to come to his house. The testator tore up the original will into tiny pieces in front of his neighbour and said: 'That good for nothing son of mine will not get a penny of my money. You are my witness.'

The testator died suddenly last week, before he had a chance to make another will, and was survived by his son and three daughters.

The testator's son has found a copy of the will in the testator's personal files and wants to know whether he will inherit his father's assets under the will.

Which of the following best describes the position in relation to the will?

A The will was not revoked when it was torn up in front of the neighbour because two witnesses would be needed for an effective revocation.

B The will was revoked when it was torn up in front of the neighbour because physical destruction of a will in front of one witness is sufficient to revoke a will.

C The will was revoked when it was torn up in front of the neighbour because physical destruction of a will with the intention to revoke is sufficient to revoke a will.

D Notwithstanding the fact that the will was torn up into tiny pieces, if its contents can be reconstructed from a copy then an order may be obtained allowing its admission to probate as a valid will.

E The will was not revoked as the testator did not make another valid will before he died.

Answer

Option C is correct as revocation of a will can be done by 'burning, tearing or otherwise destroying the same by the testator ... with the intention of revoking the same'. The will was deliberately destroyed and there was an intention to revoke on the facts.

Option A is wrong as there is no need for witnesses for the physical destruction of a will.

Option B is wrong as there is no formal requirement for witnesses although the neighbour will be able to provide evidence in relation to the testator's intention to revoke.

Option D is wrong as the reconstruction of a destroyed will is possible if it had been done by mistake or by accident but this is not the case here.

Option E is wrong as the doctrine of dependent relative revocation does not appear to apply on the facts.

Question 3

A testator died last month. His validly executed will contained the following legacy:

£40,000

'I give ~~£20,000~~ to my grandson.'

No one can remember when the legacy was altered, but the testator's initials appear in the margin adjacent to it. The testator had only one grandson and he survived the testator. The will left the rest of the estate to charity.

Which of the following best explains the grandson's entitlement under the legacy?

A He is entitled to nothing because the alteration is presumed to have been made after execution.

B He is entitled to £20,000 because the original wording is apparent.

C He is entitled to nothing because the legacy has been revoked.

D He is entitled to £40,000 because the alteration has been validly attested.

E He is entitled to nothing because the testator did not write his full signature.

Answer

Option B is correct. The alteration is presumed to have been made after execution. The alteration is invalid as it has not been properly attested, but as the original wording is apparent it will stand.

Option A is wrong. Although there is a presumption that an alteration was made after execution, this does not result in the beneficiary receiving nothing where, as here, the original wording is apparent.

Option C is wrong because revocation of the legacy would require obliteration of the original wording.

Option D is wrong because valid attestation requires the signatures (or initials) of the testator and two witnesses.

Option E is wrong. The use of a full signature would make no difference (initials are sufficient). The alteration has not been validly attested because of the absence of witnesses, but this does not result in the beneficiary receiving nothing – see comment on Option B above.

4 Intestacy

SQE1 syllabus

This chapter will enable you to achieve the SQE1 assessment specification in relation to functioning legal knowledge concerned with wills and the administration of estates.

- The validity of a will and interpretation of the contents of a will.
- The planning, management and progression of the administration of an estate.
- The law and practice relating to personal representatives and trustees in the administration of estates and consequent trusts. The rights, powers and remedies of beneficiaries of wills and consequent trusts.
- The distribution of testate, intestate and partially intestate estates.
- Section 46 Administration of Estates Act 1925.
- The statutory trusts.
- Property passing outside the estate.

Note that for SQE1, candidates are not usually required to recall specific case names or cite statutory or regulatory authorities. However, in this chapter the rules of distribution on intestacy, namely s 46 Administration of Estates Act 1925, may be referred to in the SQE1 assessments. Otherwise, in this chapter references to cases and statutory authorities are provided for illustrative purposes only.

Learning outcomes

By the end of this chapter you will be able to apply relevant core legal principles and rules appropriately and effectively, at the level of a competent newly qualified solicitor in practice, to realistic client-based and ethical problems and situations in the following areas:

- the circumstances which give rise to intestacy; and
- the distribution of the estate on intestacy.

4.1 Introduction

A survey in 2023 found that half the adults in the UK have not made a will. This may seem a surprising statistic given the advantages to be gained by making a will. However, people fail to make wills for a variety of reasons mostly revolving around ignorance of the consequences of not doing so, an unwillingness to contemplate their own death and/or simple apathy. If an individual fails to make provision for what is to happen to their estate when they die, statute does it for them in the form of the intestacy rules.

This chapter looks at:

- the operation of the intestacy rules;
- the statutory trust;
- overview of the rules of distribution;
- distribution where there is a surviving spouse or civil partner and issue;
- distribution where there is a surviving spouse or civil partner but no issue;
- distribution where there is no surviving spouse or civil partner;
- adopted children;
- illegitimate children; and
- Human Fertilisation and Embryology Act 2008.

4.2 The operation of the intestacy rules

The intestacy rules contained in the Administration of Estates Act 1925 (AEA 1925) apply to determine who is entitled to an individual's property when they die without having disposed of it by will.

The intestacy rules operate in three situations:

- Where there is no will either because the deceased never made a will at all or all wills have been successfully revoked (see **3.2**) (total intestacy).
- Where there is a will, but for some reason it is invalid (see **1.4**) or it is valid but fails to dispose of any of the deceased's estate (total intestacy).
- Where there is a valid will, but it fails to dispose of all the deceased's estate (partial intestacy). This will occur if the will simply omitted a gift of residue or if a residuary gift fails, for example because the residuary beneficiary has predeceased. In a partial intestacy the intestacy rules only apply to that part of the estate not disposed of by the will.

The intestacy rules apply to every intestacy and are mandatory. It is not possible to make any kind of provision or declaration to exclude specific people from inheriting under the rules. The only way for an individual to avoid the rules is to make a will. There are situations in which the rules can be displaced but these arise in very limited circumstances, such as by an order made under the Inheritance (Provision for Family and Dependants) Act 1975 (see **Chapter 7**).

The intestacy rules apply only to property which is capable of being left by will (see **1.2**).

Example

Sheree dies intestate, survived by her husband, Isaac, and their two children. Sheree and Isaac owned their house as beneficial joint tenants. Sheree had taken out a life assurance policy for £100,000 which is written in trust for the children, and she owned investments worth £150,000. The intestacy rules do not affect Sheree's share of the house (which passes to Isaac by survivorship) or the life policy (which passes to the children under the terms of the trust). Only the investments pass under the intestacy rules.

4.3 The statutory trust

The intestacy rules impose a trust over all the property (real and personal) in respect of which a person dies intestate (s 33 AEA 1925). That property is held on trust by the person(s) dealing with the estate - the personal representative(s) or PRs. This trust is similar to the usual express trust found in a will (see **Chapter 5**) and includes a power of sale.

The trust provides that the PRs must pay the funeral, testamentary and administration expenses (such as legal fees and any tax), and any debts of the deceased. If necessary, the PRs can sell assets from the estate in order to raise cash to pay these debts and expenses. The balance remaining (after setting aside a fund to meet any pecuniary legacies left by the deceased in the will) is the 'residuary estate' to be shared among the family under the rules of distribution set out in s 46 AEA 1925.

Although the PRs have a power of sale, they are not required to sell the assets which form the residuary estate. The PRs have power under s 41 AEA 1925 to appropriate assets in or towards satisfaction of a beneficiary's share (with the beneficiary's consent).

4.4 Overview of the rules of distribution

Although there have been intestacy laws in this country for centuries, the current regime is a product of the major revision of property law carried out by the government in the early twentieth century. It was generally accepted that the law at that time was unsatisfactory and inconsistent. In order to decide what should replace it, the government made a survey of wills to see who, on average, those who had made wills at that time had decided to leave their estate to - the 'average will'. The survey revealed that, on average, people left their estates to their family members, with the main beneficiary being the spouse. The new law was designed to reflect the 'average' will, or to put it another way the new law was based on the presumed intention of the deceased designed to effect the will which the deceased would have made if they had thought about it. The new law was incorporated into the AEA 1925. Although there have been some subsequent changes to the legislation, the essential framework remains.

In essence under the intestacy rules the estate will usually pass to the intestate's family. At first sight, this would seem appropriate. However, the division of assets between the various family members is to a large extent arbitrary. Whilst the deceased's family will benefit, their friends or favourite charities will not. The term 'family' is restricted and excludes, for example, an unmarried partner, however long the relationship.

The PRs must distribute the residuary estate in accordance with the order set out in s 46 AEA 1925. As in 1925, the primary beneficiary is a surviving spouse, but precisely who gets what is determined by the relationships the intestate had during their lifetime and the family members who survive.

4.5 Distribution where there is a surviving spouse or civil partner and issue

4.5.1 Meaning of spouse/civil partner

Under the intestacy rules, 'spouse' means the person the deceased was married to at the time of their death. For the purpose of the rules all that matters is the fact of being legally married. All spouses are treated equally, so the nature or 'quality' of the relationship is irrelevant; the couple may be living apart or, indeed, have new partners and yet still come within the definition. In *Re Park* [1954] P 89 the definition of spouse was satisfied because the couple were still legally married, irrespective of the fact that their relationship only lasted 17 days.

A former spouse is excluded from the definition, but only from the point when the divorce is actually finalised and the marriage is legally at an end.

Re Seaford [1968] P 53

The divorce case had already reached the stage of the court confirming that the wife had satisfied all the requirements to obtain a divorce. The wife's solicitors then applied to the court for the divorce to be finalised. The court order finalising the divorce was made at 10 am on 6 July. At about 11.30 am the same day, the husband was found dead in bed, having died as a result of an overdose of sleeping tablets. Medical evidence, which the judge accepted, was that the time of death could not be later than 4 am on 6 July. Therefore, the marriage had still been in existence at the time of death. Accordingly, it was held the definition of spouse was satisfied and so the wife was entitled under the intestacy rules.

In some instances, a couple may purport to enter into a marriage which is in fact void as a matter of law, for example because one party is already married or under-age. Such a marriage is said to be void ab initio (from the beginning) and is treated in law as if it had never taken place. This means that a party to a void marriage is not a spouse for the purposes of the intestacy rules.

Shaw v Shaw [1954] 2 QB 429

When the couple met, Mr Shaw said he was a widower. He proposed and they were then married. Fourteen years later Mr Shaw died intestate. It was only then that 'Mrs Shaw' discovered that for the first 12 of those years his first wife had still been alive. Consequently, the marriage was void because Mr Shaw was already married. As 'Mrs Shaw' was not his spouse she was not entitled to anything under the intestacy rules.

Some marriages are voidable (for example, because one party entered into the marriage under duress or was suffering from certain forms of mental disability). A voidable marriage is valid until such time until the court makes a nullity order. Just as in divorce, a party to a voidable marriage is a spouse for the purposes of the intestacy rules until the order is actually made.

Spouses and civil partners are treated in exactly the same way under the intestacy rules. A civil partner means the person the deceased was in a civil partnership with at the time of their death. The rules outlined above are equally applicable to civil partners.

Given that for the purpose of the rules all that matters is the fact of being legally married (or in a civil partnership), it follows that a cohabitant has no entitlement under the intestacy rules. If the intestate was living with someone outside marriage, they do not feature in the rules of distribution and have no entitlement, even if the relationship was long-standing.

4.5.2 Meaning of issue

The term 'issue' includes all direct descendants of the deceased: ie children, grandchildren, great grandchildren, etc. Adopted children (and remoter descendants) are included, as are those whose parents were not married at the time of their birth (see **4.9**). Descendants of the deceased's spouse or civil partner ('step' children) are not issue of the deceased unless adopted.

4.5.3 Entitlement

Where the intestate is survived by both spouse or civil partner and issue, the 'residuary estate' (as defined in **4.3**) is distributed as follows:

(a) The spouse or civil partner receives the personal chattels absolutely. 'Personal chattels' are defined in s 55(1)(x) of the AEA 1925 as tangible moveable property, other than any such property which–

(i) consists of money or securities for money, or

(ii) was used at the death of the intestate solely or mainly for business purposes, or

(iii) was held at the death of the intestate solely as an investment.

(b) In addition, the spouse or civil partner receives a 'statutory legacy' free of tax and costs plus interest from death until payment. The rate of interest payable is the Bank of England rate that had effect at the end of the day on which the intestate died. The 'statutory legacy' is a set amount fixed by Parliament and for deaths on or after 26 July 2023 is £322,000. If the residuary estate, apart from the personal chattels, is worth less than £322,000, the spouse receives it all (in a partial intestacy the spouse does not have to account for anything received under the will).

(c) The rest of the residuary estate (if any) is divided in half. One half is held on trust for the spouse or civil partner absolutely. The other half is held for the issue on the statutory trusts (see **4.5.5**).

The intestate's spouse or civil partner must survive the intestate for 28 days in order to inherit. If the intestate's spouse or civil partner dies within 28 days of the intestate, the estate is distributed as if the spouse or civil partner has not survived the intestate.

4.5.4 The family home

In many cases spouses or civil partners will hold their family home as beneficial joint tenants. An interest in a property held as beneficial joint tenant passes (outside the intestacy rules) by survivorship. However, if the family home is held in the intestate's sole name or as tenants in common, the intestate's interest in the home will form part of the residuary estate and therefore subject to the intestacy rules. Under the rules, the family home will not automatically pass to the surviving spouse/civil partner.

If the family home forms part of the residuary estate passing on intestacy, the surviving spouse/civil partner can require the PRs to appropriate the family home in full or partial satisfaction of their interest in the estate. In order to exercise this right, the spouse/civil partner must be living in the property. If, for example, the surviving spouse's entitlement under the intestacy rules amounts to £500,000 and the residuary estate includes the family home worth £300,000 (held in the intestate's sole name), the surviving spouse can require the home to be transferred to them in part satisfaction of their entitlement.

If the property is worth more than the entitlement of the spouse or civil partner, the spouse/civil partner may still require appropriation provided they pay the difference, 'equality money', to the estate.

The surviving spouse/civil partner must formally elect to exercise this right and notify the PRs in writing within 12 months of the grant of representation (see **Chapter 8**).

4.5.5 Applying the statutory trusts

That part of the estate which does not pass to the surviving spouse passes to the intestate's issue on 'the statutory trusts'. The statutory trusts determine membership of the class of beneficiaries, and the terms on which they take, as follows (s 47 AEA 1925):

(a) The primary beneficiaries are the children of the intestate who are living at the intestate's death. Remoter issue are not included, unless a child has died before the intestate.

(b) The interests of the children are contingent upon attaining the age of 18 or marrying or forming a civil partnership under that age. Any child who fulfils the contingency at the intestate's death takes a vested interest.

(c) If any child of the intestate predeceased the intestate, any children of the deceased child (grandchildren of the deceased) who are living at the intestate's death take their deceased parent's share equally between them, contingently upon attaining 18 or earlier marriage or formation of a civil partnership. Great grandchildren would be included only if their parent had also predeceased the intestate. This form of substitution and division, whereby each branch of the family receives an equal share, rather than each member receiving an equal share, is known as a '*per stirpes*' distribution.

(d) If children or issue survive the intestate but die without attaining a vested interest, their interest would normally fail and the estate distributed as if they had never existed. However, by virtue of an amendment to s 47 AEA 1925, if they die without attaining a vested interest but leaving issue, they will be treated as having predeceased the intestate so that they can be replaced by their own issue. To be substituted, the issue must be living at the intestate's death.

Example

Joanne dies intestate survived by her husband, Kenneth, and their children, Mark (aged 20, who has a son, Quentin) and Nina (aged 16). Their daughter, Lisa, died last year. Lisa's two children, Oliver and Paul (aged 6 and 4), are living at Joanne's death.

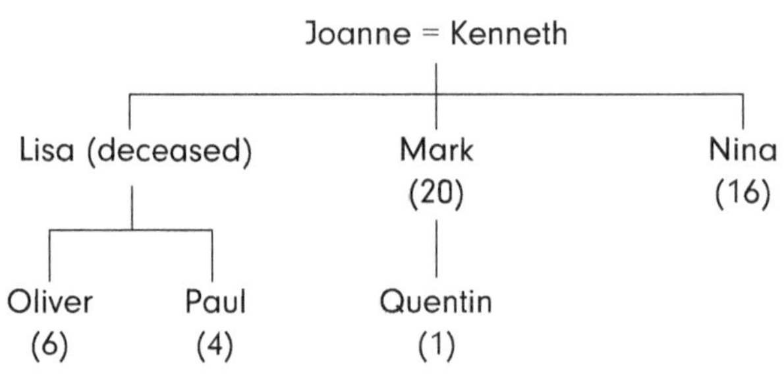

Joanne's estate consists of her share in her home, held as beneficial joint tenants with Kenneth, and other assets worth £642,000 after payment of debts, funeral and testamentary expenses. This figure includes personal chattels worth £20,000.

Distribution

Joanne's share in the house passes to Kenneth by survivorship. The rest of her estate passes on intestacy.

£	
20,000	personal chattels to Kenneth
322,000	statutory legacy to Kenneth

The remaining £300,000 is divided in half.

150,000	for Kenneth absolutely
150,000	for the issue on the statutory trusts
642,000	

The statutory trusts apply to determine the distribution between Joanne's issue as follows.

Mark and Nina, Joanne's children, are living at her death and take one share each. The share Lisa would have taken had she survived is held for her children, Oliver and Paul, in equal shares. The interests of Nina, Oliver and Paul are contingent upon attaining 18 or earlier marriage or formation of a civil partnership.

Therefore, Mark has a vested interest in one-third of the issues' half. He is entitled to £50,000 on Joanne's death. If Mark should die shortly after Joanne, his share would form part of his estate on death. Quentin has no entitlement under Joanne's intestacy.

Nina has a contingent interest in one-third of the issues' half, which will vest when she is 18 or if she marries or forms a civil partnership before 18. If Nina should die under the age of 18 and without marrying or forming a civil partnership, her interest would fail. One half of Nina's share would pass to Mark and the other half would be held for Oliver and Paul equally. However, if Nina has a child who is living on Joanne's death, the child would take Nina's place.

Oliver and Paul have contingent interests in one-sixth of the issues' half, which will vest at 18 or earlier marriage or formation of a civil partnership. If Oliver should die under the age of 18 and without marrying or forming a civil partnership (or having an illegitimate child), his share would pass to Paul (and vice versa). If both Oliver and Paul were to die under the age of 18 and without marrying or forming a civil partnership (or having an illegitimate child), their shares would be divided equally between Mark and Nina (provided she reaches 18, marries or forms a civil partnership).

Note that with effect from February 2023 the minimum age for entering a marriage/civil partnership in England and Wales rose from 16 years to 18 years.

4.6 Distribution where there is a surviving spouse or civil partner, but no issue

Where the intestate leaves a surviving spouse or civil partner but no issue, the whole estate, however large, passes to the spouse or civil partner absolutely. Other relatives, such as parents, brothers and sisters, grandparents and cousins, are not entitled.

The spouse or civil partner must survive the intestate for 28 days in order to take. If the spouse or civil partner dies within that period, the estate is distributed as if the spouse or civil partner had not survived the intestate.

4.7 Distribution where there is no surviving spouse or civil partner

4.7.1 Entitlement

Where there is no surviving spouse or civil partner, or where the spouse or civil partner dies within 28 days of the intestate, the residuary estate is divided between the intestate's relatives in the highest category in the list below:

(a) issue on the 'statutory trusts', but if none,

(b) parents, equally if both alive, but if none,

(c) brothers and sisters of the whole blood on the 'statutory trusts', but if none,

(d) brothers and sisters of the half blood on the 'statutory trusts', but if none,

(e) grandparents, equally if more than one, but if none,

(f) uncles and aunts of the whole blood on the 'statutory trusts', but if none,

(g) uncles and aunts of the half blood on the 'statutory trusts', but if none,

(h) the Crown, Duchy of Lancaster, or Duke of Cornwall (bona vacantia).

The list works on an all or nothing basis. Working from the top, if anyone falls within the category, they will receive the whole of the entitlement (divided equally if there is more than one person in the category) and those in the next and lower categories receive nothing.

4.7.2 The statutory trusts

Each category other than parents and grandparents takes 'on the statutory trusts'. This means that members of the specified class categories take the estate equally (children under 18 take their interest contingently upon attaining 18 or marrying earlier), and that issue of a deceased relative may take that relative's share. (Again, a person with an interest under the statutory trusts who dies without attaining a vested interest but leaving issue, will be treated as having predeceased the intestate so that they can be replaced by their own issue. To be substituted, the issue must be living at the intestate's death.)

This means that relatives not mentioned in s 46 (eg nephews, nieces and cousins) may inherit on intestacy if their parents died before the intestate.

Example

Tom dies intestate. He was not married to his partner, Penny, although the couple have a son, Simon, aged 13, Tom's only child. Tom's parents predeceased him, but he is survived by his only sibling, his brother, Bob, aged 40.

Tom's estate is held on trust for Simon, contingently upon attaining 18 or marrying earlier. If Simon dies before the contingency is fulfilled, Tom's estate passes to Bob absolutely.

Example

Rose, a widow aged 80, is cared for by her step-daughter, Katya (the child of her deceased husband's first marriage). Her only living blood relatives are cousins, the children of her mother's brothers and sisters. Rose dies intestate. Her estate is divided 'per stirpes' between her cousins (and the children of any cousins who predeceased her). Katya receives nothing from Rose's estate.

4.7.3 Bona vacantia

Bona vacantia means vacant or ownerless goods and under ancient common law rights, property which did not have an owner could be taken by the feudal lord. This survives today in the form of the bona vacantia rule.

Where the intestate is not survived by any of the relatives provided for under the intestacy rules the estate passes bona vacantia. This means that the estate passes to the Crown (ie the government), or the Duchy of Lancaster (if the intestate lived in Lancashire) or Duchy of Cornwall (if the intestate lived in Cornwall).

Where an estate passes bona vacantia, the Crown (through the Treasury Solicitor), the Duchy of Lancaster or Duke of Cornwall has a discretion to provide for dependants of the intestate, or for other persons for whom the intestate might reasonably have been expected to make provision. That discretion could be exercised, for example, in favour of an individual who had a close relationship with the intestate, but no entitlement under the intestacy rules such as a step-child or a cohabitant. There is an overlap here with the Inheritance (Provision for Family and Dependants) Act 1975 (see **Chapter 7**) which allows qualifying individuals to apply to court for provision from an estate. The Treasury Solicitor's policy is to require proceedings to be brought under the Act if possible as this enables all potential claimants to be involved and their respective interests weighed.

In practice it is rare for an estate to be truly bona vacantia. Modern technology and methods of communication mean that genealogists are usually able to trace some relatives. However, where funds do pass bona vacantia, the Crown hands them over to the HM Treasury to be used in the same way as money collected through taxes; the Duchies of Lancaster and Cornwall pay the money into benevolent funds which provide grants for charitable purposes.

4.8 Adopted children

Adopted children are treated for intestacy purposes as the children of their adoptive parents and not of their natural parents. If a person who was adopted dies intestate without spouse or issue, their estate will be distributed between the closest relatives in the adoptive family. An adopted child may also inherit on the intestacy of any member of their adoptive family.

The operation of the statutory trusts means that is a common occurrence on an intestacy for a minor child to have a contingent interest in an estate. It may be that such a child is subsequently adopted and thereby loses all legal connections to their natural family. Nevertheless, any contingent interest which an adopted person had immediately before the adoption in the estate of a deceased natural parent is preserved. This is a statutory exception to the rule that adopted children are treated as the child of their adoptive parents. However, the exception is limited to parents, so an adopted child will still lose a contingent entitlement to the estate of other relatives.

4.9 Illegitimate children

The intestacy rules are applied regardless of whether or not a particular individual's parents were married to each other. However, on the intestacy of an individual whose parents were not married to each other, it is presumed that the individual has not been survived by their father or by any person related to them through their father unless the contrary is shown. This presumption avoids any necessity for the PRs to make enquiries where the identity or whereabouts of the father is unknown. The presumption does not apply where the father is named on the intestate child's birth certificate.

Example

Jessica, whose parents did not marry, dies intestate. Her only known relative is a half-brother, Frank. Frank is the child of the later marriage of Jessica's mother. Nothing is known of Jessica's father or any other children he may have had. Jessica's PRs may distribute her estate to Frank relying on the presumption.

4.10 Human Fertilisation and Embryology Act 2008

The Human Fertilisation and Embryology Act 2008 deals, inter alia, with the conferring of legal parenthood in respect of children born as a result of assisted reproduction. The detail of the legislation is beyond the scope of this manual, but in simple terms it provides:

- Section 33 – a child's mother is the woman who gave birth to the child.
- Section 35 – where the mother undergoes assisted reproduction using donated sperm, and she is in a heterosexual marriage at the time of the treatment, it is her husband who is the legal father of the child (unless he did not consent to the treatment).
- Section 42 – mirrors s 35 in relation to a same-sex marriage or civil partnership so that the mother's wife or civil partner is the child's other legal parent ('second female parent').
- Section 36 – where a mother undergoes treatment at a licensed clinic using donated sperm, she can give notice that for example, her male cohabitant is to be the legal father.
- Section 43 – mirrors s 36 in relation to same-sex couples.

A person treated as a parent under the Act is treated as such for all purposes (s 48). This means that under the intestacy rules a child will be entitled to their parent's estate as 'issue' or on the intestacy of a member of that parent's family, irrespective of whether there is any genetic connection between them.

The Act also deals with children born through surrogacy. Surrogacy is essentially an arrangement by which a woman, the surrogate, carries and gives birth to a child for someone else. Usually this is for a couple, the so-called 'commissioning parents', who, for some reason, are unable to have a child of their own. The commissioning parents are able to apply to court for a parental order. The effect of the order is to confer legal parenthood exclusively on the commissioning couple. Under the intestacy rules, like adoption, the child is treated as a child of the commissioning couple for all purposes.

Summary

- The intestacy rules apply to decide who is entitled to an individual's property when they die without having disposed of it by will.
- The rules apply in respect of a total or partial intestacy.
- The rules impose a statutory trust over the estate.
- Where the intestate is survived by a spouse and issue, the spouse receives:
    - personal chattels
    - the statutory legacy of £322,000
    - half the balance (the other half passes to the issue).
- Where the intestate is survived by a spouse but no issues, the spouse receives the entire estate.

- Where there is no surviving spouse the residuary estate is divided between the intestate's relatives in the highest category below:
  - issue
  - parents
  - brothers and sisters of the whole blood
  - brothers and sisters of the half blood
  - grandparents
  - uncles and aunts of the whole blood
  - uncles and aunts of the half blood
  - the Crown, Duchy of Lancaster, or Duke of Cornwall (bona vacantia).
- Beneficiaries other than a spouse, parents and grandparents take on the statutory trusts, meaning that:
  - members of a category share equally
  - the issue of a deceased relative may take that relative's share in substitution
  - entitlement is contingent upon attaining 18 or marrying/forming a civil partnership earlier.

Sample questions

Question 1

A man died last week without leaving a will. His estate comprising assets in his sole name, after debts, is valued at £800,000, including £5,000 personal chattels. He was survived by his wife, his son aged 25 years and his daughter aged 17 years. He also has two grandchildren: a granddaughter aged two years, who is the daughter of his surviving son, and a grandson aged six years. His grandson is the only child of the man's eldest child who died six months ago.

Which of the following best explains how the estate will be distributed?

A The man's wife will only receive the statutory legacy of £322,000 and the personal chattels.

B The man's son has an interest in the estate which is contingent.

C The man's grandson has an interest in the estate which is contingent.

D The man's granddaughter has an interest in the estate which is contingent.

E The man's wife will only be entitled if she survives her husband by 14 days.

Answer

Option C is correct. The deceased died intestate survived by spouse and issue, and with an estate worth more than the statutory legacy and so some of the estate passes to the issue on the statutory trusts: the son, daughter and the issue of the pre-deceased child (ie the grandson) share, contingent on reaching 18 years of age. The grandson is under 18.

Option A is wrong because the intestacy rules provide for the spouse in these circumstances to take the personal chattels plus the statutory legacy of £322,000 plus half of the remainder absolutely.

Option B is wrong as under the statutory trusts the son has reached 18 and has a vested interest.

Option D is wrong as the granddaughter will receive nothing as her father is still alive.

Option E is wrong as the spouse will be entitled provided she survives by 28 days.

Question 2

A woman died five weeks ago without having made a will. Her only living relatives are her civil partner and the woman's daughter (aged 19). At the time of her death the woman's only assets were £10,000 in a bank account in her sole name and her interest in the house she owned with her civil partner as tenants in common. The woman's interest in the house is worth £350,000 and she had no debts.

Which of the following best describes the entitlement to the woman's estate?

A The woman's civil partner is entitled to a total of £322,000 from the estate.

B The woman's civil partner can insist on receiving the deceased's interest in the house in satisfaction of her entitlement provided that she pays equality money to the estate.

C The woman's daughter is not entitled to anything from the estate.

D The woman's civil partner and her daughter are each entitled to half of the estate.

E The woman's daughter has a contingent interest in part of the woman's estate.

Answer

Option B is correct. The entire estate passes under the intestacy rules. Having survived 28 days the deceased's civil partner receives the statutory legacy of £322,000 plus half the balance (£19,000). The remaining £19,000 goes to the deceased's daughter. The deceased's civil partner can insist on receiving the deceased's share of the house as part of the entitlement. However, as this is worth more than the total entitlement the civil partner will have to pay equality money to the estate.

Option A is wrong as the civil partner receives the statutory legacy of £322,000 plus half the balance (£19,000).

Option C is wrong as the estate exceeds the value of the statutory legacy for the civil partner and so the daughter will take some of the estate.

Option D is wrong as the civil partner takes a statutory legacy and the daughter takes half of what is left after this.

Option E is wrong as the daughter has satisfied the contingency in the statutory trusts of reaching 18 years of age and so her interest is vested.

Question 3

A woman has recently died intestate, owning assets in her sole name worth £500,000, after debts. The woman was divorced and for the past eight years has been living with her boyfriend and his daughter (aged 12 years), by his previous relationship. Both the partner and his daughter survived the woman. The woman's father died five years ago but the woman is survived by both her mother and her sister (aged 35).

Who is entitled to take a share of the woman's estate?

A The boyfriend only.

B The boyfriend's daughter only.

C The sister only.

D The mother only.

E The mother and sister only.

Answer

Option D is correct. Under the intestacy rules in the absence of a surviving spouse and issue the estate passes to parents. There is a surviving mother so she takes the whole estate.

Option A is wrong as the boyfriend is not a surviving spouse or civil partner and not included in the order of entitlement.

Option B is wrong as the daughter is not issue of the intestate.

Option C is wrong as the sister comes after parents in the order of entitlement and there is a surviving parent.

Option E is wrong as the rules only provide for sharing between relatives in the same category.

5 Will Drafting

SQE1 syllabus

This chapter will enable you to achieve the SQE1 assessment specification in relation to functioning legal knowledge concerned with wills and the administration of estates.

- Personal representatives: the appointment of executors.
- The law and practice relating to personal representatives and trustees in the administration of estates and consequent trusts.
- Revocation of wills:
  - methods of revocation
  - effect of marriage of a testator
- The interpretation of wills:
  - effect of different types of gift
  - failure of gifts
- Burden and incidence of Inheritance Tax.
- Administration of estates:
  - duties of personal representatives

Note that for SQE1, candidates are not usually required to recall specific case names or cite statutory or regulatory authorities. However, in this chapter the powers contained in ss 31 and 32 Trustee Act 1925 and the SRA Code of Conduct for Solicitors, RELs and RFLs may be referred to in the SQE1 assessments. Otherwise, references to cases and statutory and regulatory authorities are for illustrative purposes only.

Learning outcomes

By the end of this chapter you will be able to apply relevant core legal principles and rules appropriately and effectively, at the level of a competent newly qualified solicitor in practice, to realistic client-based and ethical problems and situations in the following areas:

- common provisions in a will;
- the powers and duties of executors during the administration of an estate; and
- will trusts and the powers and duties of the trustees.

5.1 Introduction

It is important for people to make wills so that after they die, their assets and possessions will pass to the beneficiaries they choose. Even with a will, a testator's intentions may be thwarted by unexpected events such as ademption or the death of a beneficiary (**Chapter 2**). A solicitor drafting a will should anticipate these eventualities and take the testator's instructions on what should happen to the property. A gift in a will may turn out to be worth a lot less than originally expected due to the need to pay inheritance tax or a mortgage (see **Chapter 9**). A testator should think about which beneficiary should be responsible for these liabilities and include appropriate provisions in the will.

Making a will also gives the testator the opportunity to select people (executors) to carry out the administration of the estate. Statute confers various powers and duties on executors and personal representatives. The will may vary the statutory powers and duties in order to facilitate the administration of the estate. A will can create an ongoing trust, eg to manage property until young beneficiaries reach a specified age. In such cases, the will should appoint trustees and consideration should be given to the possibility of varying their statutory powers and duties.

This chapter looks at:

- structure of a will;
- opening;
- revocation clause;
- appointments;
- non-residuary gifts;
- gift of residue;
- survivorship clause;
- administrative provisions; and
- attestation clause.

5.2 Structure of a will

Most firms use will drafting templates or precedents for convenience. Consequently, professionally drafted wills usually follow a uniform structure reflected in the above list of the contents of this chapter.

The following example of a simple will follows the usual structure. The will is valid, but has some shortcomings in terms of its drafting and it will therefore be used as the basis for criticism in this chapter.

Sample will

This is the Last Will and Testament of me Finlay Brand of The Old Vicarage, Church Lane, Cambridge which I make this 12th day of April 2021.

1. I revoke all former wills, codicils and testamentary dispositions.
2. I wish my body to be cremated.
3. I appoint George Marston of 3 Station Road, Cambridge to be my executor.
4. I give the gold watch which I inherited from my father to my nephew James Brand.
5. I give £10,000 to the charity Cancer UK.
6. I give The Old Vicarage to Alison Peters.
7. I give all the rest of my property after deducting debts and legacies to my sister Megan Wilson.

Signed by Finlay Brand in our	)	*Finlay Brand*
joint presence and then by us in his	)	

Hannah James	*G. James*
Hannah James	George James
2 Varsity Common	2 Varsity Common
Cambridge	Cambridge
Accountant	Nurse

5.3 Opening

The main purpose of the opening is to identify the testator and the nature of the document. The full name and address of the testator should be stated.

The date should appear within the commencement or at the end of the will. It is advisable to date a will so that the chronology can be established for the purposes of revocation (see **3.2.1**). The will is dated at the time it is executed.

If the testator intends to marry in the near future, they should state that the will is made in expectation of that marriage and that they do not wish the marriage to revoke the will (see **3.2.3**). In the absence of such a statement the will is automatically revoked by subsequent marriage. Formation of a civil partnership has the same effect.

5.4 Revocation clause

The purpose of this clause (clause 1 of the sample will above) is to indicate that all earlier wills and codicils are expressly revoked (see **3.2.1**). It is important to include a revocation clause to avoid having to search for prior wills after the testator's death.

5.5 Appointments

5.5.1 Executors (and trustees)

In Clause 2 of the sample will, Finlay Brand appoints George Marston to be his executor. One of the benefits of making a will is that the testator can choose who will be responsible for dealing with his estate.

(a) Trustees

The sample will did not create a trust and therefore, there was no need to appoint trustees as well as executors. It is sometimes sensible to create an express trust of the estate (see **5.7.2**). Where this happens, the testator should appoint persons to be trustees. It is often convenient to name the same people as both executors and trustees, although it is not essential. Such people will act as executors while they collect in the estate, pay debts and distribute the estate. When they have completed that stage, they will transfer the property that is to be held on trust to themselves to hold in the new capacity of trustee.

(b) Number of executors

In principle, there is no maximum number of executors that can be named in the will. However, there is little point in naming more than four because only a maximum of four can apply for the grant of probate to the same assets.

The minimum number is one, and this will often be sufficient for a small, simple estate where the executor is the sole or main beneficiary. (A sole executor can give a good receipt for the proceeds of sale of land held in the estate.) However, there is a risk that the sole executor may pre-decease the testator or be unable to act for some other reason. For example, if a testatrix appoints her husband to be executor but they subsequently divorce, the appointment will not have effect because it is treated as though the husband predeceased her (see **2.7.3**). It is therefore, prudent to appoint at least two executors, or name a substitute for a sole executor.

If the executors will also be trustees, it is sensible to appoint at least two so that they can give a good receipt for the proceeds of sale of any land held in the trust.

(c) Choice of executor

The testator may appoint any combination of:

- individuals who are not professionals (eg family or friends);
- solicitors or other professionals (as individuals or as a firm);
- banks or other trust corporations.

Non-professional individuals

Appointing family members or close friends whom the testator can trust will have the advantage of ensuring that persons familiar with the testator and their affairs will deal with the estate. A further advantage is that such persons are unlikely to want to charge the estate for their time spent in dealing with it. However, this advantage may be more apparent than real. If the estate is other than straightforward, it is likely that the individuals will lack the expertise necessary to complete the administration and will have to employ a solicitor. The costs of this will be paid from the estate.

Solicitors or other professionals

A solicitor or other professional will have the necessary expertise to administer the estate. Family and friends will be spared the burden at a time when they may be grieving. However, the professional executor will expect to be paid not just for expenses incurred but also for the time spent doing the work.

An individual solicitor may be appointed, but there is a risk that this person may die or retire. To avoid this possibility the firm of solicitors can be appointed. If the firm is a general partnership (ie not an LLP), it has no legal personality and so the appointment should be of the partners in the named firm. As these will change from time to time it is important to specify that it is the partners in the firm at the date of death who are appointed. Otherwise, the appointment will be of those at the date of the will and they may die or retire before the testator's death. It is usual to express the wish that only two partners will take the grant and act in the administration. It is also sensible to provide for the possibility of the firm changing its name, amalgamating or become a limited liability partnership (LLP) between the date of the will and the date of death. Usually the testator will indicate that the appointment is of the partners in the new or amalgamated firm or the members of the LLP.

Banks or other trust corporations

A testator may consider appointing a bank as executor. Most high-street banks have a trustee department, and it is able to act via the mechanism of a trust corporation. Appointing this type of executor has some similar advantages to appointing a firm of solicitors: the corporation will not die or retire, and there should be financial and some legal expertise. Disadvantages include the fact that the corporation may seem large and impersonal to the family. The charging methods of banks may also be disadvantageous, as they usually charge a percentage of the value of the estate, which can be a significant expense.

(d) Charging provisions

The rule of equity that a trustee may not profit from their trust applies both to trustees and executors. Its effect is that an executor or trustee can recover only out-of-pocket expenses from the estate or trust fund but cannot be remunerated for time spent in performing their office unless expressly authorised.

The Trustee Act 2000 made some changes to the general rule as it applies to the remuneration of so-called 'professional' trustees. Trustees act in a professional capacity if they act in the course of a profession or business which includes the provision of services in connection with the management or administration of trusts. Under s 29, professional trustees are entitled to receive reasonable remuneration for all services, even if they are services which are capable of being provided by a lay person. However, a professional trustee can only charge for their services if each other trustee has agreed in writing that they may be remunerated for the services. This means that a sole trustee will be unable to charge in reliance on s 29 and a co-trustee will be able to do so only with the permission of all co-trustees.

Wills often contain a charging clause which is an express authorisation for the professional executors/trustees to charge for their services. Such a clause commonly appears at the start of the will along with the clause appointing the executors/trustees, or it may be included together with other administrative provisions towards the end. Including an express clause is desirable in case s 29 cannot be relied upon for some reason, eg where the other appointed executors have died leaving a sole executor/trustee.

5.5.2 Guardians

Where the testator or testatrix has infant children, they should include a clause in the will appointing guardians to look after the children after the death of both parents.

5.6 Non-residuary gifts

5.6.1 Pecuniary legacies

This is a gift of money, eg clause 5 of the sample will.

5.6.2 Specific legacies

The sample will includes specific gifts in clauses 4 and 6, ie gifts of specific assets which the testator (or testatrix) owns. Strictly speaking, clause 4 is a specific 'legacy' (a gift of personalty) and clause 6 is a specific 'devise' (a gift of land). However, the term 'legacy' or 'gift' is often used for both.

If the testator does not own the specific asset at death, the gift fails ('adeems') (see **2.7.4**). The beneficiary gets nothing in place of the gifted item unless the will expressly provides for substitution. Ademption is a particular problem with legacies of shares in a named company (what will happen if the company changes its name or is taken over?) or a legacy of 'my house' or 'my car' which might be sold and replaced before death. The gift in clause 6 of the sample will would adeem if the Old Vicarage were sold before Finlay's death. The risk of ademption could have been avoided by wording the clause in a different way. For example, the will could have used more general wording such as a gift of 'my main residence at the date of my death'. This gift would not adeem if Finlay were to sell The Old Vicarage and purchase a replacement residence before his death.

The testator may leave a gift of a collection of items to several people inviting them to select an item from the estate. For example, the testator may give 'my paintings to Alice, Ben and Carl to be divided between them as they shall agree'. To prevent argument, the testator should indicate the order of choosing or provide for a means of resolving any dispute. It is normal to provide that the decision of the executors will be final. It is also wise to require the selection to be done within a time-limit to avoid delays in the administration.

5.6.3 The beneficiary

(a) Identification

Beneficiaries must be clearly identified in the will; otherwise the gift will fail for uncertainty. Accurately stating the name and address is important, and including the relationship to the testator will also help (see **2.6**).

(b) Vested and contingent gifts

Where testators wish to benefit persons who may be minors, or relatively young, they should consider whether they want to make outright or contingent gifts.

A vested gift imposes no conditions, and the beneficiary will be immediately entitled to it merely by outliving the testator. For example, 'I give £10,000 to my grandson, Oliver'. If Oliver is over 18 years of age at his grandfather's death, he receives his gift straight away. If he is under 18, the £10,000 will be held on trust for Oliver until his eighteenth birthday. Unless the will provides otherwise, his parents or guardians can give a good receipt and will hold as trustees for Oliver until his eighteenth birthday. If he dies under age 18, the money forms part of his estate.

A contingent gift imposes conditions to be satisfied before the gift can vest. The most common contingency is to require the beneficiary to reach a certain age, for example where the testator wants to give £10,000 to his grandson, Oliver, provided he reaches the age of 25. The will should appoint trustees to hold on an express trust for Oliver. Oliver will be entitled to the £10,000 only if he reaches 25. If he is under 25 when his grandfather dies, the money will be held on trust until he reaches 25. If he were to die under age 25, his estate would not be entitled to the cash, which would instead pass to the person(s) expressed to be entitled in default or, if none, with the residue of his grandfather's estate.

(c) Lapse

A beneficiary who predeceases the testator is not able to take a legacy. The legacy will normally fail or 'lapse' and will pass with residue unless the will provides for a substitute beneficiary. There are some limited exceptions (such as s 33 Wills Act 1837 – see **2.7.5**) but it is usual to include an express substitutional gift if the testator does not want the lapsed legacy to pass as part of residue.

(d) Gifts to charities

It is important to identify the charitable body accurately. This was not done in the charitable legacy in clause 5 of the sample will. To avoid argument later, the solicitor should include the address and registered charity number of the body for identification.

Some charities are run as unincorporated associations (effectively a group of people joined together with a common purpose, but, unlike a company, the association does not have separate legal personality). An issue to consider is how the executors will obtain a receipt from the charity for the gift. Without express provision stating otherwise, all members of an unincorporated association would have to sign a receipt. To avoid this, it is normal to authorise the executors to accept the receipt of an authorised officer of the charity. The clause should provide that the receipt of the person who appears to be the treasurer or other proper officer of the organisation will be sufficient. This avoids the need for the executors to check the constitution of the body to establish the identity of the proper officers.

A further problem to consider is that the charitable body may dissolve, amalgamate or change its objects before the date of death. It is useful to state that the gift is to the body 'for its general charitable purposes'. This may help establish that the gift has not failed, because those purposes can continue to be performed by another organisation, or help establish that the testator had general charitable intention and so allow the gift to be applied to a similar charity.

5.6.4 Burden of inheritance tax, costs and charges

- **Inheritance tax ('IHT')**

If the deceased's estate is large enough, IHT will be payable on the value of the estate (see **Chapter 6**). Suppose that Finlay Brand has died. The IHT on Finlay's estate is £20,000. The Old Vicarage is worth half the value of the estate and therefore accounts for half the IHT bill (namely £10,000). Which beneficiary should bear the burden of the IHT payable on The Old Vicarage? Should it be paid by Alison, the beneficiary who gets The Old Vicarage? This may mean that Alison cannot afford to keep the property. The default position is that the IHT on the individual legacies is paid out of the residuary estate (see **9.7**). In this case, the residuary beneficiary, Megan, would get £10,000 less as a result of IHT on The Old Vicarage being paid. However, the will can displace the general rule by exhibiting a contrary intention.

Examples

- *I give The Old Vicarage to Alison Peters.*

The existing clause in the sample will is silent on which beneficiary bears the burden of IHT attributable to The Old Vicarage. The general rule applies and it will be paid out of residue.

- *I give The Old Vicarage to Alison Peters* subject to tax.

The words 'subject to tax' vary the general rule. Alison bears the burden of IHT attributable to The Old Vicarage. She will have to pay £10,000.

- *I give The Old Vicarage to Alison Peters* free of tax.

  The words 'free of tax' confirm the general rule that the IHT attributable to The Old Vicarage falls on residue.

  For clarity, legacies (such as clauses 4 and 6 of the sample will) should indicate whether they are 'free of' or 'subject to' tax.

- **Costs**

There may be costs associated with the packing or transport of a specific gift. Unless the will provides otherwise, the beneficiary will bear these costs. The testator should consider if these costs will be too great for the beneficiary and if so provide that the gift is free of these costs. If such words are included, the costs will be paid from the residue of the estate.

- **Charges**

Specific devises of land give rise to a further consideration: is the property mortgaged and, if so, who will bear the burden of paying off the mortgage debt? In relation to the sample will, Finlay may have taken out a mortgage loan secured on The Old Vicarage. Does Alison inherit the mortgage debt as well as the property? Under s 35 Administration of Estates Act 1925, the mortgage debt falls on the beneficiary who receives the charged property (in this case Alison) unless the will contains a contrary direction (see **9.7**). If a testator does not want the beneficiary of the charged property to take on the mortgage debt, the devise should be expressed to be 'free of mortgage'; this will cast the burden of the mortgage debt on to residue. Thus, if the legacy had been, 'I give The Old Vicarage to Alison Peters free of mortgage', the mortgage would be paid out of residue and Megan would receive the balance.

5.7 Gift of the residue

It is important that the will contains a gift of the residue and that care is taken to ensure that it does not fail, as the result would be a partial intestacy.

5.7.1 Direction for the payment of debts and legacies

There should be an express direction for the payment of all debts, expenses and legacies to be made from the residue before it is distributed to the beneficiaries. In the absence of such a direction, the statutory order set out in the AEA 1925 will apply, and this can lead to problems (see **9.7** and **9.8**). The gift of residue in the sample will contains the direction:

> I give all the rest of my property *after deducting debts and legacies* to my sister Megan Wilson.

A further example would be:

> *Subject to the payment of my debts, funeral and testamentary expenses and legacies*, I give all my estate not otherwise disposed of to such of my brothers and sisters as may be living at my death and if more than one in equal shares.

5.7.2 Is a trust required?

Where the residue is passing outright to adult (or charitable) beneficiaries, there is no need for an express trust. However, it is not unusual to create a trust of the residue in these circumstances as it does no harm.

In family wills, common express trusts are:

- contingent trusts, conditional on the beneficiaries attaining a specified age;
- discretionary trusts (where the trustees select who, from a class of beneficiaries, is to benefit, and how much each will receive, eg 'on trust for such of my children and in such shares as my trustee shall select'); and
- trusts with successive interests, such as a trust to pay the income to the testator's or testatrix's spouse for life, remainder to the children.

Example

A contingent trust of residue

'I give all the rest of my estate not otherwise disposed of by my will to my Trustees upon trust to pay my debts, funeral and testamentary expenses and legacies and to hold the balance ('my Residuary Estate') on trust for such of my children as attain the age of 25 years and if more than one, in equal shares absolutely. If any child of mine dies before me or before attaining a vested interest, leaving children who shall attain the age of 25 years, those children shall take the share of the Trust Fund that their parent would have taken under this clause in equal shares absolutely.'

5.7.3 Avoiding partial intestacy

If a gift of residue fails, the property will pass under the intestacy rules (see **Chapter 4)**. The testator may be happy with this, but it is preferable to include substitutional gifts to cover the possibility of the primary gift failing. For example, where the residue is left to the testator's niece, there could be an express substitution of her children if she predeceases the testator. It is also worth considering a 'longstop' beneficiary to inherit if all the intended arrangements fail. The longstop beneficiary is often a charity because there is little possibility of such a gift failing.

A gift of the residue to more than one person also raises some drafting issues. For example, assume that the testator has three children, and wishes to leave them an equal share. He could leave one-third to each named child. This carries risks. He may have more children before he dies who will be excluded. Also any or all of the children may predecease him. If this were to happen, s 33 Wills Act 1837 would provide for the failed one-third share to pass to any child of the dead child; but if there were none, the failed one-third share would pass on intestacy.

Therefore, it is wiser to omit names and specific shares in the residue, and refer only to any children the testator may have at the date of death. Using the phrase 'for *such of* my children as survive me and if more than one in equal shares' will ensure that there will be a partial intestacy only if all children predecease the testator. As a result of this provision, should one child predecease the testator, the deceased child's share would pass to the other children. It is usual to further provide that if the deceased child leaves their own children, they take their parent's share. The example of the contingent trust in **5.7.2** uses this formula.

Example

*The testator's will includes a gift of residue in the same terms as the example in **5.7.2**. The testator is survived by two children, Gillian and Harry. The testator's third child, Iris, died before him. If Iris had children of her own who are living at the testator's death, they take Iris's third share contingent on attaining the age of 25. If Iris had no children, her share passes to Gillian and Harry.*

Contrast a gift of residue 'to Gillian, Harry and Iris equally'. In this case, Iris's share would lapse (unless saved by s 33 Wills Act 1837) and it would pass on partial intestacy.

5.8 Survivorship clause

Unless a will states otherwise, a beneficiary only has to be alive at the death of the testator to acquire a vested interest. This may have an unfortunate effect where the beneficiary dies a very short time after the testator. This can happen where, for example, members of the same family are involved in a common accident. Were this to happen, the testator's property would pass in accordance with the will or intestacy provisions of the deceased beneficiary (and possibly to a person the testator would not have wanted to inherit).

Example

Tarala leaves property to her married son. She dies and he dies a week later. He leaves everything to his wife.

Tarala's property will pass to her son's estate and then under his will to his wife. Tarala might well have preferred her assets to pass to beneficiaries of her own choice rather than to her son's wife.

There will also be the burden and expense of the property being part of the administration of two different estates. To give the testator more control over the destination of their property, a survivorship clause may be used as in the following example.

Example

'I give £50,000 to my son, James, if he survives by 28 days, but if he does not so survive me, then to my sister Rose.'

Alternatively, there may be a general declaration that a survivorship period is to apply to all gifts in the will, as set out below:

Example

'Any beneficiary who does not survive me by 28 days shall be treated as having died before me.'

In practice, it would also be necessary to consider the inheritance tax consequences of including, or not including, a survivorship clause but this is beyond the scope of this manual.

5.9 Administrative provisions

Personal representatives (PRs) and trustees have a number of statutory administration powers. The Administration of Estates Act ('AEA') 1925 gives certain powers to PRs and the Trustee Act ('TA') 1925 and Trustee Act ('TA') 2000 give powers to both trustees and PRs. However, it is usual to include clauses in wills extending or modifying some of these statutory powers where they are not regarded as sufficient. Even where the statutory powers are adequate, it is common to repeat them in the will so that the testator, PRs and trustees can see all the powers in one place.

A will which might give rise to a trust (for example, because there is a substitutional gift to children of a primary beneficiary who predeceases the testator) will benefit from the inclusion of extensive express administrative provisions. However, even a simple will leaving everything to adults or to a charity will benefit from some express provisions.

The administrative provisions below have been divided into those that should be considered for inclusion in any will irrespective of whether or not it might give rise to a trust, and those which should be considered only if a trust might arise.

5.9.1 Powers to include in all wills

(a) Power to charge

If the testator wishes to give the executors (and trustees) power to charge remuneration, the power can either be included as part of the appointment clause or with the other administrative provisions (see **5.5.1**). When drafting such a clause it is important to be clear whether a person engaged in *any* profession or business can charge for time spent on the administration (for example, a brain surgeon) or whether *only* a person whose profession involves administering estates and trusts can charge (for example, a solicitor or accountant).

(b) Extended power to appropriate assets without consent of legatee

Section 41 AEA 1925 gives PRs the power to appropriate any assets in the estate in or towards satisfaction of any legacy or any interest in residue provided that the appropriation does not prejudice any beneficiary of a specific legacy. For example, if the will gives a pecuniary legacy to a beneficiary, the PRs may allow that beneficiary to take chattels or other assets in the estate up to the value of their legacy, provided that these assets have not been specifically bequeathed by the will. Section 41 provides that the legatee to whom the assets are appropriated (or their parent or guardian if they are a minor) must consent to the appropriation.

It is common to remove the need for the legatee's consent. This provision is commonly included in order to relieve the PRs of the duty to obtain formal consent. Nevertheless, the PRs would informally consult the beneficiaries concerned.

(c) Power to insure assets

PRs have a duty to preserve the value of the estate. Section 19 TA 1925 gives PRs and trustees power to insure assets against all risks, to the full value of the property, and to pay premiums out of income or capital.

It is not necessary to amend the statutory provision. However, including an express provision makes life easier for lay PRs who will be able to see from the will itself exactly what they can do.

(d) Power to accept receipts from or on behalf of minors

Under the general law, an infant cannot give a good receipt for a legacy or share of the estate. However, the Children Act 1989 allows parents and guardians to give a good receipt to PRs on the infant's behalf.

There are often tensions within families and a testator or testatrix may not be happy for a parent or guardian to give a good receipt for a legacy. In such a case, the will should be drafted to leave a legacy to trustees to hold for the benefit of the minor rather than to the child directly. Alternatively, the will may include a clause allowing the PRs to accept the receipt of the child if the child is over 16 years old. The provision may be incorporated into the legacy itself or may be included in a list of powers in the will.

(e) Self-dealing

The fiduciary position of PRs and trustees prevents them from entering into any transaction where their duties and personal self-interest conflict. For example, purchasing property, which is part of the estate or the trust, would breach their fiduciary duty. An express clause in the will may permit self-dealing by the trustees. One situation where it is important to include such a clause is where the executors or trustees are also beneficiaries.

5.9.2 Powers to include for trustees

(a) Power to appropriate assets

Section 41 of AEA 1925 does not apply to trustees. It is necessary to include an express provision, equivalent to s 41, to permit the trustees to appropriate trust property towards beneficial interests arising under the trust without obtaining the consent of the beneficiary.

(b) The power to invest

Under the general law, trustees have a duty to invest trust money. The TA 2000, s 3 gives trustees a 'general power of investment' enabling them to invest as if they were absolutely entitled to the trust property themselves. This wide power excludes investment in land, other than by mortgage, but the purchase of land is permitted by s 8. In exercising the investment power, trustees are required to take proper advice and to review investments of the trust from time to time. They must have regard to the standard investment criteria, namely the suitability to the trust of any particular investment and to the need for diversification of investments of the trust.

An express investment clause can be included but is no longer necessary in most estates.

Trustees may want to delegate the management of trust investments to a financial adviser or stockbroker. The TA 2000 permits delegation. The trustee must appoint the delegate in writing and give them a written policy document setting out investment objectives and restrictions on the choice of investments. They must review the delegate's work and the policy statement from time to time.

For more detail on delegation and the trustees' investment powers, please see the **Trusts** manual.

(c) Power to purchase land

The TA 2000, s 8 gives trustees power to acquire freehold or leasehold land in the UK for 'investment, for occupation by a beneficiary or for any other reason'. When exercising their power, the trustees are given 'all the powers of an absolute owner in relation to the land'.

The statutory power does not authorise the purchase of land abroad, nor does it allow trustees to purchase an interest in land with someone else (eg a beneficiary). An express power will be needed if the trustees are to have such powers.

(d) Power to sell personalty

Trustees holding land in their trust have the power to sell it under their powers of an absolute owner under TA 2000 (see (c) above). However, there is some doubt whether trustees who hold no land and where there is no express trust for sale have power to sell personalty. For this reason, some wills may continue to impose an express trust for sale over residue. The alternative solution is to include power in the will (among the administrative provisions), giving the trustees express power to sell personalty.

(f) Power to use income for maintenance of beneficiaries

Where trustees are holding a fund for a minor beneficiary, s 31 TA 1925 gives them power to use income they receive for the minor's maintenance, education or benefit. They must accumulate any income not so used. Section 31 also requires that where a beneficiary is aged 18, the trustees have a duty to pay future income received from that beneficiary's share of the fund to that beneficiary. If the testator thinks that the age of 18 is too young to receive trust income, the will can postpone the beneficiary's right to income until a greater age.

Example

Anton's will gave his residuary estate to trustees to hold on trust for his children if they should attain the age of 25. Anton has died. He is survived by two children: Dora, who is now aged 14, and Charles, who is now aged 19.

Under s 31 TA 1925, the trustees have the power to pay all or part of Dora's share of trust income to her parent or guardian or 'otherwise apply' it for her maintenance, education or benefit. This could include paying bills (eg school fees) directly. They must accumulate any income not so applied. Dora cannot compel the trustees to use the income for her benefit because they have an absolute discretion.

As far as Charles is concerned, the trustees must pay his share of trust income to him because he is over the age of 18. However, one should check the will because it could remove Charles' right to income from the age of 18. The following is an example of a clause which would postpone Charles' right to income until he is 21; the trustees' discretion to pay or apply income for maintenance, or to accumulate any surplus would continue until Charles' 21st birthday.

'Section 31 of the Trustee Act 1925 shall apply to the income of my estate as if the age of 21 years were substituted for all references to the age of 18 wherever they occur in section 31 (references to 'infancy' being construed accordingly).'

Section 31 is covered in more detail in the **Trusts** manual.

(g) Power to use capital for the advancement of beneficiaries

Section 32 TA 1925 allows trustees in certain circumstances to give a beneficiary a payment of trust capital sooner than they would receive it under the basic provisions of the trust. There are many reasons why beneficiaries might want part of their entitlement early, such as needing help to pay university fees or to fund a deposit on the purchase of a house. The power applies only to beneficiaries who have an interest in trust capital.

Examples

The deceased's will creates a trust for 'my children if they attain the age of 21'. The deceased's son, Charles, is 18 and would like some money from the trust to help with university expenses. The trustees could make an advancement of capital to Charles because he has an interest in the trust capital.

A will creates a trust for the deceased's widow, Sarah, for life, remainder to his son, Paul. The trustees do not have the power to make an advancement under s 32 to Sarah because she does not have an interest in capital (her interest is in income). The trustees could make an advancement to Paul (because he has an interest in trust capital) but s 32 provides that they would need to obtain Sarah's written consent because she is a beneficiary with a prior interest.

Section 32 confers an absolute discretion on the trustees; therefore, the beneficiaries cannot compel them to make an advancement. For detail on the other conditions for advancements, please refer to the **Trusts** manual.

Before the Inheritance and Trustees' Powers Act 2014 came into force, advancements were restricted to one-half of the beneficiary's share of capital. This was usually extended to the whole share by a clause in the will. This common amendment was reflected in the 2014 Act – for will trusts created on a testator's death on or after 1 October 2014, trustees can make an advancement of the whole of a beneficiary's share of capital.

Where the trust creates a life interest, it is common to extend s 32 TA 1925 to permit trustees to make advancements of capital to the life tenant.

Example

Miriam is making her will; she wants to leave her estate on trust for her husband for life, remainder to her children. However, she is concerned that the trust income may not be sufficient for her husband's needs. To address this concern, the will could extend s 32 by including the following express powers for trustees in the will:

- *Power to pay or apply capital money from my residuary estate to any extent to or for the benefit of the Life Tenant.*
- *Power to advance capital money from my residuary estate to the Life Tenant by way of loan to any extent upon such terms and conditions as my Trustees may in their absolute discretion think fit.*

These provisions would permit the trustees to give or lend capital from the trust fund to the life tenant even though he has an interest only in income, not capital. Such a clause will give more flexibility to supplement the life tenant's income but the life tenant would be dependent on the discretion of the trustees.

(h) Control of trustees by beneficiaries

Section 19 of the Trusts of Land and Appointment of Trustees Act ('TLATA') 1996 provides that, where beneficiaries are *sui juris* (aged 18 or more with full capacity) and together entitled to the whole fund, they may direct the trustees to retire and appoint new trustees of the beneficiaries' choice. This means that in a case where the beneficiaries could by agreement end the trust under the rule in *Saunders v Vautier* (1841) 4 Beav 115, they now have the option of allowing the trust to continue with trustees of their own choice. The provision may be expressly excluded by the testator. If, under the terms of the trust, the position could arise where all the beneficiaries are in existence and aged over 18 but the trust has not ended, the testator may wish to prevent the beneficiaries from choosing their own trustees.

(i) Trusts of land

The TLATA 1996 gives special powers (see below) to a beneficiary under a trust of land who has an interest in possession. If, under the terms of the will, a trust of land with an interest in possession could arise, the will may amend those powers. The Act does not define 'interest in possession', so it presumably has its usual meaning; beneficiaries have an interest in possession if they are entitled to claim the income of the fund as it arises (normally either because they have a life interest, or because they are over 18 and entitled to claim income under the TA 1925, s 31).

Duty to consult beneficiaries

Trustees exercising any function relating to the land must consult any beneficiary who is of full age and beneficially entitled to an interest in possession in the land and, so far as consistent with the 'general interest of the trust', give effect to the wishes of any such beneficiary (s 11 TLATA 1996). The duty to consult may be excluded by the will and often is.

Beneficiary's rights of occupation

A beneficiary with a beneficial interest in possession, even if not of full age, has the right to occupy land subject to the trust if the purposes of the trust include making the land available for occupation by him, or if the trustees acquired the land in order to make it so available (s 12 TLATA 1996). There is no power to exclude s 12, but a declaration that the purpose of the trust is not for the occupation of land may be included in the will.

(j) Power to carry on the testator's business

Where an estate includes a business which was run by the deceased as a sole (unincorporated) trader, the powers of the PRs to run the business are limited. For example, they may only run the business with a view to selling it as a going concern and may use only those assets employed in the business at the date of death. These powers may be extended by will, although in practice PRs are unlikely to wish to involve themselves in the detailed running of a business. It may be preferable to bequeath the business by specific legacy and to appoint the legatee as a special PR of the business. It is possible to appoint an executor and limit their powers to a particular asset in the estate.

5.10 Attestation clause

All wills should contain an attestation clause reciting that the formalities required by Wills Act 1837, s 9 have been complied with (see **1.7**). The s 9 formalities require the testator to sign or acknowledge their signature in the presence of two witnesses present at the same time and the witnesses to afterwards sign (or acknowledge their signatures) in the presence of the testator. An attestation clause (such as that set out in the example below) raises a presumption of due execution.

Example

Signed by me [testator's name]

in our joint presence and then by us in [his/hers]

The attestation clause will have to be adapted if the execution of the will did not follow the standard procedure (eg if the will was signed by someone other than the testator in the testator's presence and by their direction).

5.11 Professional conduct

Solicitors drafting wills should be aware of relevant issues of professional conduct (see **Ethics and Professional Conduct**). For example, they must comply with Principles 4, 5 and 7 and act with honesty, integrity and in the best interests of clients.

5.11.1 Taking instructions from a third party

Paragraph 3.1 of the SRA Code of Conduct for Solicitors, RELs and RFLs requires:

> You only act for clients on instructions from the client, or from someone properly authorised to provide instructions on their behalf.

The wording obviously provides for the possibility of third party instructions in some circumstances. However, in the case of a will, the dangers of misunderstanding or deceit are obvious. Solicitors should not take instructions from anyone but the client for the drafting of a will. It would not be in the best interests of the client to take instructions from an intermediary.

5.11.2 Legacies to the solicitor drafting the will

Paragraph 6.1 of the SRA Code of Conduct for Solicitors, RELs and RFLs requires:

> You do not act if there is an own interest conflict or a significant risk of such a conflict.

There is obviously the potential for such a conflict where the testator wishes to benefit the solicitor. Solicitors should not prepare a will giving significant amounts to themselves, their spouses, civil partners or family members unless the client has obtained independent advice.

The SRA guidance, 'Drafting and preparation of wills', states:

> If you draft a will where the client wishes to make a gift of significant value to you or a member of your family, or an employee of your business or their family, you should satisfy yourself that the client has first taken independent legal advice with regard to making the gift.
>
> This includes situations where the intended gift is of significant value in relation to the size of the client's overall estate, but also where the gift is of significant value in itself. Paragraph 6.1 of each of the Codes requires you not to act if there is an own interest conflict or a significant risk of an own interest conflict. In a situation like this, you will usually need to cease acting if the client does not agree to taking independent legal advice.
>
> There may be some exceptions where you can continue to draft the will even if the client has not received independent legal advice; for example, if you draft wills for your parents and the surviving parent wishes to leave the residuary estate to you and your siblings in equal shares.

However, whether it is appropriate to do so will depend upon the specific circumstances of each situation, and in each case you should consider whether your ability to advise, and be seen to advise, impartially is undermined by any financial interest or personal relationship which you have.

5.11.3 Appointment of the solicitor as executor

It is common for testators to ask the solicitor drafting the will to appoint themselves to act as executor. This gives rise to a potential 'own interest conflict' because the solicitor will charge remuneration for acting as executor.

The SRA guidance, 'Drafting and preparation of wills', states:

> you must not exploit a client's lack of knowledge by leading them to believe that appointing a solicitor as an executor is essential or that it is the default position for someone making a will.
>
> Principle 7 of the Principles requires you to act in the best interests of each client. In this context this means not encouraging clients to appoint you or the business you work for as their executor unless it is clearly in their best interests to do so.
>
> In some cases it might be beneficial for a client to appoint a solicitor to act as an executor - for example, if their affairs are complex, or there are potential disputes in the family. However, in other cases there may be little or no advantage to the client - for example, if their estate is small or straightforward. A professional executor is likely to be more expensive than a lay person and the client should be advised about this.
>
> Before drafting a will which appoints you or your business (or someone else in the business) as the executor(s), you should be satisfied that the client has made their decision on a fully informed basis. This includes:
>
> • explaining the options available to the client regarding their choice of executor;
>
> • ensuring the client understands that an executor does not have to be a professional person or a business, that they could instead be a family member or a beneficiary under the will, and that lay executors can subsequently instruct a solicitor to act for them if this proves necessary (and can be indemnified out of the estate for the solicitors' fees);
>
> • recording advice that is given concerning the appointment of executors and the client's decision.

Summary

All wills contain certain common elements: opening words to identify the document, revocation of previous wills, appointment of executors (and trustees, if necessary), legacies (if required), the gift of residue, administrative powers, attestation clause and the date.

Appointment of executors

- How many?
- Appoint trustees as well if the will creates a trust
- Consider the need for a charging clause

Pecuniary legacies

- Burden of IHT

Specific legacies

- Prevent ademption?
- Burden of costs, IHT and any charges

Gift of residue

- Include a direction for payment of debts, funeral and testamentary expenses and legacies
- Is a trust required?
- Substitutional gifts are very important to avoid a partial intestacy

Beneficiaries

- Infants (Receipts clause? Vested or contingent?)
- Substitutional gift to prevent lapse?
- Charities (Identification, receipts and provision for amalgamation etc)
- Survivorship clause if testator and beneficiaries could be involved in a common accident

Attestation clause

Key statutory/express powers where there is no trust

- Charging clause
- Power to appropriate assets without the beneficiary's consent
- Power to insure
- Receipts (infant beneficiaries and charities)
- Self-dealing

Key statutory/express powers where there is a trust

- Power to appropriate assets without the beneficiary's consent
- Power to invest
- Power to purchase land
- Power to sell personalty
- Power to use trust income
- Power to make advancements of trust capital
- Clauses limiting control by beneficiaries
- Special provisions if the trust may include land or the testator's business

Sample questions

Question 1

A woman died last week. In her valid will, she gave her daughter 'the property which at my death constitutes my main residence' and she gave the residue of her estate to her son. At the date of the will, the woman owned 4 Church Mews. Before she died, she sold 4 Church Mews and bought Oak Cottage. Oak Cottage was the woman's main residence at the time of her death. The will was silent on the burden of inheritance tax ('IHT') and any mortgage on the residence.

Which of the following best describes the daughter's entitlement under the will?

A The daughter is not entitled to anything under the will because the gift of 4 Church Mews has lapsed.

B The daughter is not entitled to anything under the will because the gift of 4 Church Mews has adeemed.

C The daughter is entitled to Oak Cottage but will take it subject to IHT and any mortgage.

D The daughter is entitled to Oak Cottage and will take it free from IHT and any mortgage.

E The daughter is entitled to Oak Cottage and will take it free from IHT but subject to any mortgage.

Answer

Option E is correct.

The legacy of the house does not fail by ademption because Oak Cottage fulfils the description of 'the property which at my death constitutes my main residence'. Where the will is silent, the legatee takes the property free of IHT (which is borne by the residuary beneficiary) but subject to any charge (s 35 AEA 1925).

Option A is wrong. Lapse refers to the situation where a beneficiary predeceases the testator, which did not happen here.

Option B is wrong because the legacy was not of the residence owned at the date of the will. The wording of the gift prevents ademption unless the testatrix owned no residence at all when she died.

Option C is wrong because where the will is silent, legatees take their legacies free of IHT (it is borne by residue).

Option D is wrong because, where the will is silent, the legatee takes the property subject to any charge (s 35 AEA 1925).

Question 2

A man died last week. In his valid will, he left the residue of his estate to

'such of my children who are living at my death, and if more than one equally, PROVIDED that if any child of mine shall die before me leaving a child or children living at their death such child or children shall provided they attain the age of 18 take by substitution and if more than one in equal shares the share of my Residuary Estate which their parent would have taken had they survived me'.

The man was survived by a son, aged 30, who has no children. The man's daughter predeceased him, leaving two infant children.

Who is entitled to the residue of the man's estate?

A The son and the daughter's estate are each entitled to half of the residue.

B The son is entitled to the whole of the residue.

C The son is entitled to half of the residue. The daughter's children have vested interests in the other half of the residue.

D The son is entitled to half of the residue. The daughter's children have contingent interests in the other half of the residue.

E The son is entitled to half of the residue. The other half of the residue will pass on the man's intestacy.

Answer

Option D is correct. There is a substitutional gift for a predeceased beneficiary's share of residue. It will pass to the predeceased beneficiary's children. The interests of the daughter's children are contingent on their attaining the age of 18, and they have not done so yet because the facts say that they are infants.

Option A is wrong. The substitutional gift does not provide for the daughter's estate to take her share of the residue. This would mean that her share would pass under her will or intestacy.

Option B is wrong. The wording of the substitutional gift would only allow the son to take the daughter's share if she had no children.

Option C is wrong because, as explained above, the interests of the daughter's children are contingent.

Option E is wrong. The substitutional gift has prevented a partial intestacy.

Question 3

A woman died six months ago. She appointed her brother and sister to be her executors, left each of them £10,000 in her will and gave the residue of her estate to her partner. The will did not vary the executors' powers.

In place of the cash legacy, the brother would prefer to take one of the woman's public company shareholdings (now worth £10,000 but likely to increase in value in the near future).

Which of the following best describes the advice that should be given to the brother?

A The statutory power for executors to appropriate assets instead of a cash legacy would apply provided the woman's partner consents.

B There is no power for executors to appropriate assets to pecuniary legatees.

C The statutory power for executors to appropriate assets instead of a cash legacy would apply but, in this case, it would be a breach of the brother's fiduciary duty.

D The statutory power for executors to make advancements of capital would apply to allow the brother to give himself the shares instead of the cash legacy.

E The legacy to the brother is void because executors cannot be beneficiaries.

Answer

Option C is correct. Section 41 AEA 1925 gives PRs the power to appropriate any assets in the estate in or towards satisfaction of any legacy. However, as an executor, the appropriation would give rise to a conflict of interest, which would be a breach of the brother's fiduciary duties.

Option A is wrong. Section 41 AEA 1925 requires only the consent of the beneficiary to whom the PR is appropriating.

Option B is wrong. Section 41 has not been excluded by the will.

Option D is wrong because this is not an advancement (the payment of trust capital to a beneficiary earlier than they would otherwise be entitled).

Option E is wrong because executors (unlike witnesses) can be beneficiaries.

6 Inheritance Tax

SQE1 syllabus

This chapter will enable you to achieve the SQE1 assessment specification in relation to functioning legal knowledge concerned with wills and the administration of estates.

- The law and practice of inheritance tax in the context of lifetime gifts and transfers on death.
- Lifetime chargeable transfers.
- Potentially exempt transfers.
- Transfers on death.
- Exemptions and reliefs.
- The scope of anti-avoidance provisions.

Note that for SQE1, candidates are not usually required to recall specific case names or cite statutory or regulatory authorities. Cases are provided for illustrative purposes only.

Learning outcomes

By the end of this chapter you will be able to apply relevant core legal principles and rules appropriately and effectively, at the level of a competent newly qualified solicitor in practice, to realistic client-based and ethical problems and situations in the following areas:

- transactions which incur inheritance tax;
- inheritance tax payable on death and on lifetime transfers;
- exemptions and reliefs; and
- liability and burden of inheritance tax.

6.1 Introduction

When a person dies it is usually the case that, regardless of the way the estate passes, there will be tax consequences to consider. This chapter looks at the main tax which applies on death - Inheritance Tax (IHT). The basic aim of IHT is to impose a tax liability on estates at the time of death, so that, in effect, an individual is taxed on all the money and assets they have acquired over time. However, in order prevent tax being avoided by, for example, the individual divesting themselves of assets before they die, IHT also applies to certain transfers made during life.

This chapter looks at:

- the charge to tax;
- the main charging provisions;
- transfers on death;
- potentially exempt transfers;
- lifetime chargeable transfers;
- the effect of death on lifetime transfers;
- liability and burden;
- time for payment; and
- anti-avoidance.

6.2 The charge to tax

IHT is governed principally by the Inheritance Tax Act 1984 (IHTA 1984). As indicated above, despite its name, the tax does not apply only to death estates but can also catch transfers made during life.

There are three main occasions when IHT may be charged:

(a) Death

IHT is intended primarily to take effect on death and aims at levying a tax on the wealth that a person has acquired over their lifetime. When an individual dies, IHT is charged on the value of their estate (broadly, their assets less their liabilities) subject to various exemptions and reliefs.

(b) Lifetime gifts made to individuals within seven years prior to death

If IHT were limited to a charge on death, one way to avoid tax would be for an individual to reduce the size of their estate by making lifetime gifts; IHT is therefore also charged on certain lifetime gifts or 'transfers' if the donor dies within seven years after making them. Such gifts to individuals are called 'potentially exempt transfers', because at the time when the transfer is made no IHT is chargeable; the transfer is 'potentially exempt'. If the transferor survives for seven years, the transfer becomes exempt. If the transferor dies within that period, the transfer becomes chargeable.

(c) Lifetime gifts to a company or into a trust.

IHT might also be avoided by the use of a trust or corporate entity. A lifetime gift to a company or into a trust is immediately chargeable to IHT at the time when it is made, unless the trust is for a disabled person.

6.3 The main charging provisions

IHT is charged on 'the value transferred by a chargeable transfer' (although 'gift' is a convenient shorthand). The term 'chargeable transfer' is defined as 'a transfer of value which is made by an individual but is not an exempt transfer' (ss 1 and 2 IHTA 1984).

This charge may apply in any of the three situations outlined in **6.2**, because the term 'chargeable transfer' may refer to:

(a) the transfer on death; or

(b) a lifetime transfer which is potentially exempt when it is made but becomes chargeable because the transferor dies within seven years; or

(c) a lifetime transfer which is immediately chargeable at the time when it is made.

In each case, the method by which tax is calculated is broadly similar and may be approached by applying a sequence of logical steps.

Step 1: Identify the transfer of value

A lifetime transfer of value is any disposition which reduces the value of the transferor's estate. A gift of an asset reduces the value of the transferor's estate, whereas a sale at market value will simply exchange the asset for cash and so there will be no reduction. On death, tax is charged as if the deceased had made a transfer of value of their estate.

Step 2: Find the value transferred

For a lifetime transfer, this is the amount of the reduction in the transferor's estate.

On death, it is the value of the estate.

Step 3: Apply any relevant exemptions and reliefs

Various exemptions and reliefs exist for public policy reasons which can reduce or eliminate the IHT charge on any given transfer.

Some exemptions apply both to lifetime transfers and to the transfer on death (eg transfers to a spouse or civil partner). Others are more restricted, and many apply only to lifetime transfers (eg the annual exemption).

The main reliefs are business and agricultural property relief, which may apply both to lifetime transfers of such property and to the transfer on death.

Step 4: Calculate tax at the appropriate rate

Rates of tax

A range of tax rates apply to IHT, the lowest being zero per cent. There are two bands for which this is relevant:

(a) the nil rate band (£325,000 for 2025/26 and frozen until 2029/30) – available for all transfers of value (see **6.4.4.1**);

(b) the residence nil rate band (£175,000 for 2025/26 and frozen until 2029/30) – available only on a transfer on death where there is a 'qualifying residential interest' (see **6.4.4.2**).

The rate of tax that applies in excess of the nil rate band and the residence nil rate band (where applicable) varies according to the type of transfer (details are given in context below).

Cumulation

The nil rate band will not necessarily be available in full (or at all) for any given transfer. In order to calculate the available nil rate band on any transfer, whether during lifetime or on death, it is necessary to first look back over the seven years immediately preceding the transfer. Any chargeable transfers made by the transferor during that period must be taken into account in order to determine how much of the nil rate band remains available. This process is known as 'cumulation' and is used solely to calculate whether the nil rate band is available for any chargeable transfer. (In practice it may be necessary consider the level of the nil rate band available at the time the transfer was made, but, for ease of reference, any mention of the nil rate band in the examples in this chapter assumes that the band has always been £325,000.)

As the residence nil rate band is not available for lifetime transfers, it will be available in full on death, subject to any adjustments in relation to estates over £2 million (see **6.4.4.2**).

6.4 Transfers on death

For a transfer on death the steps outlined at **6.3** apply as follows:

6.4.1 Step 1: Identify the transfer of value

When a person dies, they are treated for IHT purposes as having made a transfer of value immediately before their death, ie there is a deemed transfer of value. The value transferred is the value of the deceased's 'estate' immediately before death.

6.4.1.1 Definition of 'estate'

A person's estate is defined as all the property to which the deceased was beneficially entitled immediately before their death, with the exception of 'excluded property' (s 5(1) IHTA 1984).

Property included within this definition falls into three categories:

(a) Property which passes under the deceased's will or on intestacy.

The deceased was 'beneficially entitled' to all such property immediately before death.

(b) Property to which the deceased was 'beneficially entitled' immediately before death but which does not pass under by will or on intestacy.

This applies to the deceased's interest in any joint property passing on death by survivorship to the surviving joint tenant(s). In most cases, the deceased will be taken to have owned an equal share in the property with the other joint tenant(s).

(c) Property included because of special statutory provisions.

By statute, the deceased is treated as having been 'beneficially entitled' to certain types of property which would otherwise fall outside the definition. These rules apply to

(i) certain trust property; and

(ii) property given away by the deceased during lifetime but which is 'subject to a reservation' at the time of death.

These categories are explained further below.

6.4.1.2 Property included in the estate by statute

Trust property

In certain circumstances, a person who is entitled to the income from a trust is treated for IHT purposes as 'beneficially entitled' to the capital which produces that income. This means that where a beneficiary who is entitled to all the income from such a trust dies, the trust fund is taxed as if it were part of the beneficiary's estate.

The type of beneficial interest covered by these provisions is known as a 'qualifying interest in possession'. To be an interest in possession, it must be an interest under which the beneficiary is entitled to claim the income from the trust property (or enjoy trust property in some equivalent way, such as living in it) with no power on the part of the trustees to decide whether or not the beneficiary should receive it. An interest in possession arising before 22 March 2006 will be a qualifying interest in possession. The rules changed on that date and where an interest in possession arises on or after 22 March 2006, it will only be a qualifying interest in possession in limited circumstances. The main example is where the interest is an 'immediate post-death interest' (IPDI). An IPDI is, broadly, an interest in possession arising on the death of the settlor under their will or intestacy.

Example

Gina died in January 2021. In her will, she left all her estate to her executors/trustees, Tom and Tessa, on trust to pay the income to Gina's son, Simon, for life with remainder to Rose absolutely. Both Simon and Rose are over 18 years old.

Tom and Tessa must invest the property to produce income. Simon is entitled to the income during his life. Tom and Tessa must pay it to him. Thus Simon, the life tenant, has an interest in possession.

When Simon dies, his rights under the trust cease. Under the terms of the trust instrument (Gina's will), Rose is now entitled to the trust fund, and Tom and Tessa must transfer all the trust property to her.

For IHT purposes, Simon had a qualifying interest in possession by virtue of it being an IPDI. Although he was entitled only to the income from the trust property and had no control over the disposition of the fund on his death, he is treated for tax purposes as 'beneficially entitled' to the whole trust fund. The fund is taxed on his death as part of his estate. The tax on the trust property will be paid from the trust fund.

Property subject to a reservation

This rule is designed to prevent people avoiding tax by parting with ownership of property but continuing to enjoy the benefit. The rule applies where the deceased gave away property during their lifetime but did not transfer 'possession and enjoyment' of the property to the donee or was not entirely excluded from enjoying the property. If property is subject to a reservation at the time of the donor's death, the donor is treated as being 'beneficially entitled' to the property.

Example

In 2017, Daumaa gave her jewellery, worth £100,000, to her daughter Effat, but retained possession of it. Daumaa dies in 2025, when the jewellery (still in her possession) is worth £120,000. Although the jewellery belongs to Effat, tax is charged on Daumaa's death as if she were still beneficially entitled to it. The jewellery, valued at £120,000, is taxed as part of Duamaa's estate. The tax on the jewellery will be borne by Effat.

6.4.1.3 Property outside the estate for IHT purposes

The definition of 'estate' turns on whether the deceased was (or was deemed to be) beneficially interested in property immediately before death. Therefore, property in which the deceased did not have such an interest falls outside the definition. Two common examples of property outside the definition are a life assurance policy once it is written in trust for a named beneficiary (because the proceeds are no longer payable to the deceased's estate) and a discretionary lump sum payment made from a pension fund to the deceased's family (because the pension trustees are not obliged to pay it to the deceased's estate).

6.4.1.4 Excluded property

Certain property which would otherwise be included in the estate for IHT purposes is defined in IHTA 1984 as 'excluded property'. Excluded property is not part of the estate for IHT purposes. One example of excluded property is a 'reversionary interest'. For IHT purposes this means a future interest under a settlement, for example an interest in remainder under a trust, created before 22 March 2006.

Example

In 2005, Faith created a settlement placing £500,000 on trust for Guy for life, remainder to Hazel absolutely. Whilst both Guy and Hazel are alive, Guy has a qualifying interest in possession and Hazel has a reversionary interest (that is excluded property).

6.4.2 Step 2: Find the value transferred

Having established which assets fall within the death estate it is then necessary to attribute a value to each of them.

6.4.2.1 Basic valuation principle

Assets in the estate are valued for IHT purposes at 'the price which the property might reasonably be expected to fetch if sold in the open market' immediately before the death (s 160 IHTA 1984).

This means that the value immediately before death of every asset forming part of the estate must be assessed and reported to HMRC. Some assets, such as bank and building society accounts, are easy to value. Others, such as shares in a private company, may be more difficult. Negotiations may be required with HMRC in order to reach an agreed valuation.

To allow for the difficulty in selling a share of jointly owned land, its value may be discounted (unless the related property rules apply - see **6.5.2**). The discount applied is normally up to 10% for commercial property and 15% for residential property, although a higher percentage may be allowed if the share in the property is very small.

The value of an asset agreed for IHT purposes is known as the 'probate value'.

6.4.2.2 Modification of the basic valuation principle

Section 171 IHTA 1984 provides that, where the death causes the value of an asset in the estate to increase or decrease, that change in value should be taken into account.

Example

Buchi has insured his life for £50,000. The benefit of the policy belongs to him (ie the policy is not written in trust). Immediately before Buchi's death, the value of the policy to him is its 'surrender value' (ie the value if he surrendered his rights back to the insurance company in return for a payment). This will be considerably less than its maturity value of £50,000. The effect of Buchi's death on the value of the policy is taken into account: its value for IHT purposes is £50,000.

6.4.2.3 Valuing quoted shares

The value of quoted shares is taken from the Stock Exchange Daily Official List for the date of death (or the nearest trading day). The list quotes two prices. To value the shares for IHT, take one-quarter of the difference between the lower and higher price and add it to the lower price. So, for example, if at the date of death, the quoted price per share is 102p/106p, the value of each share for IHT is 103p.

6.4.2.4 Debts and expenses

Liabilities owed by the deceased at the time of death are deductible for IHT purposes provided that they were incurred for money or money's worth. Therefore, debts such as gas and telephone bills may be deducted. In addition, the deceased may not have paid enough income tax on the income they received before they died; this amount may also be deducted.

The deceased's reasonable funeral expenses are also deductible.

6.4.3 Step 3: Apply any relevant exemptions and reliefs

The main exemptions applicable on death depend on the identity of the beneficiary. Reliefs depend on the nature of the property in the estate.

6.4.3.1 Spouse or civil partner exemption

Section 18 IHTA 1984 provides:

> A transfer of value is an exempt transfer to the extent that the value transferred is attributable to property which becomes comprised in the estate of the transferor's spouse or civil partner.

Any property included in the estate for IHT purposes is exempt if it passes to the deceased's spouse or civil partner under the deceased's will or intestacy or, in the case of joint property, by survivorship. (But note that if the transferor is a long-term UK resident but the transferee is not, the level of the exemption is limited to £325,000. Alternatively, the transferee can elect to be treated as a long-term UK resident for IHT purposes and so receive the full exemption.)

The rule applicable to qualifying interest in possession trusts is that IHT is charged as if the person with the right to income owned the capital (see **6.4.2.1**). This rule applies for the purpose of spouse exemption, both on creation of the trust (whether by will or on intestacy) and on the death of a life tenant.

The exemption only applies to spouses and civil partners. It does not apply to cohabitants, however long the relationship.

Holland (Executors of Holland Deceased) v IRC [2003] STC (SCD) 43

In this case an unmarried couple had lived together for 31 years. The male partner died, leaving an estate of £640,000 which passed to the female partner under the terms of his will. The female partner argued that she should be treated as a spouse for the purposes of the exemption and not to do so would be a breach of her human rights under Article 8 and Article 14. However, the Special Commissioners were not prepared to interpret s 18 to include a cohabitant and said the different treatment between cohabitants and married couples was justified. The IHT payable on the death estate was £180,000.

6.4.3.2 Charity exemption

Section 23(1) IHTA 1984 provides:

> Transfers of value are exempt to the extent that the values transferred by them are attributable to property which is given to charities.

Any property forming part of the deceased's estate for IHT purposes which passes on death to charity is exempt. The exemption most commonly applies to property which passes to charity under the deceased's will. However, if the deceased had a life interest in trust property which passes under the terms of the trust to charity, the charity exemption applies.

A similar exemption applies to gifts to certain national bodies and bodies providing a public benefit, such as museums and art galleries, and to political parties.

When large charity gifts are made by the deceased, not only is the transfer itself exempt, but it may affect the tax rate on the rest of the death estate (see **6.4.4.1**).

6.4.3.3 Business property relief

Business property relief ('BPR') (sometimes referred to as 'Business relief') operates to reduce the value transferred by a transfer of value of relevant business property by a certain percentage. In the Autumn 2024 Budget, the government announced that changes will be made to the rates below so as to restrict the availability of BPR with effect from 6 April 2026 (the change will also apply to potentially exempt transfers (see **6.5**) made on or after 30 October 2024 where the testator dies after 6 April 2026).

Relevant business property

The relief only applies where the business is 'trading' in nature (as opposed to one dealing in investments or land). The amount of relief given depends on the type of property being transferred.

(i) A reduction of 100% of the value transferred is allowed for transfers of value where the value transferred is attributable to certain defined types of 'relevant business property' (meaning that there will be no charge to IHT in respect of those assets). These are:
   (a) a business or an interest in a business (including a partnership share);
   (b) company shares that are not listed on a recognised stock exchange.

(ii) A reduction of 50% of the value transferred is allowed for transfers of value where the value transferred is attributable to any other relevant business property. They are:
   (a) company shares that are listed on a recognised stock exchange if the transferor had voting control of the company immediately before the transfer;
   (b) land, buildings, machinery or plant owned by the transferor personally but used for business purposes by a partnership of which the transferor is a member, or by a company (whether quoted or unquoted) of which the transferor has voting control.

Voting control, for these purposes, means the ability to exercise over 50% of the votes on all resolutions. In assessing whether or not a person has voting control, separate shareholdings of spouses or civil partners can, in certain circumstances, be taken as one, so that if the combined percentage of the votes gives the couple voting control then the test will be satisfied.

Time limits

To attract any relief at all, the asset or assets in question must have been owned by the transferor for at least two years at the time of the transfer or, broadly, must be a replacement for relevant business property where the combined period of ownership is two years. If property is inherited from a spouse or civil partner, the surviving spouse/civil partner is deemed to have owned the property from the date it was originally acquired by the deceased spouse/civil partner (but this rule does not apply to lifetime transfers between spouses/civil partners).

6.4.3.4 Agricultural property relief

This relief operates in a similar way to BPR. In simple terms the effect of the relief is to reduce the agricultural value of agricultural property by a certain percentage. The 'agricultural value' is the value of the property if it were subject to a perpetual covenant prohibiting its use other than for agriculture. This will be significantly less than its market value if, for example, the land has development potential (eg for housing). That part of the property's value which is over and above its 'agricultural value' will not qualify for any agricultural property relief but may qualify for business property relief if the relevant requirements are satisfied.

A reduction of 100% is allowed where either (broadly) the transferor had the right to vacant possession immediately before the transfer or where the property was subject to a letting commencing on or after 1 September 1995. A reduction of 50% is allowed in other cases. Further conditions which must also be satisfied for any relief are either that the property was occupied by the transferor for the purposes of agriculture for the two years prior to the transfer or that it was owned by the transferor for the seven years prior to the transfer and was occupied by someone throughout that period for the purposes of agriculture.

In the Autumn 2024 Budget, the government announced that restrictions will be placed on the availability of agricultural property relief with effect from 6 April 2026.

6.4.4 Step 4: Calculate tax at the appropriate rate

6.4.4.1 Nil rate band (NRB)

Generally, the position is that, if the deceased has made no chargeable transfers in the seven years before death, the rate of tax on the first £325,000 of the estate is 0% (the NRB). If the estate exceeds the NRB, IHT is normally charged on the excess at 40%. In a small number of cases, a special rate of 36% may apply. The special rate is aimed at increasing charitable giving and will apply in place of the normal 40% rate when at least 10% of a defined 'component' of a person's net estate (after deduction of other exemptions, reliefs and the available NRB) passes to charity. The special rate will rarely apply as such substantial gifts to charity are unusual in any event. Those who do wish to make a charity their main beneficiary (often because they have no close family) often leave the vast majority of their estate to that charity (and benefitting from the charity exemption) with any other gifts falling within the NRB in any event.

If the deceased died on or after 9 October 2007 having survived a spouse or civil partner, the NRB in force at the date of death of the survivor is increased by whatever percentage of the NRB of the first to die was unused by them (subject to a maximum increase of 100%).

Example

Emily, a widow, dies on 21 August 2025. Her husband Guy died 10 years earlier leaving all his estate to Emily. There was no tax to pay on Guy's death as his whole estate was spouse exempt, and his NRB was not used. Emily's estate benefits from a 100% uplift in her NRB, so that the rate of tax on the first £650,000 of her estate is 0%.

If the deceased did make any chargeable transfers in the seven years before death the cumulation principle outlined at **6.3** will apply. The effect is that the lifetime transfers use up the deceased's NRB first, reducing the amount available for the estate. Most lifetime gifts are potentially exempt from IHT and become chargeable only if the transferor dies within seven years. Less commonly, the deceased may also have made gifts in the seven years before death which were immediately chargeable to IHT at the time they were made, eg a gift into a trust. The cumulation principle applies to both types of transfer.

The 'values transferred' by such lifetime transfers must be aggregated. This means that any lifetime exemptions or reliefs which operate to reduce the value transferred are taken into account.

Example

In 2022, David made a gift to his daughter. The value transferred (after exemptions and reliefs) was £175,000.

*In August 2025 David dies, leaving his estate, valued at £200,000, to his son. The estate did not include a qualifying residential interest (see **6.4.4.2**).*

(It may help, when calculating cumulative totals, to draw a timeline showing the relevant transfers. An example is given below.)

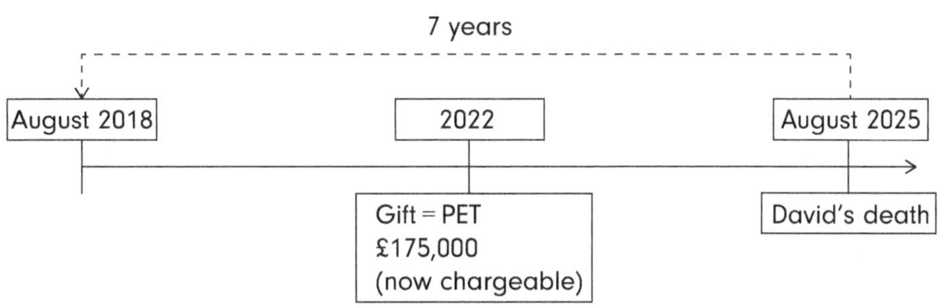

The 2022 transfer was potentially exempt from IHT but has now become chargeable. David's cumulative total is £175,000.

The nil rate band applicable to David's estate on death is	£325,000
less cumulative total	£175,000
= remaining nil rate band	£150,000
Tax on David's estate:	
£150,000 @ 0% =	nil
£50,000 @ 40% =	£20,000

For further details of the effect of the cumulation principle, see **6.7.3**.

6.4.4.2 Residence nil rate band (RNRB)

For deaths occurring after 6 April 2017, the RNRB is available in addition to the NRB. The RNRB for 2025/26 is £175,000.

For the RNRB to apply, the deceased must die owning a 'qualifying residential interest' which is 'closely inherited':

(a) A qualifying residential interest is an interest in a dwelling house which has at any time been the deceased's residence and which forms part of the deceased's estate.

(b) For a property to be 'closely inherited', it must pass to:

   (i) a child, grandchild or other lineal descendant of the deceased outright or on certain types of trust. Lineal descendants are defined as children, step-children, adopted children, foster children, or children where the deceased had been appointed as a guardian;

   (ii) the current spouse or civil partner of the deceased's lineal descendants; or

   (iii) the widow, widower or surviving civil partner of a lineal descendant who predeceased the deceased, unless such persons have remarried or formed a new civil partnership before the deceased's death.

The RNRB will apply only up to the value of the deceased's residence. When calculating the tax, the RNRB is taxed first at 0%, reducing the amount of the total chargeable estate, then, subject to cumulation, the NRB is taxed next at 0% and finally the remaining death estate at 40%.

Where the estate is valued at £2 million or more, the RNRB is reduced by £1 for every £2 over the £2 million threshold. To calculate the adjusted RNRB for an estate over £2 million, for the tax year 2025/26, the following formula may be used:

$$£175{,}000 - \frac{(\text{value of estate} - £2\text{ million})}{2} = \text{adjusted RNRB}$$

If the deceased has not used all of their RNRB, like the NRB, any unused RNRB may be claimed by a surviving spouse, even if the first spouse died before 6 April 2017.

Example

Angela dies on 4 September 2025 leaving her entire estate to her two children in equal shares. The value of her estate, after payment of debts and funeral expenses, is £1,750,000 and includes a house worth £1,250,000. Her husband, Richard, died four years earlier, leaving all his estate (worth less than £2 million) to Angela.

On Richard's death, the whole estate was spouse exempt, and the RNRB was not available to Richard's executors. As Richard has not used any of his RNRB, the amount transferred to Angela is an additional 100% of the RNRB, but at the current rate.

Therefore, when Angela dies, her executors can claim her own personal RNRB of £175,000 and Richard's unused RNRB of £175,000 (£350,000). This is the amount of RNRB current at the time of the death of the second spouse. This is in addition to the £650,000 NRB (2 x £325,000) from which Angela's estate will also benefit (see ***6.4.4.1****).*

There is a downsizing allowance to prevent (particularly older) people from holding on to unsuitable properties in order to claim the full benefit of the allowance. If, after 8 July 2015, the deceased has downsized prior to death to a less valuable property, or sold their property in order, for example, to move to a care home, the personal representatives can still claim the RNRB to which the deceased would have been entitled, provided the property would have qualified for the RNRB had it been retained, and the replacement property or other assets of an equivalent value (where the property had been sold) is left to lineal descendants.

6.4.5 Example of the application of IHT to an estate on death

Veronica dies intestate on 3 August 2025 survived by her partner William (to whom she was not married) and their children Brian (19) and Carla (22). She holds the following property:

	£
Bank accounts (in joint names with William) value of Veronica's share:	
(1) savings account	90,000
(2) current account	5,000
Life assurance policies:	
(1) payable to estate: maturity value	250,000
(2) written in trust for William: maturity value	30,000
Unquoted shares: 15% holding in a trading company (held for 10 years)	15,000
Building society account	19,000
Chattels	15,000

There are various debts, including funeral expenses, which total £4,000.

She made no substantial lifetime gifts.

Step 1: identify the transfer of value

Death is a deemed transfer of value. The death estate comprises the property to which Veronica was beneficially entitled immediately before death:

Passing on intestacy (to children): life assurance policy (1), unquoted shares, building society account, and chattels

Passing by survivorship (to William): interest in bank accounts

(Life assurance policy (2) is not included in the estate for IHT purposes because Veronica was not beneficially entitled to it immediately before her death.)

Step 2: Find the value transferred

	£	£
Passing on intestacy:		
life assurance policy (1) (full maturity value)	250,000	
unquoted shares (market value)	15,000	
building society account	19,000	
chattels	15,000	
		299,000
Joint property:		
interest in the bank accounts		95,000
		394,000
Less debts (including funeral expenses)		4,000
Value of estate (before reliefs)		390,000

Step 3: apply exemptions and reliefs

No exemptions apply to Veronica's estate as she had no spouse and left no property to charity.

The unquoted shares qualify for business property relief at 100%:

100% of £15,000	15,000
Value of estate for IHT	375,000

Step 4: calculate tax at the appropriate rate

Veronica made no lifetime gifts and so the entire NRB is available.

Calculate tax on the estate of £375,000:

on £325,000 @ 0%	nil
on £50,000 @ 40%	£20,000

6.5 Lifetime transfers: Potentially exempt transfers (PET)

The definition of a PET includes any gift made by an individual to another individual or into a disabled trust (s 3A(1A) IHTA 1984), to the extent in either case that the gift would otherwise be chargeable. This means that all lifetime gifts to an individual are 'potentially exempt' to the extent that no immediate exemption applies.

6.5.1 Step 1: Identify the transfer of value

The term 'transfer of value' includes any lifetime disposition made by a person ('the transferor') which reduces the value of his estate. In principle, therefore, any lifetime gift falls within the definition.

Certain dispositions are excluded from the definition, such as a transfer for the maintenance, education or training of the transferor's child under 18, or over that age if still undergoing full-time education or training, or for the maintenance of a dependent relative (s 11 IHTA 1984).

6.5.2 Step 2: Find the value transferred

The second step is to find the value transferred by the transfer of value. In the case of a lifetime transfer, this is the amount by which the value of the transferor's estate is 'less than it would be but for' the transfer. In other words, the value transferred is the loss in value to the estate of the transferor brought about by the transfer. The transferor's 'estate' is the aggregate of all the property to which they are beneficially entitled.

In practice, the loss to the estate will usually be the market value of the property transferred, although this does not follow in every case.

Example

Samia owns a pair of matching antique chairs. The market value of the pair together is £80,000, but individually each one is worth £25,000. If Samia were to give away one chair to her son, the loss to her estate would be calculated as follows:

	£
Value of pair	80,000
Less value of remaining chair	25,000
Loss to estate	55,000

The related property rules (which also apply on death) are designed to prevent tax avoidance in relation to a group or set of assets. The rules apply most often to property transferred between husband and wife.

Example

Bryn owns a pair of matching vases. The market value of the pair together is £50,000, but individually each one is worth £15,000. Bryn decides to give one of the vases to his husband, Chris (an exempt transfer to a spouse). Without the related property rules Bryn and Chris would each then own one vase worth £15,000.

However, because Bryn and Chris are married the two vases are related property. Under the related property valuation rule, the value of each vase is the appropriate portion of the value of the pair, ie half of £50,000 which is £25,000. If Bryn was then to give away his vase (or if it passed as part of his estate) the value transferred would be £25,000.

6.5.3 Step 3: Apply any relevant exemptions and reliefs

As seen at **6.3**, a gift is potentially exempt only to the extent that it would otherwise be chargeable. At the time when a lifetime gift is made it may be clear that an exemption applies. Some lifetime exemptions, however, may apply to only part of a lifetime transfer, so that the excess is potentially exempt.

The main exemptions and reliefs applicable on death apply also to lifetime transfers. In addition, there are some further exemptions which apply only to lifetime transfers.

6.5.3.1 Spouse or civil partner and charity exemptions

These exemptions, outlined at **6.4.3.1** and **6.4.3.2**, apply to lifetime transfers as well as to the transfer on death. So, any lifetime gift to the transferor's spouse or civil partner or to charity is exempt, even if the transferor dies within seven years.

6.5.3.2 Business and agricultural property relief

The reliefs set out at **6.4.3.3** and **6.4.3.4** apply to reduce the value transferred by transfers of business or agricultural property made during lifetime as well as on death. However, where there has been a lifetime transfer, followed by the death of the transferor within seven years, the BPR given at the time of the lifetime transfer will be withdrawn unless the transferee still owns the business property at the date of the transferor's death (or, if earlier, the transferee's own death).

6.5.3.3 Order of application of exemptions and reliefs

Spouse or civil partner and charity exemptions are applied before reliefs, since their effect is to make the transfer wholly exempt. If, for example, a transferor gives relevant business property to their spouse, BPR is academic – the transfer is exempt.

The 'lifetime only' exemptions (see **6.5.3.4**), however, may apply to only part of a transfer. Since the reliefs apply to reduce the value transferred, they should be applied before such exemptions are considered.

6.5.3.4 Lifetime only exemptions

The annual exemption

The annual exemption applies to the first £3,000 transferred by lifetime transfers in each tax year. Any unused annual exemption may be carried forward for one year only, so that a maximum exemption of £6,000 may be available. The current year's exemption must be used before the previous year's exemption can be carried forward.

Example

On 1 May 2023, Annie gives £3,000 to her son Ben. The transfer falls within Annie's annual exemption for 2023/24 and is exempt. Annie does not make any further gifts until 1 May 2025.

On 1 May 2025, Annie gives £7,000 to her daughter Claire. Annie may apply her annual exemption for 2025/26 and may carry forward her unused annual exemption for 2024/25. Thus £6,000 of the transfer is exempt at the time of the gift. (The remaining £1,000 will be 'potentially exempt', as explained below.)

If a transferor makes more than one transfer of value in any one tax year, then the exemption is used to reduce the first transfer. Any unused exemption is set against the second and any further transfers until it is used up.

Small gifts

Lifetime gifts in any one tax year of £250 or less to any one person are exempt. This exemption cannot be set against a gift which exceeds £250.

Normal expenditure out of income

A lifetime transfer is exempt if it can be shown that:

(a) it was made as part of the transferor's normal expenditure; and

(b) it was made out of the transferor's income; and

(c) after allowing for all such payments, the transferor was left with sufficient income to maintain their usual standard of living.

A typical example (provided the requirements are satisfied) would be a regular payment from a parent to a child studying at university to assist with living expenses.

Gifts in consideration of marriage

Lifetime gifts on marriage are exempt up to:

(a) £5,000 by a parent of a party to the marriage;

(b) £2,500 by a remoter ancestor of a party to the marriage (eg a grandparent); and

(c) £1,000 in any other case.

6.5.3.5 Potentially exempt status

Any value remaining after exemptions and reliefs have been applied at step 3 is potentially exempt. The transfer will become chargeable *only* if the transferor dies within seven years. The transferor does not need to take any action at the time when such a lifetime transfer is made, and if they survive for seven years it will automatically become exempt. However, if the transferor dies within the seven-year period, the transfer becomes chargeable and must be assessed as such. (For further explanation of the effect of death within seven years, see **6.7.2**.)

Example

On 1 March 2025, Abriana gives £130,000 to her sister, Chiara. She has made no previous lifetime gifts. The disposition is a transfer of value because the value of Abriana's estate is reduced. The value transferred is £130,000, the loss to Abriana's estate.

	£
Value transferred	130,000
Less: annual exemptions for 2024/25 and 2023/24	6,000
Potentially exempt transfer	124,000

No tax is payable at the time of the gift. Abriana has made a PET. If Abriana survives until 1 March 2032, the PET will become completely exempt. If Abriana dies before that date, the PET will become a chargeable transfer.

6.6 Lifetime transfers: Lifetime chargeable transfers (LCTs)

Any lifetime transfer which does not fall within the definition of a PET (see **6.5**) is immediately chargeable as a 'lifetime chargeable transfer' (LCT). The main example is a lifetime transfer made on or after 22 March 2006 into any trust (other than a disabled trust) or to a discretionary trust or company (whether made before, on or after 22 March 2006). The charge to IHT on lifetime creation of trusts is part of a wider regime under which further charges to tax arise during the existence of the trust and on its ending. The details of these further charges are beyond the scope of this manual. The examples below refer to transfers into trusts: in each case it is assumed that the trusts are not disabled trusts.

Where an individual makes an LCT, the IHT calculation begins with application of the first three steps as described at **6.5.1**, **6.5.2** and **6.5.3**. Once relevant exemptions and reliefs have been applied (except the small gifts exemption which is not available to LCTs), the balance is chargeable to IHT and tax must be calculated by applying step 4.

The rates of tax applicable to LCTs are:

(a) 0% on the first £325,000 (the nil rate band); and

(b) 20% on the balance of the chargeable transfer (this rate being half the rate for transfers which are chargeable on death).

Chargeable transfers made in the seven years before the current chargeable transfer reduce the nil rate band available to that current transfer. In other words, the value transferred by chargeable transfers made in the seven years before the current chargeable transfer must be 'cumulated' with that transfer (whilst the transferor is alive, any PETs made are ignored for cumulation purposes because they may never become chargeable).

Example

In this example, it is assumed that Venetia has used up her annual exemptions in each relevant tax year.

On 1 May 2025, Venetia transfers £50,000 to the trustees of a trust.

She has previously made the following lifetime chargeable transfers (after applying relevant annual exemptions):

1 May 2017 £100,000

1 May 2020 £280,000

She has made no other lifetime transfers (and makes no more in the current tax year).

To calculate the IHT due on the chargeable transfer of £50,000, the values transferred by any chargeable transfers made in the seven years prior to 1 May 2025 must be 'cumulated'.

(Remember that it may help when calculating cumulative totals to draw a time line, showing the relevant transfers. An example is given below.)

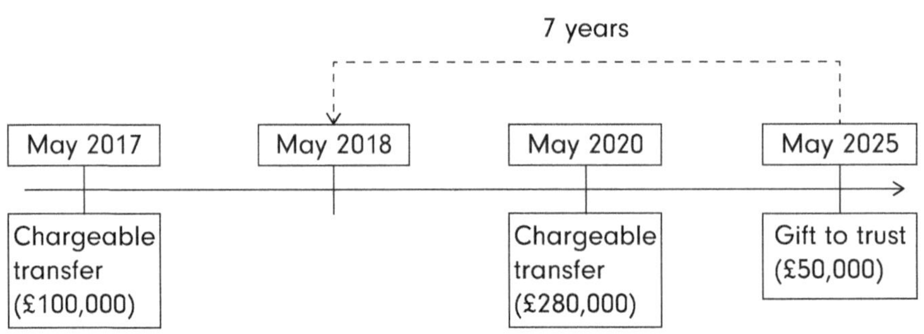

Venetia's cumulative total consists of the £280,000 transferred on 1 May 2020 (less than seven years before the present transfer).

The transfer of £100,000 was made more than seven years ago and can be ignored.

	£
NRB	325,000
less cumulative total	280,000
= remaining NRB	45,000

Tax on current chargeable transfer of £50,000:

£45,000 at 0% = nil

£5,000 at 20% = £1,000

Note that only chargeable transfers are relevant for cumulation. If the May 2020 transfer had been an outright gift of cash, it would have been a PET and not chargeable (as Venetia is still alive). It would not have been relevant for cumulation purposes, and the whole nil rate band would be available in relation to the 2025 gift to the trust.

Each transfer has its own cumulation period. If a new transfer is made, it is necessary to re-calculate the cumulative total (see **6.7.3** for an example).

6.7 Effect of death on lifetime transfers

6.7.1 Introduction

The death of a transferor may result in a charge (or additional charge) to IHT on any transfers of value which the transferor has made in the seven years immediately preceding their death, whether those transfers were PETs or LCTs when they were made. First, PETs made in that period become chargeable and the transferee will be liable for any IHT payable. Secondly, the IHT liability on LCTs made in that period is recalculated and the trustees will be liable for any extra tax payable. In either case, as the liability arises on death, the rate of tax, once the NRB and, if relevant, the RNRB are exceeded, is 40%.

Once the transfers that must be (re)assessed have been identified by checking the seven-year period before the transferor's death, each of those transfers must be analysed chronologically, starting with the transfer furthest back in time and working through the transfers (ending with the calculation of IHT on the death estate). If a transfer was originally a PET, the rules are those set out at **6.7.2**; if it was an LCT, the rules at **6.7.3** are used.

6.7.2 Effect of death on PETs

Potentially exempt transfers are defined and explained in **6.5**. There is no liability on a PET at the time of the transfer, and it will become wholly exempt if the transferor survives for seven years after the transfer. Many gifts will therefore escape a charge to IHT.

A PET will become chargeable *only* if the transferor dies within seven years of making the transfer.

6.7.2.1 Steps 1–3

As seen at **6.5**, the first three steps are applied to determine the size of the PET. Business property relief and/or agricultural property relief may apply to reduce the value transferred, provided that the transferee still owns the business or agricultural property.

6.7.2.2 Step 4: Calculate tax at the appropriate rate

The final step is to identify the rate or rates of tax applicable to the transfer in question. In order to do this, it is necessary to establish the transferor's cumulative total of transfers at the time of the PET, as this will reduce the available NRB. The cumulative total will be made up of:

(a) any LCTs made in the seven years *before the PET being assessed* (even if the LCT was made more than seven years before the transferor's death – therefore a taxpayer who makes an LCT may have to survive for 14 years before it ceases to have any impact); and

(b) any other PETs made during the seven years *before the PET being assessed* which have become chargeable as a result of the transferor's death.

Example

Gina gave the following gifts of cash to her children:

1 September 2019	£200,000 to Claire
25 June 2023	£200,000 to James

Gina died on 30 August 2025 leaving her estate (consisting of her house and bank accounts worth a total of £400,000) to the two children equally. She had made no other significant gifts.

Both gifts were PETs which have now become chargeable as Gina has died within seven years.

(1) Tax on the 2019 PET	£
Loss to estate	200,000
Annual exemptions 2019/20; 2018/19	6,000
	194,000

Gina had made no chargeable transfers in the seven years before 1 September 2019 so her NRB was intact.

Tax on £194,000 @ 0% Nil

(2) Tax on the 2023 PET	£
Loss to estate	200,000
Annual exemptions 2023/24; 2022/23	6,000
	194,000

Gina's cumulative total of chargeable transfers made in the seven years up to 25 June 2023 was £194,000 (the 2019 transfer to Claire). Only £131,000 of Gina's NRB remains.

Tax on £194,000

£131,000 @ 0%	Nil
£63,000 @ 40%	£25,200 (payable by James)

(3) Tax on Gina's estate: The house is a qualifying residential interest which has been closely inherited, so Gina is entitled to the RNRB of £175,000.

Gina's NRB has been used up by the two chargeable transfers in the last seven years.

Tax on £175,000 @ 0%

Tax on £225,000 @ 40% £90,000 (payable by Gina's PRs from the property passing to the children).

6.7.2.3 Tapering relief

Where a PET has become chargeable, tapering relief is available if the transferor survives for more than three years after the transfer. The relief works by reducing any *tax payable* on the PET.

Tax is reduced to the following percentages:

(a) transfers within three to four years before death: 80% of death charge

(b) transfers within four to five years before death: 60% of death charge

(c) transfers within five to six years before death: 40% of death charge

(d) transfers within six to seven years before death: 20% of death charge

Example

1 January 2019 Leonora makes a gift of £96,000 to Isadora

Leonora's cumulative total before the gift is made is £325,000

1 July 2025 Leonora dies

Effect of death:	£
Transfer of value	96,000
Less: Annual exemptions 2018/19; 2017/18	6,000
PET (which is now chargeable)	90,000

Rate of tax: Cumulative total £325,000 so all £90,000 is in the 40% band

£90,000 @ 40%	36,000

Tapering relief applies. Leonora died within six to seven years of the PET so 20% of this figure is payable

Tax payable by Isadora 20% of £36,000	7,200

6.7.3 Effect of death on LCTs

If a transferor dies within seven years of making an LCT, the IHT payable must be recalculated and more IHT may be payable by the trustees. The tax bill may be increased not only because the full death rate of IHT will now apply, but also because PETs made *before* the LCT may have become chargeable. They will increase the cumulative total and so reduce the NRB applicable to the LCT.

6.7.3.1 Steps 1–3

As described at **6.6**, the first three steps apply to find the value transferred by the LCT that is chargeable to tax. It will be necessary to check whether any reliefs claimed at step 3 when the LCT was made (such as BPR) are still available.

6.7.3.2 Step 4: calculate tax at the appropriate rate

Inheritance tax is recalculated in accordance with the rates of tax in force at the transferor's death if these are less than the rates in force at the time of the transfer; if not, the death rates at the time of the transfer are applied (the lower 36% charity rate is not applicable).

The cumulative total relevant to the LCT will determine how much (if any) of the NRB is available. The cumulative total is made up of:

(a) any other LCTs made in the seven years *before the LCT being assessed* (even if such earlier LCTs were made more than seven years before the transferor's death); and

(b) any PETs made during the seven years *before the LCT being assessed* which have become chargeable as a result of the transferor's death.

Each transfer that becomes chargeable or rechargeable has its own cumulation period, which means that a taxpayer who makes an LCT may have to survive for 14 years before it ceases to have an impact.

Example

Jasmin dies in November 2025. During her lifetime, she made the following gifts. In December 2018, she gave her son £100,000 in cash and, in January 2012, she transferred £300,000 to a discretionary trust for the benefit of her grandchildren.

(Assume that Jasmin used her annual exemption each year.)

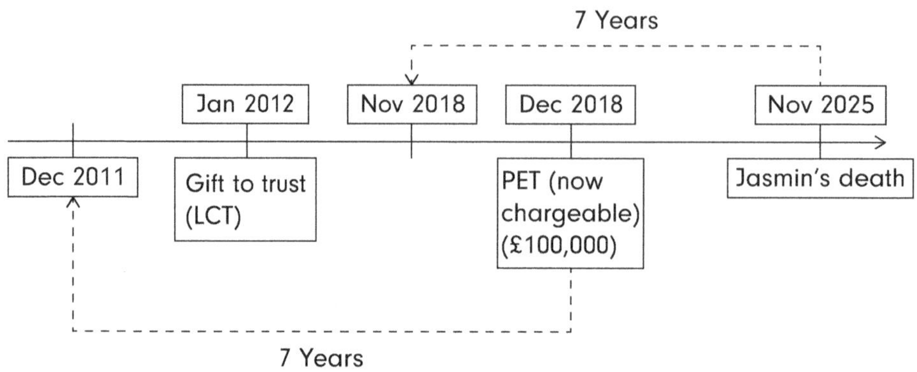

The December 2018 PET is just within seven years of Jasmin's death, and has now become chargeable. As a result, it now has its own cumulation period, so it is necessary to look back seven years from December 2018, when the PET was made, to see if any chargeable transfers were made during that period. The January 2012 LCT is just within the seven years from December 2018 and must be cumulated. As a result, there is only £25,000 NRB left for the December 2018 PET.

Notes:

(a) As Jasmin survived for more than seven years from the January 2012 LCT, it is not rechargeable. It is only relevant for cumulation purposes.

(b) Had the January 2012 transfer been a PET, as Jasmin survived for more than seven years, it would never have become chargeable, and so would not be taken into account when calculating the cumulative total.

(c) The cumulative total for the death estate, looking back seven years from November 2025, is £100,000, ie the amount taken by the PET which has become chargeable. The January 2012 LCT has no effect on the death estate as it is outside the seven years before Jasmin's death.

6.7.3.3 Tapering relief and credit for IHT already paid

Once the IHT on the LCT has been recalculated, and if more than three years have elapsed between the transfer and the subsequent death, tapering relief applies to reduce the recalculated tax (using the rules set out at **6.7.2.3**). Credit is then given for any IHT paid on the LCT at the time it was made but if the recalculated bill is lower than the original amount paid (which may occur if tapering relief is available) no tax is refunded.

Example

On 1 May 2022, George transferred £381,000 into a trust on condition that the trustees must pay the IHT. He had made no other lifetime gifts.

(a) On 1 May 2022, George made an LCT.

	£
Value transferred	381,000
Less: Annual exemptions 2022/23; 2021/22	6,000
	375,000
Calculate tax.	
£325,000 @ 0%	nil
£50,000 @ 20%	10,000
Tax payable by trustees	£10,000

(b) George dies on 1 September 2025, within seven years of the LCT.

Recalculate tax at death rates.

£325,000 @ 0%	nil
£50,000 @ 40%	£20,000

George died between three and four years after the transfer, so apply tapering relief

80% of £20,000	16,000
Less: tax already paid (see part (a))	10,000
Further tax payable by trustees	6,000

6.8 Liability and burden

6.8.1 Meaning of 'liability' and 'burden'

The rules that follow concern the question of who is liable to account to HMRC for the payment of IHT and who bears the burden of the tax. HMRC is concerned with obtaining payment of the tax (ie liability). Payment will usually be obtained from people who are not beneficially entitled to the property but who hold property in a representative capacity (ie PRs and trustees). Those who ultimately receive the property are concurrently liable with such representatives, but in most cases tax will have been paid before the beneficiaries receive the property. The concept of 'burden' concerns who ultimately bears the burden of the tax. The testator can change the statutory rules on the burden by making express provision in the will. However, the statutory rules on liability cannot be varied.

6.8.2 The estate rate

The term 'estate rate' means the average rate of tax applicable to each item of property in the estate. When tax on the estate has been calculated, it may be necessary for various reasons to work out how much of the tax is attributable to a particular item of property in the estate. For example:

(a) since tax on certain types of property, such as land, may be paid in instalments, the PRs must calculate how much of the tax relates to that property;

(b) the PRs may not be liable to pay all the tax on the estate. If the estate for IHT purposes includes trust property, the trustees are liable to pay the tax attributable to that property;

(c) the will may give a legacy 'subject to tax' so that the recipient has the burden of tax relating to that legacy.

The principle is that tax is divided between the various assets in the estate proportionately, according to their value. This may be applied by calculating the average rate of tax on the estate as a percentage, ie the 'estate rate'. For example, if the deceased's nil rate band was completely used up by lifetime transfers, the 'estate rate' would normally be 40%. However, it is not always necessary to calculate the estate rate as a percentage; instead, the amount of tax on a particular item of property in the estate may be calculated by applying to the value of that property the proportion which the total tax bill bears to the total chargeable estate.

Example

Graham, who has made no lifetime transfers, leaves a house, valued at £210,000, to his brother, Henry, subject to payment of IHT, and the rest of his estate, valued at £190,000 net, to his nephew, Ian.

Tax on Graham's estate:	£325,000 @ 0%	nil
	£75,000 @ 40%	£30,000

The 'estate rate' is:

$$\frac{\text{£30,000 (total tax bill)}}{\text{£400,000 (total chargeable estate)}} \times 100 = 7.5\%$$

Henry pays tax on the house:

$$\text{£210,000} \times \frac{\text{£30,000}}{\text{£400,000}} = \text{£15,750}$$

Ian pays tax on the residue:

$$\text{£190,000} \times \frac{\text{£30,000}}{\text{£400,000}} = \text{£14,250}$$

The same result would be achieved if the estate rate of 7.5% was applied to the value of the house and residue respectively.

6.8.3 Liability for IHT on death

6.8.3.1 The PRs: tax on the non-settled estate

The PRs are liable to pay the IHT attributable to any property which 'was not immediately before the death comprised in a settlement' (s 200 IHTA 1984). This includes:

(a) the property which vests in the PRs (ie the property which passes under the deceased's will or intestacy); and

(b) property (other than trust property) which does not pass to the PRs but is included in the estate for IHT because the deceased was beneficially entitled to it immediately before death (eg joint property which passes by survivorship).

Thus the PRs are liable to pay the IHT on joint property even though that property does not vest in them. Their liability is, however, limited to the value of the assets they received in respect of the estate, or would have received but for their own neglect or default.

Concurrently liable with the PRs is 'any person in whom property is vested ... at any time after the death or who at any such time is beneficially entitled to an interest in possession in the property' (s 200(1)(c) IHTA 1984). This means that tax on property passing by will or intestacy may in principle be claimed by HMRC from a beneficiary who has received that property. Similarly, HMRC may claim tax on joint property from the surviving joint tenant. In practice such tax is normally paid by the PRs and it is relatively unusual for HMRC to claim tax from the recipient of the property.

6.8.3.2 The trustees: tax on settled property

If the estate for IHT purposes includes any property which was 'comprised in a settlement' immediately before the death, the trustees of the settlement are liable for IHT attributable to that property. This principle is relevant where the deceased had a qualifying interest in possession under a trust (see **6.4.1.2**). Again, any person in whom the trust property subsequently vests or for whose benefit the trust property is subsequently applied is concurrently liable with the trustees.

Example

In 2002, Ruth's father died leaving shares now worth £300,000 on trust for Ruth for life with remainder to Arthur. Ruth dies leaving property worth £200,000 which passes under her will to her niece, Tessa. The trust fund is taxed as part of Ruth's estate as she had a qualifying interest in possession for IHT purposes. She had made no lifetime transfers.

Tax on Ruth's death

£325,000 @ 0%	nil
£175,000 @ 40%	£70,000

The trustees are liable to pay the tax on the trust fund (calculated according to the estate rate):

$$£300,000 \times \frac{£70,000}{£500,000} = £42,000$$

Arthur, the remainderman, is concurrently liable if any of the trust property is transferred to him before the tax has been paid.

Ruth's PRs are liable to pay the tax on Ruth's free estate (the remaining £28,000).

6.8.3.3 Additional liability of PRs

Property which the deceased gave away during lifetime is treated as part of the estate on death if the transferor reserved a benefit in the property which they continued to enjoy immediately before death (see **6.4.1.2**). The transferee of the gift is primarily liable to pay tax attributable to the property. However, if the tax remains unpaid 12 months after the end of the month of death, the PRs become liable for the tax.

6.8.4 Liability for IHT on PETs

Where a person dies within seven years of making a PET, the transfer becomes chargeable and IHT may be payable. The transferee is primarily liable but, again, the PRs become liable if the tax remains unpaid 12 months after the end of the month of death.

The liability of the PRs is limited to the extent of the assets they actually received, or would have received but for their neglect or default. However, PRs cannot escape liability on the grounds that they have distributed the estate and so they should ideally delay distribution until IHT on any such lifetime gifts has been paid.

6.8.5 Liability for IHT on LCTs

6.8.5.1 Trustees pay

The transferor is primarily liable for IHT, although HMRC may also claim the tax from the trustees. In practice, the trustees often pay IHT out of the property they have been given.

6.8.5.2 Transferor pays: grossing up

If the transferor pays, the amount of tax will be more than it would be if the trustees paid.

This is because IHT is charged on the value transferred, ie the loss to the transferor's estate brought about by the gift. If the transferor pays, the loss is increased by the amount of tax he pays.

Example

Henrietta transfers £80,000 in cash to trustees of a trust. Earlier in the tax year, she gave them £331,000 in cash. She has made no previous chargeable transfers.

The annual exemptions for this tax year and last have already been used by the gift of £331,000 and her cumulative total stands at £325,000. All the current transfer will be taxed at 20%.

If trustees pay IHT:

The loss to her estate is £80,000. Tax payable is 20% of £80,000, which is £16,000.

If Henrietta pays IHT:

The total loss to her estate (ie the value transferred) is £80,000 plus the IHT payable on that transfer.

Therefore, in order to ascertain the value transferred, it is necessary to calculate what sum would, after deduction of tax at the appropriate rate (ie 20%), leave £80,000 (ie the transfer must be grossed up).

Gross up £80,000 at 20%

$$£80{,}000 \times \frac{100}{80} = £100{,}000$$

The gross value transferred is £100,000.

Calculate tax on £100,000:

£100,000 @ 20% = £20,000

The tax payable by Henrietta is more than the tax payable by the trustees.

However, if she pays, the trustees are left with the full amount of the property transferred, £80,000, as opposed to £64,000 if they pay.

6.8.5.3 Additional liability following the transferor's death

If additional IHT becomes due on an LCT following the transferor's death, the rules for those liable for the additional tax are set out in IHTA 1984, s 199 (as summarised at **6.8.4** above).

6.8.6 Burden of IHT

Unlike liability, the question of where the burden of tax should fall is one for the transferor to decide. For example, the burden of tax could fall on the transferees of any gifts (including PETs and LCTs) or the transferor could choose to relieve them of that burden by paying any IHT themselves on lifetime gifts and directing that any IHT arising following death be paid from the residue of the estate. If the will is silent, then the default position essentially is that the IHT on property which vests in the PRs is payable as a testamentary expense, and that on property held as beneficial joint tenants is borne by the surviving joint tenant (see **9.7.2.3**).

6.9 Time for payment

6.9.1 Death estates

6.9.1.1 The basic rule

The basic rule is that IHT is due for payment six months after the end of the month of death (although PRs will normally pay earlier in order to speed up the administration of the estate as any IHT due must be paid before the grant of representation can be obtained; see **Chapter 8**).

If the tax due is not paid on time, interest runs on the outstanding amount.

6.9.1.2 The instalment option

Some property, such as land and certain types of business property, attracts the instalment option. Any tax attributable to instalment option property may be paid in 10 equal yearly instalments, the first falling due six months after the end of the month of death. The tax on the estate is apportioned using the estate rate to find how much tax is attributable to the instalment option property.

The instalment option applies to:

(a) land of any description;

(b) a business or an interest in a business;

(c) shares (quoted or unquoted) which immediately before death gave control of the company to the deceased;

(d) unquoted shares which do not give control if either:

  (i) the holding is sufficiently large (a holding of at least 10% of the nominal value of the company's shares and worth more than £20,000); or

  (ii) HMRC is satisfied that the tax cannot be paid in one sum without undue hardship; or

  (iii) the IHT attributable to the shares and any other instalment option property in the estate amounts to at least 20% of the IHT payable on the estate.

6.9.1.3 Interest

Where the instalment option is exercised in relation to tax on shares or any other business property or agricultural land, instalments carry interest only from the date when each instalment is payable. Thus, no interest is due on the outstanding tax provided that each instalment is paid on the due date.

In the case of other land, however, interest is payable with each instalment (apart from the first) on the amount of IHT which was outstanding for the previous year.

6.9.1.4 Sale

If the instalment option property is sold, all outstanding tax and interest becomes payable.

6.9.2 PETs

Any IHT on a PET that has become chargeable is due six months after the end of the month of death. The instalment option outlined above may be available depending on the circumstances.

6.9.3 LCTs

6.9.3.1 At the time of the transfer

Any IHT on LCTs made after 5 April and before 1 October in any year is due on the 30 April in the following year. Inheritance tax on LCTs which are not made between those dates is due six months after the end of the month in which the LCT is made.

6.9.3.2 Following subsequent death within seven years

Any additional IHT on the reassessment of an LCT following the transferor's death is due six months after the end of the month of death.

Again, the instalment option may be available.

6.10 Example of the rules on liability, burden and timing

Xander, who was divorced, dies on 4 May 2025, leaving an estate on which the total IHT due is £150,000. His taxable estate (of £800,000) comprises instalment property (a house) worth £240,000 and non-instalment property worth £560,000 (of which £200,000 is Xander's share of a joint bank account held with this brother, Zak). Xander left a valid will, leaving the residue of his estate to his nephew, but which makes no mention of the burden of IHT.

Liability

The executors of Xander's estate are liable for the entire IHT due of £150,000.

Burden

As the will makes no contrary provision, the default rule is that the IHT on the share of the joint bank account is borne by Zak as the surviving joint tenant:

$$£200{,}000 \times \frac{£150{,}000}{£800{,}000} = £37{,}500$$

IHT on the property passing via the will is paid from the residuary estate as a testamentary expense:

$$£600{,}000 \times \frac{£150{,}000}{£800{,}000} = £112{,}500$$

Timing

The house qualifies as instalment option property:

$$£240{,}000 \times \frac{£150{,}000}{£800{,}000} = £45{,}000$$

This tax can be paid in 10 equal annual instalments, with the first instalment of £4,500 payable on 30 November 2025 (six months after the end of the month of death).

6.11 Anti-avoidance

Historically individuals largely arranged their affairs so as to avoid paying tax unnecessarily and be free from comment or criticism. However, eventually the development of highly complex and lucrative schemes which enabled wealthy individuals and commercial enterprises to escape the payment of tax generated a good deal of publicity, with the result that public opinion somewhat turned against tax avoidance. Parliament responded by putting in place measures designed to stop tax avoidance which could be described as 'abusive' or 'exploitative'. However, it must be stressed that legitimate tax planning remains permissible.

6.11.1 Disclosure of tax avoidance schemes (DOTAS)

IHT is one of the taxes subject to the regulations on DOTAS. The regulations require certain schemes to be disclosed to HMRC. The point of disclosure is to provide HMRC with information at an early stage thereby allowing time to assess the scheme and, if necessary, to introduce measures to counteract it.

To constitute a 'notifiable arrangement' and therefore fall within the regulations, in essence the main purpose, or one of the main purposes, of the arrangements must be to enable a person to obtain one or more of a list of specific advantages in relation to IHT (a tax advantage), eg a reduction in the value of a person's estate, and the arrangements must involve one or more contrived or abnormal steps without which a tax advantage could not be obtained. HMRC guidance says that 'normal and straightforward' IHT planning is not notifiable.

HMRC has the power to impose penalties for a failure to comply with the regime.

6.11.2 General anti-avoidance rule (GAAR)

IHT is subject to GAAR. GAAR is intended to enable HMRC to counteract 'abusive' tax arrangements.

In essence, an arrangement is a 'tax arrangement' for the purpose of GAAR if, having regard to all the circumstances, it would be reasonable to conclude that the obtaining of a tax advantage was the main purpose (or one of the main purposes) of the arrangement. A tax arrangement is 'abusive' if the entering into or carrying out of the arrangement cannot reasonably be regarded as a reasonable course of action (the double reasonableness test). It is for HMRC to show that an arrangement is abusive.

Where a taxpayer seeks to claim a tax advantage under a scheme that falls foul of GAAR, HMRC may counteract the advantage and, if appropriate, impose a penalty.

Summary

- The main occasions of charge to IHT are:

  (a) on death on the value of an individual's estate;

  (b) on lifetime gifts made by one individual to another made within seven years prior to death;

  (c) on lifetime gifts to a company or into a trust.

  Lifetime gifts to an individual are only chargeable to IHT if the donor dies within the seven years after making the gift. At the time such a gift is made it is a 'potentially exempt transfer' (PET). It becomes exempt if the donor survives for seven years or chargeable if he dies during that period.

  Lifetime gifts into a trust or to a company are immediately chargeable to IHT at the time they are made. They are known as 'lifetime chargeable transfers' (LCTs).

- There are four steps to be used to calculate liability to IHT.

  Step 1: Identify the transfer of value

  On death this means the value of the estate, ie all the property to which the deceased was beneficially entitled.

  For lifetime transfers this means any transaction which reduces the value of the transferor's estate. This includes any gift or a sale at an undervalue.

  Step 2: Find the value transferred

  On death this means the value of the property in the estate, valued at open market value.

  For lifetime transfers this means the amount by which the transferor's estate has been reduced as a result of the transfer.

  Step 3: Apply exemptions and reliefs

  Transfers to spouse or charity are exempt whether in lifetime or on death.

  Some exemptions apply only to lifetime transfers. These include annual exemption (£3,000 pa), small gifts, marriage gifts and gifts made as normal expenditure out of income.

  Business property relief applies to reduce the value transferred by a transfer of certain types of business property by 100% or 50%. This may apply to transfers made in lifetime or on death.

  Step 4: Calculate tax at the appropriate rate

  If the estate includes a qualifying residential interest which is closely inherited, tax is charged at 0% on the first £175,000 (the residence nil rate band).

  Tax is then charged at 0% on the first £325,000 of other transfers (the nil rate band).

  In order to calculate IHT on any transfer, chargeable transfers made during the preceding seven years must be taken into account. Such transfers will reduce the nil rate band available for the current transfer.

  The balance of the transfer in excess of the nil rate band is taxed at 40% (or, rarely, 36%) if the transfer is on death or 20% for LCTs.

- Potentially exempt transfers (PETs) made within seven years of the transferor's death become chargeable as a result of death. The rate of tax is 40%, but the amount of tax is tapered if the transferor survived for more than three years after the transfer.
- If a transferor dies within seven years of making an LCT, tax must be recalculated at death rates, applying taper if the death was more than three years after the transfer.

Sample questions

Question 1

A man has been making various lifetime transfers for the past 10 years. Each year on 7 April he has given £50,000 from his savings to his son. He also gives each of his three grandchildren £100 on their birthdays (which are in September and October). Additionally, in May of this tax year he put £300,000 into a discretionary trust for the benefit of his grandchildren.

Which of the following best describes the man's inheritance tax position in relation to the transfers made in this tax year?

A He has made potentially exempt transfers of £47,000.

B He has made potentially exempt transfers of £50,000.

C He has made potentially exempt transfers of £50,300.

D He has made lifetime chargeable transfers of £350,000.

E He has made lifetime chargeable transfers of £350,300.

Answer

Option A is correct. The £100 to each of the grandchildren is covered by the small gifts exemption. The transfer into the discretionary trust is immediately chargeable and is not a potentially exempt transfer (PET). The first £3,000 of the transfer to the son is exempt which leaves £47,000 as a PET.

Option B is wrong as it has not deducted the annual exemption.

Option C is wrong as it has added in the £300 gifts covered by the small gifts exemption and not deducted the annual exemption.

Option D is wrong as it has included the potentially exempt transfer as chargeable and has not deducted the £3,000 annual exemption.

Option E is wrong as it has included the £300 gifts covered by the small gifts exemption and the potentially exempt transfer as chargeable and has not deducted the £3,000 annual exemption.

Question 2

A testator made a valid will six months ago which included the following gifts of company shares:

'I give to my nephew all my shares in AB plc.'

'I give to my niece all my shares in XY plc.'

'I give to my daughter all my shares in DEF Limited.'

The testator died last week. All of these beneficiaries survived the testator, and the testator owned all of the above-mentioned shares.

The shares in AB plc were purchased 18 years ago and represent a 30% shareholding in the company, which makes clothing and is listed on the London Stock Exchange. The shares in XY plc were purchased 10 years ago and represent a 10% shareholding in the company, which makes vehicles and is also listed on the London stock exchange. The shares in DEF Limited were inherited from the testator's father 25 years ago and represent a 45% shareholding in the testator's family private company which makes bathroom fittings.

Which of the following best explains whether these gifts qualify for business property relief for inheritance tax?

A All three gifts will attract business property relief at the rate of 100%.

B The gift of shares in AB plc and XY plc will both attract business property relief at the rate of 50% and the gift of shares in DEF Limited will attract business property relief at the rate of 100%.

C The gift of shares in AB plc and the gift of shares in DEF Limited will both attract business property relief at the rate of 50% but the gift of shares in XY plc does not qualify for the relief.

D All of the three gifts will attract business property relief at the rate of 50%.

E The gift of shares in AB plc and XY plc do not qualify for business property relief but the gift of shares in DEF Limited will attract business property relief at the rate of 100%.

Answer

Option E is correct as in order to qualify for business property relief the shares must be owned for at least two years before death and the company must be a trading company (satisfied for all of the shares) but if the shares are in a company listed on a recognised stock exchange, the owner must have had voting control of the company, which is not the case here. This is not required for an unquoted company, where the relief is 100%.

Option A is wrong as although the unquoted shares attract 100% relief, the quoted shares only attract 50% if they give the owner control of the company.

Option B is wrong as the unquoted shares attract 100% relief, and the 30% holding does not give voting control of AB plc.

Option C is wrong as although XY plc shares do not attract any relief, neither do the AB plc shares and the unquoted shares attract 100% relief.

Option D is wrong as the unquoted shares attract relief at 100% and the quoted shares do not attract any relief as they do not give voting control.

Question 3

A man, who never married or formed a civil partnership, died owning the following assets, which he left to his friend: a yacht (worth £500,000), bank accounts (worth £200,000), and chattels (worth £70,000). The deceased had debts and funeral expenses totalling £20,000. The only lifetime transfer made by the deceased was a 21st birthday gift of £15,000 to his niece one year before he died. At the relevant time the nil rate band was £325,000 and annual exemption £3,000.

What is the amount of inheritance tax payable on the deceased's estate?

A £170,000.

B £176,000.

C £173,600.

D £174,800.

E £181,600.

Answer

Option C is correct as the chargeable estate is £750,000. The potentially exempt transfer to the niece, after deducting two annual exemptions, is £9,000 and so there is only £316,000 nil rate band available, leaving the remaining £434,000 to be taxed at 40% = £173,600.

Option A is wrong as it has not included the effect of the potentially exempt transfer on the nil rate band.

Option B is wrong as it has omitted the annual exemptions in relation to the potentially exempt transfer.

Option D is wrong as it has included only one annual exemption.

Option E is wrong as it has not deducted debts from the value of the estate.

7 Family Provision and Post-death Variations

SQE1 syllabus

This chapter will enable you to achieve the SQE1 assessment specification in relation to functioning legal knowledge concerned with wills and the administration of estates.

- The planning, management and progression of the administration of an estate including claims under the Inheritance (Provision for Family and Dependants) Act 1975.
- The law and practice relating to personal representatives and trustees in the administration of estates and consequent trusts. The rights, powers and remedies of beneficiaries of wills and consequent trusts.
- Claims against estates under the Inheritance (Provision for Family and Dependants) Act 1975:
    - time limit
    - applicants
    - ground
    - liabilities of personal representatives and their protection.

Note that for SQE1, candidates are not usually required to recall specific case names or cite statutory or regulatory authorities. However, in this chapter, the ability of certain categories of people to apply to the court to claim part of an estate on the ground that the will/intestacy did not make reasonable provision for them is governed by the Inheritance (Provision for Family and Dependants) Act 1975. This Act may be referred to in the SQE 1 assessment. Otherwise, references to cases, statutory and regulatory authorities in this chapter are provided for illustrative purposes only.

Learning outcomes

By the end of this chapter you will be able to apply relevant core legal principles and rules appropriately and effectively, at the level of a competent newly qualified solicitor in practice, to realistic client-based and ethical problems and situations in the following areas:

- potential applicants for family provision;
- the process by which the court exercises its discretion under the Inheritance (Provision for Family and Dependants) Act 1975;
- protection of personal representatives against personal liability to successful family provision applicants; and
- rights of beneficiaries to vary the disposition of the deceased's estate post-death together with any associated inheritance tax (IHT) and capital gains tax (CGT) consequences.

7.1 Introduction

The jurisdiction of England and Wales is somewhat unique in that people are free to leave their property to whoever they want on death. This contrasts with other jurisdictions such as France and Scotland. Legal systems based on Roman law have forced heirship laws which means that a certain proportion of a deceased's estate will go to their family regardless of the deceased's wishes.

However, it would be wrong to say that citizens of England and Wales have complete testamentary freedom due to the Inheritance (Provision for Family and Dependants) Act 1975. Testators are free to leave their property to whoever they like but, after they die, certain categories of people can apply to the court to claim part of the estate on the ground that the will did not make reasonable provision for them (such claims are often referred to as 'family provision'). Claims can also be made where the deceased died intestate. It is not presumed that the intestacy rules make reasonable provision in all cases.

Family provision is not the only way of claiming part of a deceased's estate. People who are disappointed with the amount they receive under a will should consider whether the will is valid (see **Chapter 1**). It might be possible to mount a challenge on the ground that the will was not executed properly or that the testator lacked capacity or knowledge and approval. If the challenge succeeds, the applicant may benefit under an earlier will or on intestacy.

After a person has died, their beneficiaries might decide voluntarily that they wish to rearrange the dispositions in the deceased's will or on intestacy. This might be prompted by a desire to save inheritance tax (IHT) or to benefit another member of the family who is in greater need. Beneficiaries can make a post-death variation or disclaimer of their entitlement.

This chapter looks at:

- Inheritance (Provision for Family and Dependants) Act 1975; and
- post-death variations and disclaimers.

7.2 Inheritance (Provision for Family and Dependants) Act 1975 ('the Act')

The Act allows certain categories of people who may be aggrieved because they have been left out of a will, or are not inheriting on an intestacy, to apply to the court for a benefit from the estate following the testator's or intestate's death. The Act may also be used by a person who has received some benefit under the will or intestacy but is dissatisfied with the amount of the inheritance.

The Act applies only where the deceased died domiciled in England and Wales.

7.2.1 Categories of applicant

The following persons can make a claim:

(a) the spouse or civil partner of the deceased;

(b) a former spouse or civil partner of the deceased who has not remarried (except where, on the making of the final order of divorce/dissolution or nullity, the court made an order barring the former spouse or civil partner from making a claim);

(c) a child of the deceased (whatever the child's age);

(d) any person treated by the deceased as a child of the family in relation to any marriage or civil partnership of the deceased, or otherwise in relation to any family in which the deceased at any time stood in the role of a parent (eg a step-child or child of a cohabitee);

(e) any person who, immediately before the death of the deceased, was being maintained by the deceased either wholly or in part. A person is 'maintained' if 'the deceased was making a substantial contribution in money or money's worth towards the reasonable needs of that person, other than a contribution made for full valuable consideration pursuant to an arrangement of a commercial nature';

(f) any person who, during the whole of the period of two years ending immediately before the date when the deceased died, was living:

(i) in the same household as the deceased, and

(ii) as the husband, wife or civil partner of the deceased.

Each category is considered in more detail below.

(a) The spouse or civil partner of the deceased

It is perhaps unsurprising that the deceased's spouse or civil partner is able to make a claim.

(b) A former wife, husband or civil partner of the deceased who has not remarried

Applications by a former spouse or civil partner are quite rare. Usually, a financial settlement will have been agreed or imposed on the divorce. The divorce court often orders that the former spouse cannot claim family provision against the other spouse's estate under the Act. Such a bar would obviously prevent a claim.

(c) A child of the deceased

For the purposes of the Act, adopted children are regarded as the children of their adoptive parents. Category (c) does not include step-children although they may come within category (d).

Applications by infant children are uncontroversial. It is more difficult for adult children to succeed. In *Re Coventry* [1979] 2 WLR 853, Oliver J stated that applications for family provision by 'able-bodied and comparatively young men in employment and able to maintain themselves must be relatively rare' and need to be approached 'with a degree of circumspection'. If the adult child is in employment and likely to have earning capacity for the foreseeable future, it is unlikely that their application will succeed without some special circumstance such as:

- a moral obligation owed by the deceased;
- the adult child having a disability;
- the adult child working for the deceased for many years for a low wage; or
- the child making sacrifices in order to care for the deceased.

However, a claim by an adult daughter succeeded in *Illot v Blue Cross* [2017] UKSC 17 (see **7.2.3** below).

(d) Any person (not being a child of the deceased) who was treated by the deceased as a child of the family;

Category (d) covers people who are not the deceased's legal children but where the deceased acted as a parent towards them. Step-children have succeeded under this category although they have to prove that the deceased acted as a parent towards them.

In Re Callaghan *[1985] Fam 1, the applicant was a married man, aged 47, with a family of his own. He applied for family provision from his step-father's estate, who had died intestate. The deceased started living with the applicant's mother when the applicant was a teenager. They lived together for over 20 years before marrying. The deceased had treated the applicant as his own son throughout. It was held that the applicant could make a claim as a child of the deceased's family. It was relevant that the deceased treated the applicant's children as his grandchildren, he placed confidence in the applicant regarding his financial affairs and relied on the applicant to look after him in his last illness.*

(e) Any person (not listed above) who immediately before the death of the deceased was being maintained either wholly or partly, by the deceased

Category (e) is designed to catch anyone who does not fall into the other categories but can establish financial dependency on the deceased. The requirement is that they were maintained wholly or partly by the deceased. The Act provides that a person is 'maintained' if the deceased was making 'a substantial contribution in money or money's worth towards the reasonable needs of the applicant otherwise than for full valuable consideration pursuant to an arrangement of a commercial nature'.

Jelley v Iliffe [1981] 2 WLR 80

The applicant was a widower who went to live with Mrs Iliffe for the last eight years of her life. She gave him rent-free accommodation, cooked and washed for him. He did the garden and household jobs. They pooled their pensions to pay the bills. The applicant sought provision from Mrs Iliffe's estate on the basis that she had been maintaining him. The Court of Appeal accepted that he could bring a claim in category (e). Providing rent-free accommodation was a substantial contribution to his reasonable needs (especially as he was a pensioner) and therefore, amounted to maintenance.

(*Jelley v Iliffe* preceded the introduction of a separate category for cohabitants which was added in 1996. Before 1996, cohabitants had to prove that they came into the maintenance category.)

The timing of the maintenance, 'immediately before death', is not to be construed literally. In *Jelley v Iliffe*, the Court of Appeal made it clear that the phrase referred to the general arrangements for maintenance which had existed during the deceased's lifetime. The question was whether there was a settled basis or arrangement between the parties as regards maintenance. A temporary break in maintenance immediately prior to death (eg while the deceased was in hospital) does not prevent a claim.

The maintenance must not be part of a commercial arrangement. So a housekeeper or live-in carer could not claim in this category. Even though they might get rent-free accommodation, they provide consideration pursuant to a contract to carry out household duties or provide care.

(f) Any person who lived in the same household as the deceased and as their husband, wife or civil partner during the whole period of two years ending immediately before the deceased's death

Cohabitants who have not formalised their relationship by marriage or the formation of a civil partnership can apply under this category if they satisfy three conditions:

- they must have been living in the same household as the deceased;
- as the husband, wife or civil partner; and
- this must have been for the whole of the two years immediately preceding the deceased's death.

Taking each of these requirements in turn.

- **Same household**

  'Living in the same household' means living together as one unit. It would not include the situation where a couple is living under one roof but as two entities.

  In *Gully v Dix* [2004] 1FLR 918 Ward LJ said '... the relevant word is "household" not "house" ... Thus they will be in the same household if they are tied by their relationship. The tie of that relationship may be made manifest by various elements, not simply their living together under the same roof, but the private and public acknowledgement of the mutual protection and support that binds them together'.

- **As husband/wife or civil partner**

  The applicant and the deceased must have lived together as if they were spouses or civil partners. The question is whether a reasonable person with normal perceptions would regard them as living together as husband and wife or civil partners. The absence of sexual relations does not preclude the court from making this finding. The relationship as a couple must be openly acknowledged.

- **Two years immediately before death**

  A temporary separation such as if the deceased was in hospital or a care home for a period before death will not disqualify the cohabitant. The court considers whether a reasonable person would regard them as living as husband and wife or civil partners. There has to be some degree of permanence and commitment in the relationship.

Gully v Dix [2004] 1 FLR 918

The applicant and the deceased lived together for 27 years. The deceased had a drink problem and the applicant had on a number of occasions walked out temporarily as a result of his behaviour, although she had always gone back to him. She walked out after another drunken incident when he threatened her with a knife. They were apart for three months. Then he died. He had left messages with the applicant's daughter asking her to come back, but the daughter did not pass on the messages. The Court of Appeal held that the applicant should be regarded as having cohabited with the deceased for the requisite two years immediately before his death. 'The couple had a substantial and enduring relationship akin to marriage which had lasted for 27 years' and the applicant continued to be part of the 'household' irrespective of the fact that she had lived elsewhere for three months. Crucially, on the facts the relationship had not ended – he wanted her back and she would have gone back had she known about the messages.

7.2.2 Time limit

Applications must be made within six months from the date of the grant of representation. The reason for having a time limit is that it would be unfair to delay indefinitely the distribution of the estate to the beneficiaries due to a possible claim for family provision. An application can be made before the grant is issued.

A potential applicant can make an online or postal search of the probate records to discover whether a grant has already been issued. It is also possible to make a 'standing search' which ensures that the applicant is notified of any grant which issues in the following six months.

The court has a discretion to extend the time limit for a family provision application but it will only permit an extension if there is good reason for the delay. The court will consider the merits of the applicant's claim for provision, how promptly the applicant sought permission, whether the estate has already been distributed, whether the personal representatives or beneficiaries had notice within the time limit of a possible claim and whether the applicant would have another remedy if permission were refused (such as suing their solicitor in negligence).

Re Salmon [1981] Ch 167

The deceased left nothing to his widow in his will. The widow made a claim for family provision even though she had been separated from the deceased for 34 years. She missed the six months' time limit by 4½ months. The court refused to extend the time limit. The widow's solicitor had not warned the personal representatives that he was instructed to make a claim and the estate had already been distributed to the beneficiaries. The solicitor admitted that he had forgotten about the deadline. The inference from the judgment is that the judge expected the widow to obtain redress by suing her solicitor for negligence.

7.2.3 The ground for a claim and the guidelines

(a) Ground

The only ground for a claim is that 'the disposition of the deceased's estate effected by his will or the law relating to intestacy, or a combination of his will and that law, is not such as to make reasonable financial provision for the applicant'. The first step is to determine whether the estate makes reasonable financial provision for the applicant. This is an objective test; it is not a question of whether the deceased was reasonable. The burden is on the applicant to show that the test is satisfied. There are two standards for judging 'reasonable financial provision':

(i) 'The surviving spouse standard' allows a surviving spouse or civil partner such financial provision as is reasonable in all the circumstances 'whether or not that provision is required for his or her maintenance'. A relevant factor is how much the spouse or civil partner might have expected on a divorce.

(ii) 'The ordinary standard' applies to all other categories of applicant and allows 'such financial provision as it would be reasonable in all the circumstances ... for the applicant to receive for his maintenance'.

'Maintenance' is not defined in the Act, but case law has established that it connotes payments which enable the applicant to discharge the cost of their daily living at whatever standard of living is appropriate to them. It therefore addresses payments required to meet recurring expenses, such as rent, heating and food bills.

The limitation to maintenance in the ordinary standard means that a person who is able to pay for their living expenses out of their own resources will not obtain an award.

(b) Guidelines

The Act contains guidelines to assist the court in determining whether the will and/or intestacy makes reasonable financial provision for the applicant. (These are set out in s 3 of the Act and are therefore often referred to as the s 3 guidelines or s 3 factors.) The common guidelines should be considered for every applicant. There are also special guidelines for each category of applicant. In order to assess whether the applicant is likely to be successful, it is necessary to consider how the relevant guidelines apply to the facts. When considering the common and special guidelines, the court takes into account the facts at the date of the hearing.

The common guidelines set out in the Act are:

(i) the financial resources and needs of the applicant, other applicants and beneficiaries of the estate now and in the foreseeable future;

(ii) the deceased's obligations towards any applicant or beneficiary;

(iii) the size and nature of the estate;

(iv) the physical or mental disability of any applicant or beneficiary;

(v) anything else which may be relevant, such as the conduct of the applicant.

Some of these common guidelines are considered in more detail below.

- **The financial resources and needs of the applicant, other applicants and beneficiaries of the estate now and in the foreseeable future**

  The court balances the needs and resources of the applicant against the needs and resources of the beneficiaries and all those with a claim on the estate. It will take into account their earning capacity and their financial obligations and responsibilities. The court should also consider the effect of any order on any state benefits the applicant receives.

- **The deceased's obligations towards any applicant or beneficiary**

  These obligations include legal obligations (such as the duty of a parent to maintain their infant child) and moral obligations.

Example

A woman died. In her will she left everything she owned to her husband. They had an understanding that when he died, he would give all the woman's property to their daughter. After the woman's death, the husband remarried and when he died, he left his entire estate (including his first wife's property) to his second wife.

The daughter makes a claim for family provision against the husband's estate. A court is likely to regard the husband as having been under a moral obligation to leave his first wife's property to their daughter.

- **The size and nature of the estate**

  It is easier to make a successful claim against a large estate. The smaller the estate, the more difficult it is to provide for all the beneficiaries and claimants and the courts do not want to encourage claims where the costs would swallow up a large part of the estate.

Re Coventry [1980] Ch 461

An adult son's application for family provision from his late father's estate was refused. The estate was small and the beneficiary was the deceased's widow who was living in difficult financial circumstances. The applicant son was able-bodied and in employment, albeit not particularly lucrative employment. The estate was too small to satisfy everyone's needs and the scales tipped towards the deceased's widow.

- **Anything else which may be relevant including conduct**

  A testator may leave written reasons for excluding the applicant from their will. The reasons may be in the will itself (and become public when the will is admitted to probate) or in a separate document. The court has a discretion as to how much weight to attach to the reasons. In *Illot v Blue Cross Properties and others* [2017] UKSC 17, the Supreme Court held that the deceased's wishes were relevant factors which fell to be considered alongside the other factors.

  The guideline specifically refers to conduct. An example of extreme conduct, which may have a very significant impact on how much the claimant would receive, would be if the claimant had killed the deceased. If a beneficiary under a will is criminally responsible for the testator's death, their entitlement under the will is forfeit (see **2.7.7**). However, they can still bring a claim for family provision. Another example of conduct which has affected the award is a prolonged period of estrangement between the applicant and the deceased.

The special guidelines set out in the Act vary with the category of applicant. For example, where the applicant is the surviving spouse or civil partner, the court takes into account the applicant's age and contribution to the welfare of the family (including looking after the home or caring for the family), the duration of the marriage or civil partnership and the likely financial settlement if the marriage or civil partnership had ended in divorce or dissolution rather than death. On an application by a child of the deceased the applicant's education or training requirements are considered. Where the application is by a cohabitant, the court should take account of the applicant's age, the length of the period of cohabitation and the contribution made by the cohabitant to the welfare of the family (including looking after the home or caring for the family).

Ilott v Blue Cross Properties and others [2017] UKSC 17

This case is a good example of the application of the guidelines to a claim by an adult child.

Melita Jackson died leaving her estate of £486,000 to three animal charities. Her daughter, Heather, had left home at 17 to live with a man of whom Melita disapproved. The mother and daughter were estranged for the next 26 years and never reconciled. Melita drafted a statement explaining her decision to exclude Heather. Heather had five children and lived in straightened circumstances. She lived with her husband and children in a house rented from a Housing Association and they were dependent on state benefits to meet basic living expenses. Heather claimed family provision.

The ordinary standard of provision (reasonable provision for the applicant's maintenance) applied. The Supreme Court said that maintenance 'did not extend to any or everything which it would be desirable for the applicant to have' and must 'import provision to meet the everyday expenses of living'. Claims by adult children who are capable of earning their own living, needed to be approached with caution. In the case of an adult applicant living independently, proof of a need and their relationship to the deceased may not be sufficient; there had to be some sort of moral claim or special circumstance established by the applicant in addition to the mere fact of blood relationship.

Under the s 3 guidelines, the Supreme Court took account of the applicant's financial needs and resources as well as those of the charity beneficiaries which depended on donations and legacies from the public. The effect which an order would have on the applicant's state benefits was also relevant. The relationship between the testatrix and her daughter, the prolonged period of estrangement and the testatrix's wishes expressed in her statement also fell to be considered under 'anything else which may be relevant including conduct'. The Supreme Court awarded Heather £50,000.

7.2.4 Orders

Having carried out an objective assessment and concluded that the estate has not made reasonable financial provision, the next step is to determine the amount and nature of the provision which should now be made.

The court has wide powers to make orders against the 'net estate' of the deceased, including orders for periodical payments, lump sum payments or the transfer of specific property to the applicant. The court will take the relevant guidelines into account when determining what orders to make.

The 'net estate' against which an order can be made includes not only property which the deceased has, or could have, disposed of by will, but also the deceased's share of joint property passing by survivorship if the court so orders.

In making an order for family provision, the court will declare how the burden of the order is to be borne, ie which beneficiary is to lose part or all of the property they would otherwise have taken.

For IHT purposes, the altered disposition of the estate is treated as taking effect from death. The IHT paid on death may have to be recalculated, eg if the order increases the amount passing to the deceased's spouse, more of the estate will attract the spouse exemption.

7.2.5 Anti-avoidance

In order to avoid a successful claim for family provision, a person might be tempted to give away their property in their lifetime so that on their death, it does not form part of their 'net estate' against which orders can be made. This ploy would be fruitless because the court can, for instance, avoid gifts made less than six years before death with the intention of defeating a claim under the Act. As a result of the court making such an order, the property in question would be included in the 'net estate' from which a claim could be satisfied.

7.2.6 Protecting the PRs

If PRs distribute the estate within six months of the grant and the court allows a claim for family provision, the PRs will be personally liable to satisfy the claim if insufficient assets remain in the estate (see **9.4.3**). PRs should be advised not to distribute the estate until six months have elapsed from the issue of the grant. Then, if a court permits an application out of time, the PRs will not be liable personally, but the applicant may be able to recover property from the beneficiaries.

7.2.7 Flowchart

The following flowchart summarises how to assess whether a family provision claim is likely to be successful.

Advising on a family provision claim

Did the deceased die domiciled in England and Wales?

↓

Does the applicant fall within a category of applicant?

(a) the spouse or civil partner of the deceased
(b) a former spouse or civil partner of the deceased who has not remarried
(c) a child of the deceased
(d) a child of the family
(e) any person who, immediately before the death of the deceased, was being maintained by the deceased either wholly or in part
(f) any person who, during the whole of the period of two years ending immediately before the date when the deceased died, was living in the same household as the deceased as the husband, wife or civil partner of the deceased

↓

Is the applicant within the time limit?
6 months from the grant

↓

Has the will/intestacy made reasonable provision for the applicant?
Spouse - reasonable provision whether or not needed for maintenance
Other applicants - reasonable provision for maintenance

Apply guidelines

General guidelines

(i) the financial resources and needs of the applicant, other applicants and beneficiaries of the estate now and in the foreseeable future;

(ii) the deceased's moral obligations towards any applicant or beneficiary;

(iii) the size and nature of the estate;

(iv) the physical or mental disability of any applicant or beneficiary;

(v) anything else which may be relevant, such as the conduct of the applicant.

Special guidelines according to category of applicant

↓

Orders

- Periodical payments, lump sum payments or the transfer of specific property to the applicant
- Made against 'net estate' (could include deceased's interest in joint property)

7.3 Post-death variations and disclaimers

Despite the terms of the will or the operation of the intestacy rules, after a person dies it is possible for the beneficiaries to alter what happens to the estate. There are various reasons why a post-death variation or disclaimer might be desirable. For example:

(a) A beneficiary may feel that a member of the family has been unfairly excluded or needs a larger legacy. Maybe circumstances have changed since the testator made his will. Adult beneficiaries may decide that they would prefer their legacy to go to their children.

(b) Where a person is threatening to bring a claim for family provision, a voluntary variation of the deceased's will or distribution on intestacy in favour of the claimant may secure an out-of-court settlement and avoid the stress, acrimony and expense, of a court case.

(c) The will or distribution on intestacy may not be tax-efficient and a variation of the terms could achieve a considerable saving of IHT and/or capital gains tax (CGT).

7.3.1 Types of arrangement

Property can be redirected in a number of ways. The following are the most common examples:

(a) A lifetime gift by the beneficiary of an inheritance under a will or under an intestacy

For example, Jack is given a house in his late father's will. Jack already has a house and would like his father's property to go to his son, Ben. Jack could accept the devise of the house and then make a lifetime gift of the house to Ben.

(b) Post-death disclaimers

Disclaimers amount to a rejection of the assets inherited under the will or the intestacy law or by survivorship (see also **2.7.6**). The disclaimed assets then pass as though the original beneficiary had predeceased. Disclaimers are, therefore, appropriate only if, following the rejection, the property passes to the person whom the original beneficiary intends to benefit.

Example

Amir's will gives a legacy of £100,000 to Zainab and residue to Maz.

If Zainab disclaims her legacy, it will be treated as though she predeceased. Therefore, it would form part of residue and the £100,000 would go to Maz. If she does not want it to go to Maz, a disclaimer is not appropriate.

There are other limitations on disclaimers; a beneficiary cannot disclaim part of a gift and cannot disclaim once they have accepted a benefit from the gift.

(c) Post-death variations

The restrictions on disclaimers do not apply to post-death variations. A beneficiary who varies a benefit *can direct* where benefit is to go and on what terms. So in the above example, Zainab could effect a variation and direct that the legacy is to go to her daughter, Shamime. In effect, the original beneficiary re-writes the deceased's will or intestacy rules. Variations can also be used to redirect the deceased's interest in joint property which passes by survivorship.

The original beneficiary who effects the variation must be aged 18 or more and have mental capacity. If the beneficiary is not legally capable of effecting the variation, an application could be made to the court. Under the Variation of Trusts Act 1958, the court has the power to consent for infants and people who lack capacity and cannot consent for themselves, provided the variation is for their benefit. However, applications to the court are expensive and time-consuming. Nevertheless, an application might be justified if, for example, it would achieve a considerable tax saving.

7.3.2 IHT considerations

Example continued

Amir's will gives a legacy of £100,000 to Zainab and residue to Maz.

Amir's estate is large enough to attract IHT. If Zainab disclaims her legacy she would be regarded as making a lifetime transfer of value (a PET) to Maz (see ***6.5****). If she varies the legacy in favour of Shamime, this too would be regarded as a PET by Zainab.*

Amir's death ——→ (IHT) Zainab ——→ (PET) Maz/Shamime

The PET would become chargeable if Zainab were to die within seven years. This could mean that the £100,000 would be taxed twice: once on Amir's death and then a second time on Zainab's PET. Even if there is no IHT to pay on Zainab's lifetime transfer because it falls within her nil rate band, it still has a tax effect because there would be less of her nil rate band available for her death estate.

To overcome the taxation problem described above, s 142 Inheritance Tax Act 1984 (IHTA1984) allows variations to be 'read back' into the will. In these circumstances, it is as if the testator gave the legacy direct to the new beneficiary.

Certain conditions have to be satisfied for the variation or disclaimer to be read back to the deceased's death. The conditions are that the disclaimer or variation:

(a) is in writing and signed by the original beneficiary;

(b) is within two years of the deceased's death; and

(c) is not made for a consideration in money or money's worth.

In addition, variations must state that s 142 IHTA 1984 is to apply.

Example continued

Zainab uses s 142 to vary the will so that the legacy is left to Shamime. It is as if Amir gave the £100,000 direct to Shamime.

Amir's death ——→ (IHT) Shamime

There would be no PET by Zainab and no risk of a second charge to IHT.

In Zainab's case, the variation did not result in a change to the IHT bill on Amir's estate. Some variations do – for example, if Amir's will gave everything to his wife and she varied in favour of their children, the spouse exemption for Amir's estate would be lost. If this would lead to inheritance tax on Amir's estate, then it would be preferable not to read back the variation and to treat the variation as a PET by Amir's wife. Each case should be assessed individually. If more IHT is payable as a result of a variation, the deceased's personal representatives must join in the written variation.

7.3.3 CGT considerations

A disclaimer or redirection of an inheritance could also give rise to CGT. Broadly, CGT is charged on 'disposals' of assets (not cash). Disposals include sales and lifetime gifts of assets but not transfers on death. On a disposal, CGT is charged on any gain (ie the increase in the value of the asset since the person acquired it). CGT is covered in more depth in **9.9.5**.

A disclaimer or variation within two years of the deceased's death can be read back to the deceased's will for CGT purposes so that there is no disposal by the original beneficiary and no CGT charge. The conditions which must be satisfied to have a disclaimer or variation read back to the deceased's death are similar to those in relation to IHT.

Example

In his will, a father leaves a painting to his daughter. At the father's death, the painting is valued at £100,000. One year later, when the painting is worth £130,000, the daughter decides to give the painting to her son.

A lifetime gift or post-death variation would be regarded as a disposal by the daughter. Her gain is £30,000, which, subject to available exemptions and reliefs, would attract CGT.

If the conditions are satisfied, the daughter could elect to have a post-death variation read back to the father's will. There would be no CGT. The daughter's son would be deemed to acquire the painting on his grandfather's death at a value of £100,000.

Summary

Family provision

- Family members and dependants can ask the court to alter the disposition of the deceased's estate if they feel that reasonable financial provision has not been made for them. The relevant legislation is contained in the Inheritance (Provision for Family and Dependants) Act 1975.
- Orders are made at the court's discretion by application of the s 3 guidelines.
- PRs should not distribute the estate within six months of the grant to avoid personal liability to a successful applicant.

Post-death variations and disclaimers

- A beneficiary can redirect cash or property which they have inherited on death by disclaimer or variation:
    - A disclaimed benefit passes as though the beneficiary predeceased
    - A variation allows the beneficiary to control who receives the benefit.
- In order to read back to the deceased's death for IHT and/or CGT so that it is treated as though the deceased gave the property direct to the new beneficiary the disclaimer or variation must be made:
    - in writing;
    - within two years of the deceased's death;
    - not for consideration in money or money's worth; and
    - in the case of a variation, it must contain an election that it is to be read back for IHT and/or CGT.
- If not read back:
    - For IHT, there would be a deemed transfer of value on the deceased's death and a PET by the beneficiary.
    - For CGT, assuming that the benefit comprises an asset and not cash, there would be a disposal by the beneficiary which may give rise to a CGT charge if the asset has risen substantially in value since the deceased's death.

Sample questions

Question 1

A woman died last week. In her valid will, she gave her entire estate to a charity. She left her husband 18 months ago and went to live with her same-sex partner ('her partner') with whom she has cohabited ever since. The partner paid the rent for their accommodation and most of their household expenses. The woman is survived by her husband, her partner and a step-son, who is her husband's child by a former marriage.

Which of the following best describes potential applicants under the Inheritance (Provision for Family and Dependants) Act 1975?

A The partner could claim in the cohabitant category.

B The partner could claim on the basis that the woman maintained her.

C The step-son could claim as the woman's child.

D The step-son might be able to claim as a child of the woman's family.

E The husband could claim as a former spouse who has not remarried.

Answer

Option D is correct. The step-son might be able to bring a claim as a person (not being a child of the deceased) who was treated by the deceased as a child of the family. It will depend on whether the woman acted as a parent towards him.

Option A is wrong because the partner had not lived with the woman for two years immediately before her death.

Option B is wrong because the woman did not make a substantial contribution towards the partner's reasonable needs. Rather, the partner was maintaining the woman.

Option C is wrong because step-children are not regarded as a person's 'children'.

Option E is wrong because the woman and her husband were not divorced. (He could claim as a spouse in the first category.)

Question 2

A man died seven months ago. He died intestate. No grant has been obtained yet. The man and his wife were beneficial joint tenants of a house and bank account. He also owned a car and some clothes in his sole name. The man and his daughter quarrelled seven years ago and have not seen each other since. The daughter, who is a teacher, intends to claim family provision.

Which of the following best explains whether her claim is likely to be successful?

A The daughter will be unsuccessful because the only assets which she can claim against are the car and the clothes and the courts discourage applications in small estates.

B The daughter will be unsuccessful because she is out of time.

C The daughter will be unsuccessful unless she can show some special circumstance, such as a moral obligation owed by the deceased, and that she needs financial help with her day-to-day living expenses.

D The daughter will be unsuccessful because she cannot show that she was maintained by the deceased immediately before his death.

E The daughter is likely to succeed because the deceased should have made reasonable provision for her whether or not needed for her maintenance.

Answer

Option C is correct. The courts have rejected claims by adult children who cannot show some special circumstance. The standard of reasonable financial provision under the Act would be the ordinary standard of reasonable provision for maintenance. Thus, any provision would be to meet daily living expenses and the court will reject her claim if she has the resources to meet these expenses herself.

Option A is wrong. The court could order that the net estate, against which orders can be made, should include the man's interest in a joint tenancy of the house and bank account.

Option B is wrong because the time limit is six months from the grant and a grant has not been obtained in the man's estate. In any event, the court can extend the time limit.

Option D is wrong. The daughter can bring her claim as a child of the deceased and would not have to use the maintenance category.

Option E is wrong. The standard for an applicant who is not a spouse is the ordinary standard of reasonable provision for maintenance.

Question 3

A woman died six months ago, having used all of her nil rate band in her lifetime. She left her holiday cottage to her sister and the rest of her £1 million estate to her brother. The sister wants to pass the cottage to her daughter.

Which of the following is the best way for the sister to achieve her wishes?

A The sister should make a lifetime gift of the cottage to her daughter.

B The sister should disclaim her right to the cottage.

C The sister should make a variation passing the cottage to her daughter and elect to have the variation read back to the woman's death for IHT purposes.

D The sister should make a variation passing the cottage to her daughter but she should not elect to have the variation read back to the woman's death for IHT purposes because it would result in more IHT becoming payable on the woman's estate.

E The sister should make a variation passing the cottage to her daughter. It should be made in writing, within two years of the woman's death and it must be signed by the sister, the brother and the woman's PRs.

Answer

Option C is correct. A variation read back to the woman's death is the best option for IHT purposes. No additional IHT will be payable on the woman's estate (a non-exempt beneficiary is replaced by another non-exempt beneficiary). The election would mean that the sister would not be regarded as making a PET which could become chargeable if she were to die within seven years.

Option A is wrong. The lifetime gift would be regarded as a PET and would become chargeable if the sister were to die within seven years. This is not desirable especially because the cottage has already incurred IHT on the woman's death.

Option B is wrong. A disclaimer would not pass the cottage to the sister's daughter. The cottage would pass as though the sister had predeceased and the brother would inherit it as part of residue.

Option D is wrong. As explained above, an election to have the variation read back would not result in more IHT becoming payable on the woman's estate.

Option E is wrong because only the original beneficiary (the sister) needs to sign the variation. The signature of the brother is unnecessary as are the signatures of the PRs (in the latter case because no additional IHT would be payable on the woman's estate). The other conditions stated in Option E are correct.

8 Administration: Obtaining the Grant of Representation

SQE1 syllabus

This chapter will enable you to achieve the SQE1 assessment specification in relation to functioning legal knowledge concerned with wills and the administration of estates.

- The planning, management and progression of the administration of an estate.
- Grants of representation:
  - need for a grant of representation
  - the relevant provisions of the Non-Contentious Probate Rules
  - application procedure
  - valuation of assets and liabilities
  - excepted estates
  - methods of funding the initial payment of inheritance tax

Note that in the SQE1 assessments, candidates are not usually expected to recall specific case names or cite statutory or regulatory authorities. However, in this chapter, the following may be referred to in the SQE1 assessment:

- inheritance tax form (number IHT400);
- Non-Contentious Probate Rules (NCPR) 1987, Rules 20 and 22; and
- forms PA1P and PA1A.

Otherwise, references to cases, statutory and regulatory authorities are provided for illustrative purposes only.

Learning outcomes

By the end of this chapter you will be able to apply relevant core legal principles and rules appropriately and effectively, at the level of a competent newly qualified solicitor in practice, to realistic client-based and ethical problems and situations in the following areas:

- whether a grant of representation is required, the type of grant and possible applicants;
- whether an inheritance tax ('IHT') form should be submitted;
- the date for payment of IHT and funding the initial payment;
- probate papers required to obtain the grant; and
- the effect of a grant of representation.

8.1 Introduction

When a person dies, the personal representatives ('PRs') or the deceased's family often seek a solicitor's advice on winding up the estate.

The family may be unaware that in many cases, it will be necessary to obtain a grant of representation, an official document confirming the PRs' authority to act. PRs have to gain control of the deceased's assets so that they can realise or sell them, if necessary, in order to pay the deceased's debts and pecuniary legacies (see **Chapter 9**). Before asset holders, such as banks, building societies and insurance companies, will release funds to the PRs, they usually require proof that the PRs have been properly appointed. Similarly, in order to sell most assets, the PRs must prove to the purchaser that they (the PRs) have title to the assets. The document which confirms the PRs' authority and their title to the deceased's assets is the grant of representation. Applications for grants are made to His Majesty's Courts and Tribunals Service Probate ('HMCTS'). Solicitors are often instructed to implement the procedure for obtaining the grant.

In larger estates, IHT may be payable. A solicitor can advise on whether this is the case, whether it is necessary to send an account (IHT400) to HMRC, and whether some of the IHT has to be paid before the grant is obtained.

This chapter deals with the process of obtaining the grant of representation and dealing with IHT. In particular, it looks at:

- initial assessment;
- IHT account IHT400;
- paying the IHT;
- Forms PA1P and PA1A;
- executors applying for the grant of probate;
- administrators applying for the grant of letters of administration with the will annexed; and
- administrators applying for the grant of (simple) letters of administration.

8.2 Initial assessment

8.2.1 The PRs

(a) Identify the PRs

The PRs will be either the deceased's executors or intended administrators. 'Personal representative' is a generic term which covers both.

The following diagram shows how to identify the PRs in the common scenarios listed on the left-hand side.

The deceased left a valid will which appoints executors, one or more of whom is able and willing to act.	→	**Executors** will obtain a **grant of probate** (using form PA1P). See **8.6**.
The deceased left a valid will but there are **no** persons able or willing to act as executors.	→	**Administrators** will obtain a **grant of letters of administration with the will annexed** (using form PA1P). NCPR 1987, r 20 determines who the administrators will be (usually the residuary beneficiary). See **8.7.1**.
The deceased left no will or no valid will.	→	**Administrators** will obtain a **grant of (simple) letters of administration** (using form PA1A). NCPR 1987, r 22 determines who the administrators will be (usually the main beneficiaries on intestacy). See **8.8.1**.

(b) Number of PRs

One PR may obtain a grant and act alone. This is so even if the estate includes land which may be sold during the administration, because one PR can give the purchaser a good receipt for the sale proceeds. In contrast, where trustees sell land, the purchaser will insist on a receipt from all the trustees being at least two in number or a trust corporation.

One difference between executors and administrators is that two administrators are usually required where one of the beneficiaries is an infant ('a minority interest') or only has a life interest. This is the case whether the grant is one of simple letters of administration or letters of administration with the will. In contrast, one executor can always act alone in these cases.

(c) Authority of PRs before the grant

An executor derives authority to act in the administration of an estate from the will. The grant of probate confirms that authority. It provides conclusive evidence of the title of the executors to the deceased's assets and of the validity and contents of the will. Although the executor has full power to act from the time of the deceased's death, the executor will be unable to undertake certain transactions (eg sale of land) without producing the grant as proof of entitlement to act. Similarly, the deceased's bank and other institutions will not release the money to the PRs without sight of the grant.

Administrators (with or without the will) have very limited powers before a grant is made. Their authority stems from the grant which is not retrospective to the date of death. The grant of letters of administration vests the deceased's property in the administrators. It provides conclusive evidence of the administrators' title to the deceased's assets and of the validity and content of any will.

8.2.2 The beneficiaries

It is important to obtain any will made by the deceased and check it carefully to make sure that it is valid and admissible to probate. If it is not, there will be an intestacy and an application will be made for a grant of simple letters of administration. To ensure that the will is admissible, it is necessary to check the following:

- the will is the last will of the testator;
- that it has not been validly revoked;
- that it is executed in accordance with the Wills Act 1837, s 9; and
- that it contains an attestation clause which indicates that the will was executed in accordance with the requirements of the Wills Act 1837 and raises a presumption of 'due execution'.

If there is a will, the solicitor must establish the identity of the beneficiaries and the nature and extent of their entitlements (eg whether as legatee or as residuary beneficiary). The solicitor will also check whether any of the gifts in the will have failed due to, eg lapse or ademption (see **2.7**). If the deceased has died intestate, the solicitor will establish which members of the family have survived, so that they can advise on the distribution of the estate in accordance with the rules discussed in **Chapter 4**.

To comply with the obligations imposed by the UK General Data Protection Regulation, solicitors must inform beneficiaries that they are holding personal data on them, the purposes for which the data will be used and the rights of the beneficiaries as data subjects.

8.2.3 Obtain details of the deceased's property and debts

The solicitor will ask the PRs for details of the deceased's assets and obtain any associated documents such as building society passbooks and share certificates. From these details, it is possible to begin to assess the size of the deceased's estate, and any IHT liability.

The valuation of assets for IHT is dealt with at **6.4.2**. The IHT valuation is also used for probate purposes. The balances on the deceased's bank and building society accounts and the amount due on any life policies can be obtained by writing to the asset holders. Assets are usually valued at their open market value, but special rules apply to related property and the valuation of quoted shares (see **6.5.2** and **6.4.2**). An estate agent/auctioneer can be asked to value the deceased's residence or other land and the contents of the house. A valuation of unquoted shares should be obtained from an accountant.

8.2.4 Assets for which a grant is not required

A grant enables the PRs to prove their authority to deal with the deceased's assets which pass under the will or the intestacy rules. However, it is possible to access some assets without a grant, which is particularly useful where the deceased's family needs funds immediately for paying IHT or for discharging other bills. If the whole estate comprises these assets and nothing else, there is no need for a grant at all. The assets which can be realised without the grant are covered in (a), (b) and (c) below.

(a) Assets which may pass to the PRs without a grant

- **Administration of Estates (Small Payments) Act 1965**

  Orders made under this Act permit payments to be made to persons appearing to be beneficially entitled to the assets without production of the grant. This facility is not available if the value of the asset exceeds £5,000 and, as the payments are made at the discretion of the institutions concerned, it is not possible for PRs to insist that payments should be made.

If payment is refused, the PRs will have to obtain a grant before the asset can be collected. Subject to these points, payments can be made in respect of, for example:

- money in the National Savings Bank and Trustee Savings Bank (but not in other bank accounts);
- National Savings Certificates and Premium Bonds; and
- money in building societies and friendly societies.

- **Chattels**

  Moveable personal property, such as furniture, clothing, jewellery and cars, can normally be sold without the PRs having to prove formally to the buyer that they are entitled to sell such items.

- **Cash**

  Usually, the PRs do not require a grant when taking custody of any cash found in the deceased's possession (ie found in the home of the deceased as opposed to deposited in a bank or other account). Although it should be noted that whilst banks and building societies vary in their approach, in practice most are prepared to release relatively small amounts without requiring a grant.

(b) Assets not passing through the PRs' hands

These assets do not pass under the deceased's will or intestacy and therefore do not vest in the PRs. Consequently, the grant is irrelevant.

- **Joint property**

  On death, any interest in property held by the deceased as beneficial joint tenant with another (whether it is an interest in land or personalty, eg a bank account) passes by survivorship to the surviving joint tenant. As it does not pass through the PRs, any grant is irrelevant. The survivor can get the property transferred into their sole name merely by producing the deceased's death certificate to the relevant institution (eg the deceased's bank or the Land Registry). Since it is common for married couples and civil partners to own property jointly, there are many occasions where a grant is not required for this reason.

  (Conversely, if the property is held by persons as beneficial tenants in common, the share of each tenant in common passes on their death to their PRs for distribution under the will or intestacy, and a grant will be required.)

(c) Assets not forming part of the deceased's estate

- **Insurance policies assigned or written in trust**

  The deceased may have insured their life but assigned the proceeds or written them in trust for others. The beneficiary can obtain the proceeds of the policy simply by producing the deceased's death certificate to the insurance company. A grant is not required since the money does not form part of the deceased's estate. The proceeds do not attract IHT because the deceased had no beneficial interest in the policy and therefore they are not part of the transfer of value on death (**6.4.1.3**). Such a policy is particularly advantageous, as the proceeds make tax-free provision for dependants of the deceased and can be obtained immediately following the death.

- **Pension benefits**

  Death in service benefits under a pension scheme are often payable to persons to be selected at the discretion of the pension fund trustees. Payments are made to the beneficiaries on production of the death certificate. A grant is not required, since the pension benefits do not pass under the deceased employee's will or intestacy. This is another method of making tax-free provision for dependants, and such provision can also be obtained immediately following the death.

8.2.5 Assessment of the IHT position

Once details of all the deceased's assets have been gathered and a value attributed to them, it is possible to calculate the IHT (if any) payable on the estate.

As a separate matter, it will also be necessary to work out whether it is necessary to submit an IHT account to HMRC or whether it is an excepted estate (see **8.3** for the qualifying conditions for excepted estates in respect of deaths on or after 1 January 2022).

If IHT is payable, some of it is likely to be due before the grant is obtained (see **8.4**). Before the PRs apply for the grant, they send the IHT account IHT400 to HMRC (or IHT401 for a person domiciled outside the UK) and pay any IHT due before the grant to HMRC. HMRC will write to or email the PRs confirming receipt and processing of the IHT400 and providing a unique code and details of the estate values which will be required when submitting the grant application to HMCTS.

Where IHT is payable before the grant, it will be necessary to find ways of funding the IHT, given that it is not possible to gain access to most of the deceased's assets without production of the grant (see **8.4**).

8.2.6 Preparing the application for the grant

(a) The application and fee

Applications by legal professionals for a grant of probate must be made online (apart from a few limited exceptions, eg where the application is to prove a copy of the will).

Applications for grants of letters of administration (with or without the will) are made by post but can be made online if certain conditions are fulfilled (for example, where there is only one applicant, they are the only person entitled to the estate and certain other prerequisites are satisfied).

Postal applications are made by sending a completed form PA1P if there is a will (ie for grants of probate or letters of administration with the will annexed) or a PA1A where there was no will.

Further details of the forms and applications appear below at **8.5-8.8**.

The same fee is payable irrespective of whether the application is made on paper or online. The fee for paper applications is paid by cheque. In the case of online applications made by professionals, the firm must open a 'HMCTS Payment by Account' from which payment is taken automatically when the application is submitted.

The fee is currently £300 where the estate exceeds £5,000. There is no fee if the estate is £5,000 or less. Applicants automatically receive one free copy of the grant. Extra copies can be requested and cost £1.50 each.

(b) Additional documents required

In order to obtain the grant, it will be necessary to send the deceased's will and codicil, if any, to HMCTS.

In some cases, before issuing the grant, HMCTS may require further evidence of the validity of any will. Evidence can take the form of an affidavit sworn before a solicitor who is not acting for the PRs or a witness statement verified by a statement of truth. Solicitors normally use precedents as a starting point for drafting these documents. To some extent the need for such further evidence can be anticipated from a close examination of the will as indicated by the following:

- Evidence of due execution and/or capacity

If there is no attestation clause, or the clause is in some respect defective, or there are circumstances raising doubt about the execution of the will, HMCTS will require evidence, preferably from an attesting witness, to establish that the will has been properly executed.

If there is doubt about the mental capacity of the testator to make the will, the affidavit of a doctor may be necessary. In such cases, it is helpful if a doctor examined the testator to ascertain whether they had sufficient capacity at the time the will was made.

- Evidence as to knowledge and approval

There may be doubt as to whether the testator was aware of the contents of the will when they executed it. This may arise where the will was signed by someone other than the testator due to illiteracy or frailty of the testator, or because of suspicious circumstances, for example where the person who prepared the will for the testator benefits substantially by its terms.

In any of these circumstances, the attestation clause should have been suitably adapted, ideally by indicating that the will was read over to the testator or was independently explained to the testator. In the absence of this, HMCTS will require to be satisfied that the testator had knowledge and approval of the contents of the will. The evidence is provided by means of an affidavit or witness statement made by someone who can speak as to the facts. Normally, this will be one of the attesting witnesses, but it could be an independent person who explained the provisions of the will to the testator.

- Evidence as to remote witnessing

Where the will was executed during the currency of the remote witnessing rules (see **1.7.1**) and the witnesses were not physically present when the testator signed or acknowledged the will but watched via a video link, questions as to formalities, capacity and knowledge and approval are more likely to arise than in cases of conventional execution. Unless the attestation clause has been amended to give details of such matters, it is likely that evidence in the form of an affidavit or witness statement will be required from the witnesses or anyone else who was present (remotely or physically).

- Evidence of plight and condition

If the state of the will suggests that it has been interfered with in some way since execution, the registrar will require further evidence by way of explanation. This may arise:

(i) where the will has been altered since its execution;

(ii) where there is some obvious mark on the will indicating a document may have been attached to it (eg the marks of a paper clip, raising a suggestion that some other testamentary document may have been attached); or

(iii) where the will gives the appearance of attempted revocation (eg where it is torn).

Generally, the explanation required will take the form of an affidavit or witness statement of plight and condition made by some person having knowledge of the facts.

- Lost will

A will which was known to have been in the testator's possession but which cannot be found following the death is presumed to have been destroyed by the testator with the intention of revoking it. Although it is possible to rebut the presumption.

However, if the will has been lost or accidentally destroyed, probate may be obtained of a copy of the will, such as a copy kept in the solicitor's file, or a reconstruction. In such a case, application should be made to the registrar, supported by appropriate evidence in the form of an affidavit or witness statement from the applicant for the grant of probate.

(c) Summary of procedure for obtaining the grant

IHT 400 required	Excepted estate
• Send IHT 400 to HMRC and pay any IHT due before the grant. Wait for HMRC to provide unique code and asset values	• Apply for grant online or send PA1P or PA1A as appropriate to HMCTS
• Apply for grant online or send PA1P or PA1A as appropriate to HMCTS • Send to HMCTS: ◦ the deceased's will and codicil, if any ◦ additional evidence (eg of due execution) ◦ probate fee	• Send to HMCTS: ◦ the deceased's will and codicil, if any ◦ additional evidence (eg of due execution) ◦ probate fee

8.3 IHT account IHT400

If the estate is not an 'excepted estate', the PRs will prepare an IHT400 (IHT401 for a person domiciled outside the UK) and whichever of the supporting schedules are relevant to the estate. For example, if the deceased made lifetime gifts, the PRs must complete schedule 403 which deals with lifetime gifts.

The IHT400 is an inventory of the assets to which the deceased was beneficially entitled and of their liabilities, and is the form for claiming reliefs and exemptions and calculating the inheritance tax payable. It should be delivered within 12 months of the end of the month in which the death occurred. Usually, PRs aim to deliver the account within six months of the end of the month of death to comply with IHT time limits for the payment of interest. Until the account is submitted, no grant of representation can be issued.

Where IHT is payable, it is necessary to apply for a reference number before submitting the IHT400. Application may be made online or by post using schedule IHT422.

If the estate is excepted, PRs do not submit any IHT form to HMRC. Information as to value of the estate is included on the forms submitted to the HMCTS which is passed on to HMRC. HMRC has 60 days from the issue of the grant of representation to ask for additional information. If no such request is made, the estate receives automatic clearance. If an estate which initially appears to be excepted is subsequently found not to be so, the PRs must submit the IHT400 within six months of the discovery.

8.3.1 Excepted estates – conditions for deaths on or after 1 January 2022

The precise requirements for qualifying as an excepted estate are set out in the Inheritance Tax (Delivery of Accounts) (Excepted Estates) Regulations 2004. They have become extremely complex. It may be easier to focus on the broad description of the requirements rather than on the detail.

There are three categories of excepted estate:

(a) Category 1 – 'small' estates

Broadly, estates falling into this category are those where the gross value of the estate for IHT purposes, plus the value of any 'specified transfers' and 'specified exempt transfers' (defined below) in the seven years prior to death, does not exceed the current nil rate threshold. The gross value of the estate is the value before deduction of debts and exemptions and reliefs.

The nil rate threshold or band ('NRB') is presently £325,000 but can be increased if the deceased's spouse or civil partner predeceased without using all or part of their NRB (see **6.4.4**). The NRB in force at the death of the survivor is increased by whatever percentage of the NRB of the first spouse to die was unused by them. Note, however, that it is only possible to use the NRB of one spouse or civil partner.

In full, the Regulations for **'small excepted estates'** require the following:

(a) the deceased was a long-term UK resident immediately before their death;

(b) the value of the estate is attributable wholly to property passing:
- (i) under his will or intestacy,
- (ii) under a nomination of an asset taking effect on death,
- (iii) under a single settlement in which he was entitled to an interest in possession in settled property, or
- (iv) by survivorship in a beneficial joint tenancy or, in Scotland, by survivorship in a special destination;

(c) of that property:
- (i) not more than £250,000 represents property which, immediately before that person's death, was settled property; and
- (ii) not more than £100,000 represents property situated outside the United Kingdom;

(d) the deceased made no chargeable transfers in the seven years before death other than specified transfers (defined below) where the aggregate value transferred (ignoring business or agricultural relief) did not exceed £250,000; and

(e) the aggregate of:
- (i) the gross value of the deceased's estate, plus
- (ii) the value transferred by any specified transfers (defined below), plus
- (iii) the value transferred by any specified exempt transfers (defined below), did not exceed the nil rate threshold for the deceased, increased to take account of any nil rate band transferred from one deceased spouse or civil partner.

'Specified transfers' for Categories 1 and 2

These are chargeable transfers of cash, personal chattels or tangible moveable property, quoted shares or securities, or an interest in or over land (unless the land becomes settled or is subject to a reservation of benefit) made in the seven years before death. This means that if someone makes a gift which does not fall within this category in the seven years before death (for example, a transfer of unquoted shares), the estate cannot be excepted under Categories 1 or 2.

When valuing the specified transfers, business and agricultural property relief is ignored so the unrelieved value has to be taken into account.

'Specified exempt transfers' for Categories 1 and 2

These are transfers of value made during the seven years before death which are exempt under one of the following exemptions:

(a) s 18 (transfers between spouses (or civil partners));

(b) s 23 (gifts to charities);

(c) s 24 (gifts to political parties);

(d) s 24A (gifts to housing associations);

(e) s 27 (maintenance funds for historic buildings, etc); or

(f) s 28 (employee trusts).

Gifts which are exempt under the normal expenditure out of income exemption are treated for this purpose as chargeable if they exceed £3,000 in any one tax year.

Example 1

Adam has just died. His will leaves his estate to his wife, Brenda, and daughter, Clare, in equal shares. He was a long-term UK resident and had made no lifetime transfers.

	£
His estate consists of:	
House owned jointly with Brenda (Adam's half share)	80,000
Building society a/c (sole name)	100,000
Personal chattels	2,000
Life interest in a trust fund set up in his father's will (value of capital assets)	30,000
	212,000
Debts (funeral bill and credit cards)	(2,000)
	210,000

This is a Category 1 ('small') excepted estate. The gross value of Adam's estate (before deduction of debts and exemptions and reliefs) is £212,000, which is under the NRB. Looking at the more detailed requirements, the value of settled property (ie trust property in which he had a life interest) does not exceed £250,000 and there were no lifetime gifts. The PRs will not submit IHT400. The probate application will contain information confirming that it is an excepted estate.

Example 2

Fred has just died leaving his estate to his two children. His wife, Gemma, died last year and left everything to Fred.

Fred's gross estate is £600,000 and consists of a house and money in the bank. He has made no lifetime gifts.

This is a Category 1 ('small') excepted estate because Fred's nil rate threshold is increased for the purpose of the excepted estates regulations to £650,000 as a result of inheriting the whole of Gemma's nil rate band.

(Had Gemma left a legacy of £32,500 to her grandson, 90% of Gemma's nil rate band would have transferred. Therefore, Fred's estate would still qualify as an excepted small estate because his gross estate would still be less than the aggregate NRB of £617,500.)

(b) Category 2 – 'exempt' estates

These are estates where the bulk of the estate attracts the spouse (or civil partner) or charity exemption. More particularly:

- the *gross* value of the estate (plus specified transfers and specified exempt transfers made in the seven years before death) must not exceed £3 million; and

- the *net chargeable* estate after deduction of liabilities and spouse and/or charity exemption (plus specified transfers and specified exempt transfers made in the seven years before death) must not exceed the nil rate band.

As with Category 1 estates, a transferred nil rate band can increase the nil rate threshold for this purpose.

In full, the Regulations for **'exempt excepted estates'** require the following:

(a) the deceased was a long-term UK resident immediately before their death;

(b) the value of the estate is attributable wholly to property passing:

  (i) under his will or intestacy,
  (ii) under a nomination of an asset taking effect on death,
  (iii) under a single settlement in which he was entitled to an interest in possession in settled property, or
  (iv) by survivorship in a beneficial joint tenancy or, in Scotland, by survivorship in a special destination;

(c) of that property:

  (i) chargeable trust property included in the estate does not exceed £250,000 and the total amount of trust property including exempt amounts does not exceed £1 million; and
  (ii) not more than £100,000 represents property situated outside the United Kingdom;

(d) the deceased made no chargeable transfers during the period of seven years ending with his death other than specified transfers (defined below) where the aggregate value transferred (ignoring business or agricultural relief) did not exceed £250,000;

(e) the aggregate of:

  (i) the gross value of that person's estate, plus
  (ii) the value transferred by any specified transfers (defined above) made by that person, plus
  (iii) the value transferred by any specified exempt transfers (defined above), did not exceed £3 million;

(ea)there is property left after deduction of liabilities to pass to spouse or charity; and

(f) the aggregate of:

  (i) the value of the estate after deducting allowable liabilities, spouse and charity exemptions, plus
  (ii) specified transfers (defined above), plus
  (iii) specified exempt transfers (defined above),

  did not exceed the nil rate threshold, increased to take account of any nil rate band transferred from a deceased spouse or civil partner.

Example

Davina has just died. Her will leaves £50,000 to her son, Ernst, and the residue to her husband, Fernando. She was a long-term UK resident. Her only specified transfer was made two years ago when she gave £200,000 to Ernst.

	£
Her estate consists of:	
House owned jointly with Fernando (half share)	£1,400,000
Quoted investments	100,000
Bank and building society accounts	50,000
Personal chattels	15,000
Specified transfer	200,000
There are:	
Debts (funeral bill and credit cards)	(5,000)

This is a Category 2 ('exempt') excepted estate. The gross value of the estate, plus the value of specified transfers in the seven years prior to death does not exceed £3 million; Davina did not make chargeable lifetime transfers in the seven years before her death which exceeded £250,000; the net estate after deduction of liabilities and the spouse exemption, together with the value of specified transfers and specified exempt transfers in the seven years prior to death does not exceed the current nil rate threshold of £325,000.

(c) Category 3 – 'non-domiciled' estates

The third category is where the deceased was not a long-term UK resident at any time on or after 6 April 2025 and was not domiciled or treated as domiciled in the United Kingdom at any time after that date, and owned only limited assets in the United Kingdom.

(d) Procedure for excepted estates

PRs provide no information directly to HMRC. Instead, they include the following on their applications for a grant:

(i) the deceased's full name and date of death; and

(ii) a declaration:

- that the estate is an excepted estate; and
- whether they are claiming against the estate the unused proportion of the IHT nil rate band of a pre-deceased spouse or civil partner (the transferable nil rate band); and

(iii) the following three IHT estate values:

- the gross value of the estate for IHT plus any specified transfers and specified exempt transfers made by the deceased in the seven years before their death;
- the net value of the estate for IHT less any allowable debts;
- the net qualifying value of the estate, that is, the net value of the estate for IHT less any spouse, civil partner or charity exemptions.

HM Courts and Tribunals Service will have one month to pass the information to HMRC.

Personal representatives of those who are not long-term UK residents will have to provide rather more information. HMRC will select a random sample to review within 60 days of the application for a grant. In addition, it 'will use other information sources to identify those estates nearer to the IHT threshold' where it feels that there is a risk that IHT may be payable.

8.3.2 IHT400

An IHT400 must be used whenever the deceased was a long-term UK resident immediately before their death and the estate is not an 'excepted' estate.

The PRs send the completed IHT400 and relevant supporting schedules to HMRC. The PRs (or their solicitor) use the form to calculate the amount of any IHT payable and they also pay any IHT due before the grant (**8.4**). HMRC will write to/email the applicant providing a unique code and details of the estate values which must be included in the grant application. The application cannot be submitted to HMCTS until the code and the values have been received.

8.4 Paying the IHT

8.4.1 Date for payment

The general rule is that IHT is due six months after the end of the month in which the deceased died (see **6.9**). For example, if a person dies on 10 January, inheritance tax is due on 31 July. However, certain types of property such as land and some types of business property (see **6.9.1.2**) attract the instalment option which means that there is the right to pay by 10 annual instalments.

The following table shows when the IHT on the various components of an estate is due.

IHT on non-instalment option property	→	IHT is due within six months of the end of the month in which the death occurred. Late payments attract interest. **BUT IHT on non-instalment option property must be paid before the grant.**
IHT on instalment option property	→	If PRs do not elect for instalments: IHT must be paid before the grant (or within 6 months of the end of the month of death, if earlier). If PRs elect to pay by instalments: The first instalment is due within 6 months of the end of the month of death. The other nine instalments are due at annual intervals.

The IHT payable on the estate is apportioned between the instalment and non-instalment option property using the estate rate formula described in **6.8.2**.

Example

Jane, who never married or formed a civil partnership, died on 8 November leaving her entire estate to her sister. Jane owned a house, worth £400,000, and personalty (comprising her savings in banks and building societies and small shareholdings in various quoted companies) worth a total of £200,000. Jane had no debts and made no lifetime gifts.

Do any of Jane's assets attract the instalment option?

The house is instalment option property. The other assets are non-instalment option. (Note that the quoted shares do not attract the instalment option because they did not give Jane control (more than 50% of the shares) of the companies.)

How much IHT is payable?

Jane's chargeable estate is £600,000.

The first £325,000 is taxed at 0%

The balance of £275,000 is taxed at 40% = £110,000

When is the IHT on the non-instalment option property payable?

*IHT on the non-instalment option property (£200,000) payable before the grant is calculated as follows. (See the formula for apportioning IHT using the estate rate in **6.8.2.**)*

$$£200{,}000 \times \frac{110{,}000 \text{ (IHT)}}{600{,}000 \text{ (chargeable estate)}} = £36{,}667$$

When is the IHT on the house payable?

If the PRs elect to pay IHT on the house (£73,333) by instalments, it need not be paid before the grant. The first instalment will be due six months after the end of the month of death and the remaining instalments will be due at annual intervals thereafter.

Instalments of IHT on land carry interest whether or not they are paid on time. If the land is sold, all the remaining instalments become payable forthwith.

8.4.2 Funding the IHT

Funding IHT payable before the grant is problematic. The institutions holding the deceased's assets, such as banks and building societies, usually want to see the grant before they will release the money.

Some options for raising IHT before the grant are set out below.

(a) Direct payment scheme

HMRC has reached an agreement with banks, building societies, investment management firms, pension and life insurance providers on a procedure allowing PRs to arrange payment of IHT to HMRC directly from the deceased's accounts or for assets to be sold and the proceeds paid to HMRC.

The scheme is voluntary on the part of the institution.

The procedure is as follows:

- The PRs must provide whatever identification the relevant institution requires. They should do this well in advance of applying for a grant so as to avoid any unnecessary delay in the application.
- The PRs complete a separate IHT423 for each institution from which money is to be transferred.
- The PRs send each IHT423 to the relevant institution at the same time that they send the IHT400 and supporting schedules to HMRC. The IHT423 includes an IHT reference number provided by HMRC to allow HMRC to match up the payment with the correct estate.
- The institution will send the money direct to HMRC.

The process is not quick, so where there is an urgent need for a grant, PRs will want to find an alternative source of funding.

Solicitors often make private arrangements with banks and building societies under which the bank or building society transfers funds directly to HMRC from the deceased's accounts. This is a relatively quick and easy method of funding.

(b) Life assurance

Where the proceeds of an insurance policy on the deceased's life are payable to the estate, the life assurance company, like a bank, may be willing to release funds to pay the IHT directly to HMRC.

(c) Assets realisable without production of the grant

By applying the Administration of Estates (Small Payments) Act 1965 (see **8.2.4**), assets may, in some cases, be realised without production of a grant. The maximum value of any one asset that may be realised is £5,000. The Act gives a discretion to the institution to allow assets to be realised in this way. Where an estate is large or complex, this discretion will often not be exercised.

(d) Loans from beneficiaries

Wealthy beneficiaries may be prepared to fund the tax from their own resources, on condition that they will be repaid from the deceased's estate once the grant issues. Alternatively, beneficiaries may already have received assets as a result of the death which they are prepared to use to pay the tax, such as money from a jointly held bank account, or the proceeds of a life policy assigned to them during the deceased's lifetime.

(e) Bank borrowing

Banks which do not participate in the voluntary scheme will still usually lend against an undertaking to repay the loan given by the PRs. A bank may also require an undertaking from the solicitor to repay the loan from the proceeds of the estate. Whether or not the solicitor is a PR, any undertaking should be limited to 'such proceeds as come into the solicitor's control'. Undertakings to pay money should be carefully worded so as to ensure payment is not due from the solicitor personally.

Bank borrowing is expensive, because the bank will charge an arrangement fee and interest on the amount borrowed. Money borrowed should be repaid at the earliest opportunity so as to honour any undertaking and to stop interest running. Income tax relief is available to the PRs for interest paid on a separate loan account in respect of IHT payable on personalty vesting in them.

(f) National Savings and Government stock

Payment of tax may also be made from National Savings Bank accounts or from the proceeds of National Savings Certificates, and, in certain circumstances, from British Government stock.

(g) Heritage property in lieu of tax

Taxpayers can offer HMRC an asset in lieu of tax (IHTA 1984, s 230(1)). The Secretary of State must agree to accept such assets and the standard required of such objects is very high. The item must be 'pre-eminent for its national, scientific, historic or artistic interest'.

(h) Obtaining a grant on credit

Where the PRs can demonstrate that they are genuinely unable to pay the IHT in advance, HMRC will allow the grant to be obtained on credit.

8.5 Forms PA1P and PA1A and online applications

Paper applications for a grant must be made on Forms PA1P or PA1A. The forms are fairly self-explanatory and can be found on the Government's website. The applicants will be the PRs although the form is often completed by their legal adviser.

The PA1P is used where the deceased left a valid will. It will lead to a grant of probate (if there are executors appointed by the deceased's will who are able and willing to act) or a grant of letters of administration with the will annexed (where the deceased left a valid will but, for some reason, there are no executors able or willing to take a grant of probate). The PA1A is for use where the deceased did not leave a valid will and died intestate. The two PA1 applications are similar but differ in points of detail.

Online applications require the same information as the paper forms. HMCTS is increasingly moving to online applications. Lay applicants can use paper application forms but are encouraged to apply online. In contrast it is obligatory for professionals to apply online unless the application falls within an exception. The exceptions include:

- a grant of administration including a grant of administration with will annexed;
- a second grant of probate in respect of the same estate;
- a grant where the person entitled has been convicted of murder or manslaughter of the deceased or has otherwise forfeited the right to apply;
- a grant in respect of a foreign will;
- a grant accompanied by an application to prove a copy of the will;
- a grant, where all those entitled are deceased, to any of their legal personal representatives.

At present, therefore, applications by professionals for letters of administration (with or without a will) do not have to be made online. However, these applications can be made online if certain conditions are fulfilled, for example, where there is only one applicant, and they are the only person entitled to the estate.

Where applications are made online, supporting documentation, such as the death certificate, original will and HMRC forms have to be sent separately to HMCTS where they are scanned. The scans are then sent to the caseworkers who manage the application process.

The purpose of the application is to establish the basis of the applicants' right to take the grant (for example, in the case of applications by executors, it identifies the applicants as the persons named as executors in the will and confirms that the will is valid).

The forms have the following points in common.

8.5.1 Applicants

The forms identify the applicants. Where there is a will, if any applicant's name as written in the will differs from their name as it appears on their identification papers such as their passport, both names must be included on the form.

8.5.2 The deceased

The forms identify the deceased by their name, address, date of birth and date of death, together with their marital status and their permanent place of residence at the date of death. If the deceased was known by more than one name, all names must be included if the deceased held assets in the other name. The other names will then be included on the grant. There is no need to include another name if no assets were held in that name.

8.5.3 Settled land

The forms ask whether there was any land vested in the deceased, which was settled previously to their death and which remained settled land notwithstanding their death. These settlements are relatively unusual as, since the Trusts of Land and Appointment of Trustees Act 1996, no new Settled Land Act settlement can be created.

8.5.4 Applications as an attorney

It is quite common for persons to apply for a grant as an attorney on behalf of the person entitled to take out the grant (for example where the person entitled is elderly).

Where a person lacks capacity to manage their own affairs, medical evidence may be required as well as the enduring or lasting power of attorney appointing the applicant to act.

Where no attorney has been appointed and there are no persons entitled in the same degree to take out a grant, a grant will be made to another person for the use and benefit of the incapacitated person.

8.5.5 IHT form and probate estate

The final set of questions relates to the value of the deceased's assets.

The applicant must state whether an IHT400 was completed and, if so, insert the unique code and the estate values provided by HMRC.

If it was not because the estate was excepted, the following details must be provided:

(i) the gross value of the estate for IHT plus any specified transfers and specified exempt transfers made by the deceased in the seven years before their death;

(ii) the net value of the estate for IHT less any allowable debts;

(iii) the net qualifying value of the estate, that is, the net value of the estate for IHT less any spouse, civil partner or charity exemptions.

The PRs must also specify the gross and net figures for the estate *passing under the grant*. This determines the probate fee payable. The estate passing under the grant (or the 'probate value') comprises only the property vesting in the PRs. Thus, it excludes the deceased's interest in joint tenancies, life policies assigned or written in trust, discretionary lump sums under pension schemes and trust property in which the deceased had a life interest.

The probate value is not the same as the IHT value of the estate because property which does not pass under the grant, such as trust property in which the deceased had a life interest and joint property devolving by survivorship, is included in the IHT estate. Business and agricultural property relief may reduce the IHT value of the estate, but such reliefs are irrelevant for probate purposes.

The gross estate passing under the grant is the value before deducting debts. The net estate passing under the grant is value after deduction of debts and the funeral account. The gross figure must be given because the personal representatives undertake to duly administer the estate, which includes the payment of debts; therefore, they must refer to gross figures not merely to net ones.

Example

Netta dies leaving the following assets:

Asset	£
House (owned as tenants in common with husband) Value of Netta's share	400,000
Holiday cottage (owned as joint tenants with her daughter) Value of Netta's share	100,000
Shares in various quoted companies	200,000
Cash in accounts in sole name	50,000
Life Assurance Policy assigned to Netta's son 10 years ago	70,000

Netta's debts and the funeral account amount to £20,000. Her valid will leaves her interest in the house to her husband and the residue of her estate to her children.

The probate value of Netta's estate (the property passing under her will)

Gross probate value: £400,000 + £200,000 + £50,000 = £650,000

Net probate value (deduct debts and funeral account): £650,000 - £20,000 = £630,000

The value of Netta's estate for IHT

Gross estate for IHT: £400,000 + £100,000 + £200,000 + £50,000 = £750,000

Net chargeable estate for IHT (or 'net qualifying value of the estate' for IHT) (deduct debts, exemptions and reliefs): £750,000 - £20,000 (debts) - £400,000 (spouse exemption) = £330,000

8.5.6 Legal statements

Both forms end with a statement of truth. The applicants confirm that they will administer the deceased's estate in accordance to law, and that the content of the form is truthful. They also acknowledge that criminal proceedings for fraud may be brought against the signatories if it is found that the evidence provided is deliberately untruthful or dishonest, as well as revocation of the grant.

The statement of truth is followed by a simple signature section where each applicant signs, inserts their name and adds the date. Where the applicant is legally represented and the legal representative (usually a probate practitioner) is authorised by the applicant to sign on their behalf, the legal representative signs next to their name with either a typed or handwritten signature. However, the grant will issue in the name of the applicant given within the applicant section of the form.

8.6 Executors applying for a grant of probate

The executors will apply on Form PA1P.

8.6.1 Identification of the will

The original will and any codicils must be sent to HMCTS. The dates of the will and codicils must be entered on the form and details must be provided of any foreign wills in case they revoke the UK will. The form asks whether the deceased married or formed a civil partnership after making the will for the same reason.

8.6.2 Entitlement to the grant

Where executors are appointed by a valid will, they have the best right to take a grant which will be a grant of probate. In the PA1P, the executors confirm the date of the will and any codicils and that they have not been revoked by a subsequent marriage or civil partnership.

The appointment of executors is not affected by the fact that the will may fail to dispose of some, or all, of the deceased's estate.

Example

Diana has just died. Her will appoints Eric as her executor and leaves her entire estate to Freda. Freda died before Diana whose estate will therefore be distributed according to the intestacy rules. Eric is alive and prepared to act as executor. Eric will apply for a grant of probate using a PA1P.

8.6.3 Number of executors

One executor may obtain a grant and act alone, even if the estate includes land or there are infant beneficiaries.

Example

Fiona has just died. Her will appointed her husband, Gary, and her adult son, Henry, as her executors and divided her estate equally between them. Before her death, Fiona and Gary divorced. Under s 18A Wills Act 1837, the appointment of Gary as executor and the gift to him fails. Henry will take out the grant of probate alone. (If the will had appointed Gary as the sole executor, the grant would be a grant of letters of administration with the will annexed.)

8.6.4 Executor lacking capacity to act

A person appointed as an executor by the will but who, at the testator's death, lacks capacity to make decisions, cannot apply for the grant. The other executors will take the grant. Where the only executor lacks capacity, their attorney appointed under an enduring or lasting power of attorney can take the grant in their place.

Where one of several executors is a minor, the other(s) being adults, probate can be granted to the adult executor(s) with power reserved to the minor to take a grant at a later date (for an explanation of 'power reserved', see **8.6.5**). If the administration of the estate has not been completed by the time the minor attains 18 years, an application for a grant of double probate can be made to enable the former minor to act as executor alongside the other proving executor(s).

Where the minor is the only executor appointed by the will, someone must take the grant on behalf of the minor as it would be impracticable to leave the testator's estate unadministered until the executor reaches 18 years. A grant of letters of administration with will annexed for the use and benefit of the minor will be made, usually to the parent(s) or guardian(s) of the minor, until the minor attains 18 years. On obtaining majority, the executor may apply for a cessate grant of probate if the administration has not been completed.

Example

Darren's will appoints his wife, Patricia, and his daughter, Quennie, to be his executors and gives his entire estate to Quennie.

When Darren dies, Quennie is aged 16.

Quennie is too young to take a grant of probate. Patricia will take the grant alone with power reserved to Quennie. One executor can act even where there is an infant beneficiary.

8.6.5 Renunciation

Persons appointed as executors may renounce their right to take the grant. Rights as executor then cease and the administration of the estate proceeds as if the executor had never been appointed.

Executors can renounce only if they have not intermeddled in the estate. Intermeddling consists of doing tasks a PR might do, for example selling the deceased's chattels. By intermeddling, executors accept their appointment. Once executors have intermeddled, they must take the grant because they are treated as having accepted office.

A renunciation must be made using Form PA15, signed by the person renouncing (the signature must be witnessed), and the renunciation must be filed with HMCTS. This is normally done by the PRs who are applying for a grant when they lodge their application.

Executors who are also appointed as trustees will remain trustees despite renouncing the executorship. They will have to disclaim the trusteeship as well if they want to act in neither capacity.

8.6.6 Power reserved

There is no limit on how many executors can be appointed by the will, but probate will be granted to a maximum of four executors in respect of the same property. Power may be reserved to the other(s) to take out a grant in the future if a vacancy arises.

Example

Alan's will appoints B, C, D, E and F to be his executors. All are willing and able to act. C, D, E and F apply for a grant of probate. 'Power is reserved' to B. If F dies before the administration is complete, B can then apply for a grant. B must apply if he wishes to act; there is no automatic substitution.

A person appointed as one of two or more executors may not wish to act initially but may not want to take the irrevocable step of renouncing the right to a grant of probate.

Example

Dennis appoints Bella and Charles as his executors. When Dennis dies, Bella is working in Germany but is due to return to England in 12 months' time. Bella does not feel that she should act as executor whilst abroad and is happy to let Charles act alone initially, but she does want to help in the administration if it has not been completed by the time she returns to England.

Charles should apply for the grant 'with power reserved' to Bella to prove at a later stage. In the PA1P Charles will confirm that he has notified Bella of the application for the grant.

It is possible to obtain a grant limited to part only of the estate. This is frequently done where particular expertise is required. For example, an author's will might appoint literary executors to deal with their books and general executors to deal with everything else. Up to four executors can take the grant limited to the deceased's writings, and up to four can take the grant dealing with the rest of the estate.

8.7 Administrators applying for a grant of letters of administration with the will annexed

If there is a valid will but no executor able and willing to act, the appropriate grant is letters of administration with will annexed. This is the case whether or not the will disposes of the whole of the testator's property. Examples of where a grant of letters of administration with the will annexed is appropriate include: where the will does not appoint executors, or they have all predeceased or renounced or where the will appointed the deceased's spouse as the sole executor but they divorced before the deceased's death.

8.7.1 Entitlement to the grant – NCPR 1987, r 20

The order of priority of the person(s) entitled to a grant of letters of administration with will annexed is governed by NCPR 1987, r 20. The rule states as follows:

> Where the deceased died on or after 1 January 1926 the person or persons entitled to a grant in respect of a will shall be determined in accordance with the following order of priority, namely:

(a) the executor ...;

(b) any residuary legatee or devisee holding in trust for any other person;

(c) any other residuary legatee or devisee (including one for life) or where the residue is not wholly disposed of by the will, any person entitled to share in the undisposed of residue (including the Treasury Solicitor when claiming bona vacantia on behalf of the Crown), provided that:

  (i) unless a registrar otherwise directs, a residuary legatee or devisee whose legacy or devise is vested in interest shall be preferred to one entitled on the happening of a contingency, and
  (ii) where the residue is not in terms wholly disposed of, the registrar may, if he is satisfied that the testator has nevertheless disposed of the whole or substantially the whole of the known estate, allow a grant to be made to any legatee or devisee entitled to, or to share in, the estate so disposed of, without regard to the persons entitled to share in any residue not disposed of by the will;

(d) the personal representative of any residuary legatee or devisee (but not one for life, or one holding in trust for any other person), or of any person entitled to share in any residue not disposed of by the will;

(e) any other legatee or devisee (including one for life or one holding in trust for any other person) or any creditor of the deceased, provided that, unless a registrar otherwise directs, a legatee or devisee whose legacy or devise is vested in interest shall be preferred to one entitled on the happening of a contingency;

(f) the personal representative of any other legatee or devisee (but not one for life or one holding in trust for any other person) or of any creditor of the deceased.

Each applicant is listed in priority in r 20. A person in a lower-ranked category may apply only if there is nobody in a higher category willing and able to take the grant. The applicant must explain the basis of their own entitlement to the grant by explaining why nobody in a higher category is applying (this is called 'clearing off') and also why they are entitled. An example might be: 'I am one of the residuary legatees and devisees named in the will. The deceased did not appoint a residuary legatee and devisee in trust.'

Each category is considered below:

'(a) The executor ...'

An executor appointed in the will has the best right to a grant. If there is no executor able and willing to act, it is necessary to go down the list in Rule 20.

'(b) Any residuary legatee or devisee holding in trust ...'

Example

Arthur has died leaving a will. Although he failed to appoint executors, he left his residue to Brian and Claire to hold on trust for Debbie. Brian and Claire are the residuary legatees (or devisees, depending on the type of trust property) holding on trust and so they have first right to a grant.

In the application, they will have to explain that 'no executor was appointed in the will' and they are 'the residuary legatees holding on trust named in the will'.

'(c) Any other residuary legatee or devisee ...'

Example

Amanda has died leaving a will appointing Boris as her executor and trustee and giving the residuary estate on trust for Carol absolutely, ie Carol is the residuary legatee and devisee.

Carol can apply for a grant only if Boris is unable or unwilling to act. She must explain why Boris is not taking a grant of probate, eg by saying, 'the executor and trustee named in the will has predeceased the deceased' and state that she is the residuary legatee and devisee named in the will.

'... or ... any person entitled to share in the undisposed of residue'

If a partial intestacy arises because the will fails to dispose of all or part of the residuary estate, those people entitled to the residue by virtue of the intestacy rules may apply for a grant under NCPR 1987, r 20. In the application, they will explain why nobody in higher ranked categories in Rule 20 are taking the grant, why there is an intestacy and why they are entitled as beneficiaries on the intestacy.

Example

Damien's will appoints Errol to be his sole executor and (subject to three legacies) gives the residue of the estate to Errol. Errol died last month and Damien has just died. Damien's closest living relative is his mother, Florence.

As the sole residuary beneficiary has predeceased the deceased (and the gift is not saved by any substitutional gift), the residue is undisposed of and will be distributed according to the intestacy rules. Damien has left no spouse or civil partner and no issue but is survived by his mother, Florence, who is next entitled to the property. She will be entitled to take the grant of letters of administration with the will annexed under NCPR r 20. In the application, she will explain that the executor and residuary legatee and devisee predeceased the deceased. This clears off people higher up the list in Rule 20 and also explains why there is an intestacy. To establish her entitlement to the residue on intestacy, she will explain her relationship to the deceased and the fact that, as he left no surviving spouse, civil partner or issue, she (a parent) is entitled to the undisposed of property.

'(d) The personal representative of a deceased residuary legatee or devisee ...'

Category (d) covers residuary beneficiaries who survive the testator to take a vested interest in the estate but then die without having taken the grant. The beneficiary's PR may apply for the grant. This is because the gift under the will forms part of the beneficiary's estate and needs to be collected by their PR.

Example

Gazala died last week leaving a will appointing Hafsa as executrix and giving the residuary estate to Imran absolutely. Hafsa has predeceased Gazala; Imran died yesterday. Imran's will appoints Jamila as his sole executrix and beneficiary.

Jamila may apply for a grant of letters of administration with will annexed to Gazala's estate. To do so, Jamila must clear off Hafsa and Imran by saying, 'the sole executrix predeceased the deceased and the sole residuary legatee and devisee named in the said will survived the deceased and has since died without having proved the said will and I am the executrix of the deceased residuary legatee and devisee'.

'(e) Any other legatee or devisee ... or any creditor of the deceased ...'

This category covers any other beneficiary under the will, for example a specific devisee who has been left the deceased's house, or a pecuniary legatee who has been left money by the deceased. It also covers creditors of the deceased.

'(f) The personal representative of any other legatee or devisee ... or of any creditor ...'

This category works on the same principles as category (d) above.

8.7.2 Beneficiary with vested interest preferred

Where there is more than one person of equal rank but one has a vested and one a contingent interest in the estate, the court generally prefers an application by the beneficiary with the vested interest.

Example

Kalima's will leaves her residuary estate to her two children, Laila and Masoud, contingent on their attaining 25 years of age. There is no executor appointed in the will and at Kalima's death Laila is 30 years old and Masoud 23 years old.

Laila and Masoud can make a joint application, but if they were to apply separately the court would prefer Laila because Masoud's interest is still contingent.

8.7.3 Minors

Minors (infants) cannot act as administrators with will annexed, nor can they apply for a grant. Other people entitled in the same category as the minor will apply. If there are no such persons, the minor's parent(s) or guardian(s) may apply for a grant 'for the minor's use and benefit' on their behalf. The grant is limited until the minor attains the age of 18.

8.7.4 Number of administrators

Where there is a life interest, or property passes to a minor (whether the interest is vested or contingent), the court normally requires a minimum of two administrators to apply for the grant. A question in the application asks whether there are any minor beneficiaries, in which case two administrators will be required.

Example

Abhijeet has just died leaving a valid will which:

(a) appoints Balinder his executor;

(b) gives £1,000 to Fraz (aged 6) contingent on reaching 21;

(c) gives the residue of his estate to Pardeep and Parminder.

If Balinder renounces probate, at least two people must apply for a grant of letters of administration because there is a minority interest (ie the legacy to Fraz). Pardeep and Parminder have the best right to take a grant.

Example

Quentin's will fails to appoint an executor. He leaves his estate to his wife Rose for life, the remainder to his adult son, Sam.

Two administrators are required because of Rose's life interest. Rose and Sam should both apply.

Example

Tahir's will gives a pecuniary legacy to a charity and leaves his residuary estate to his friend, Una. The will appoints Una to be the sole executrix. Una has predeceased Tahir. Tahir is divorced and has three children, Varisha (21), Wahid (19), and Zafir (15).

Tahir therefore dies partially intestate. By virtue of the intestacy rules his children take the residuary estate on the statutory trusts.

Two administrators are required because part of the estate goes to Zafir who is a minor. Varisha and Wahid should both apply.

If there are several people entitled to act as administrators, then, as with executors, the grant will not issue to more than four of them in relation to the same property (Senior Courts Act 1981, s 114). It is not possible for an administrator to have power reserved to prove at a later stage.

Where two or more people are entitled in the same degree, a grant can be made on the application of any one of them without notice to the other or others.

Example

Jenny dies leaving her residuary estate by will to her two adult brothers, Ken and Larry. Jenny's will does not appoint an executor. Larry does not wish to act.

Ken can apply for a grant alone. This does not affect Larry's beneficial entitlement to half the estate.

8.7.5 Renunciation

Any person entitled to apply for a grant of letters of administration with will annexed can renounce in the same way as an executor (though using a Form PA16), except that an administrator does not lose the right to renounce by intermeddling. Renunciation does not affect any beneficial entitlement of the administrator or any appointment as a trustee.

8.8 Administrators applying for a grant of (simple) letters of administration

Form PA1A is completed where the deceased died without a valid will and so is totally intestate.

8.8.1 Entitlement to the grant

The person or persons entitled to the grant are listed in NCPR 1987, r 22 as set out below. The order is the same as the order of entitlement on intestacy (see **Chapter 4**). Thus, the beneficiaries on intestacy take the grant.

NCPR 1987, r 22

(1) Where the deceased died on or after 1 January 1926, wholly intestate, the person or persons having a beneficial interest in the estate shall be entitled to a grant of administration in the following classes in order of priority, namely:

(a) the surviving spouse or civil partner;

(b) the children of the deceased and the issue of any deceased child who died before the deceased;

(c) the father and mother of the deceased;

(d) brothers and sisters of the whole blood and the issue of any deceased brother or sister of the whole blood who died before the deceased;

(e) brothers and sisters of the half blood and the issue of any deceased brother or sister of the half blood who died before the deceased;

(f) grandparents;

(g) uncles and aunts of the whole blood and the issue of any deceased uncle or aunt of the whole blood who died before the deceased;

(h) uncles and aunts of the half blood and the issue of any deceased uncle or aunt of the half blood who died before the deceased.

(2) In default of any person having a beneficial interest in the estate, the Treasury Solicitor shall be entitled to a grant if he claims bona vacantia on behalf of the Crown.

(3) If all persons entitled to a grant under the foregoing provisions of this rule have been cleared off, a grant may be made to a creditor of the deceased or to any person who, notwithstanding that he has no immediate beneficial interest in the estate, may have a beneficial interest in the event of an accretion thereto.

For the avoidance of doubt, step-children and step-brothers and sisters are not entitled to any property on intestacy and therefore, cannot take a grant.

Brothers and sisters of the whole blood have the same two parents as the intestate. Brothers and sisters of the half blood have one parent in common with the intestate; in other words they are half brothers and sisters.

Example

Susan has been married twice. By Tom she had two children, Una and Victoria, and by Arshad she had a son, Wisan

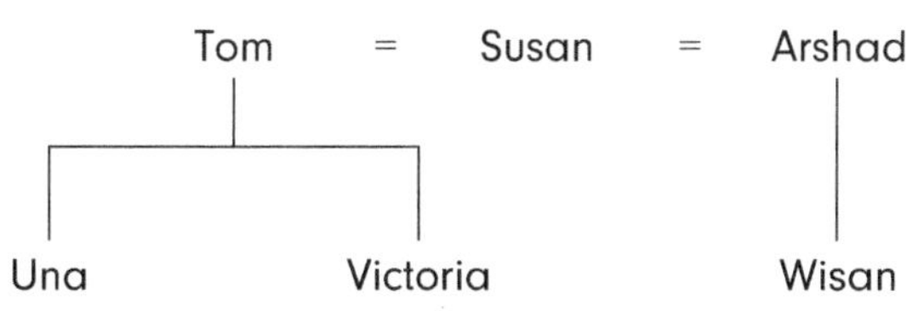

Una and Victoria are sisters of the whole blood.

Wisan is their brother of the half blood.

Uncles and aunts of 'the whole blood' are full brothers or sisters of the deceased's parents. Aunts and uncles of the half blood are half brothers and sisters of the deceased's parents.

Each category is listed in priority in NCPR 1987, r 22. People in the lower categories can take the grant only if there is nobody in the higher categories. In Form PA1A, the applicants establish their entitlement to the grant by:

- explaining why nobody in the higher categories in Rule 22 is taking the grant (this is called 'clearing off'). This may simply be a case of stating that there were no relatives in the higher categories. In Form PA1A the applicant has to state as a matter of course whether the deceased left a surviving spouse or civil partner and which other relatives in the Rule 22 categories survived; and
- stating the applicants' relationship to the deceased.

Unless the applicant is the Treasury Solicitor or a creditor, they must have a beneficial interest in the estate (or would have such an in interest if there was an accretion to the estate) by virtue of the intestacy rules.

Example

Chandra, who is unmarried, dies intestate survived by her mother and one brother.

Only the mother can apply for the grant because she is solely and absolutely entitled to Chandra's estate under the intestacy rules. In the PA1A, the applicant will clear off higher categories in Rule 22 by saying that the deceased did not leave a surviving spouse, civil partner, children or grandchildren and establish her right to the grant by describing her relationship as parent.

Example

David dies intestate survived by his wife, Eve, and adult son, Fred. Excluding personal chattels, David's estate is valued at £500,000.

As Eve and Fred share the estate by virtue of the intestacy rules, Eve and Fred can apply for the grant. If Fred applies alone, he will need to clear off Eve by saying, for example, that she has renounced.

Example

The facts are the same as in Example 2 but David's estate is £190,000. Prima facie, Fred would seem to have no interest and would therefore be unable to apply for a grant if Eve failed to do so. But Fred can apply in these circumstances on the basis that if additional assets were found in David's estate, Fred would then share the estate with Eve. In other words, he would be beneficially entitled if there were an accretion to the estate. It is irrelevant that David's estate never actually increases above £190,000. Again, Eve ranks in priority.

8.8.2 Minors

Minors cannot act as administrators, neither can they apply for a grant. The same procedure as discussed at **8.8.3** applies.

8.8.3 Number of administrators

The grant will issue to a maximum of four administrators. If there are more than four people with an equal entitlement, it is not possible to have 'power reserved' to a non-proving administrator.

Where two or more people are entitled in the same degree, a grant can be made on the application of any one of them without notice to the other(s).

A minimum of two administrators is generally required where the intestacy creates minority interests through property being held for minors on the 'statutory trusts'. The court may dispense with the need for two administrators in special circumstances.

Example

John dies intestate leaving personal chattels and other assets worth £400,000. He is survived by his wife, Kala, and children, Laksha (20) and Madesh (16).

Kala and Laksha must take the grant. Two administrators are needed because the intestacy creates a minority interest. Madesh cannot be an administrator because he is a minor.

Example

Nigel dies intestate, a bachelor without issue. Both his parents are dead. He is survived by his sister, Olive, together with Quentin and Rachel, who are the children of his deceased brother, Peter.

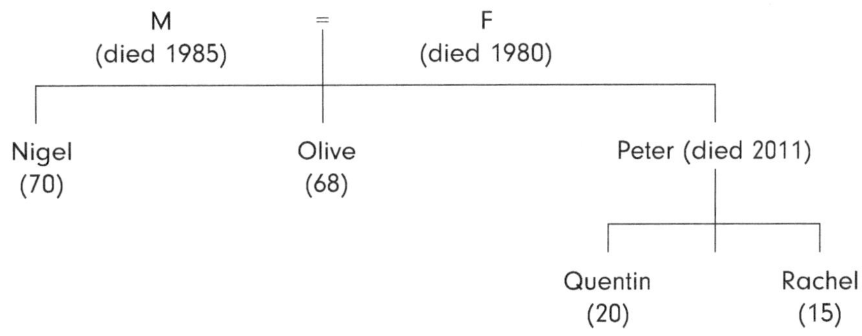

Olive, Quentin and Rachel share the estate under the intestacy rules. Both Olive and Quentin must apply for the grant of letters of administration because Rachel is a minor.

8.8.4 Renunciation

A person entitled to a grant under NCPR 1987, r 22 can renounce their right to the grant in the same way as an administrator with the will annexed. Renunciation does not affect any beneficial entitlement of the administrator.

Summary

- When a person dies, someone must deal with the administration of the estate. Those who take on this task are referred to generically as 'personal representatives' (PRs). They may be executors or administrators.
- Executors are appointed by the will and take a grant of probate.
- If there is a valid will but no executor able and willing to act, the grant will be one of letters of administration (with the will annexed). Priority is governed by Rule 20 of the Non-Contentious Probate Rules 1987.
- If there is no valid will, the grant will be one of (simple) letters of administration. Priority is governed by Rule 22 of the Non-Contentious Probate Rules 1987.
- Some assets (eg joint property, life policies assigned or written in trust during the deceased's lifetime) do not pass through the hands of the PRs. They are not part of the 'probate value' of the estate and can be realised or transferred without a grant.
- If the estate is not 'excepted', PRs must submit an IHT400 (if the deceased was a long-term UK resident) to HMRC and pay any IHT due before obtaining the grant. If the estate is excepted, the PRs make declarations about the IHT value of the estate and the fact that it is excepted in the application for the grant.
- IHT must be paid before the grant is obtained (except that PRs can elect to pay IHT on instalment option property by 10 annual instalments).
- The following should be sent to the HMCTS:
  - a Form PA1P or PA1A (or an online application) completed by the PRs explaining their right to take a grant
  - any will and codicils
  - additional evidence of validity of any will where necessary
  - probate fee
  - any renunciations of the right to act
- One executor is always sufficient. Two administrators are required if there is a minority or life interest.

Sample questions

Question 1

A woman died last week. In her valid will, she appointed her solicitor as her executrix and, apart from a pecuniary legacy of £25,000 to her adult nephew, she left her estate to be divided between her brother and sister.

The solicitor predeceased the woman. Everyone else mentioned in the will survives. The woman's husband also survived her.

Which of the following best describes who will be entitled to take a grant of representation and which type of grant is appropriate?

A The nephew has the best right to take a grant of letters of administration with the will annexed.

B The brother and sister will be entitled to take a grant of letters of administration with the will annexed.

C The brother and sister will be entitled to take a grant of probate.

D The husband can take a grant of (simple) letters of administration.

E The husband can take a grant of letters of administration with the will annexed.

Answer

Option B is correct.

The grant will be a grant of letters of administration with the will annexed because the deceased left a will but no executor is able to act. Under NCPR 1987, Rule 20, residuary beneficiaries (the brother and sister) have the best right to the grant under category (c).

Option A is wrong. The nephew does not have the 'best right' because, compared with the brother and sister, he is lower down the list in Rule 20. He appears in category (e).

Option C is wrong. Only executors appointed in the will can take a grant of probate.

Option D is wrong. A grant of (simple) letters of administration is not appropriate because the woman did not die intestate; she left a valid will.

Option E is wrong because the husband does not fall into any of the categories of applicant in Rule 20.

Question 2

A man died three months ago. His estate included a house worth £600,000. The rest of his assets (comprising chattels, a bank account and small holdings of shares in quoted companies) are worth £600,000. The inheritance tax (IHT) payable on the estate is £350,000. The man's PRs are ready to apply for the grant of representation.

How much IHT will the man's PRs have to pay before they get the grant?

A None of it, if they elect to pay by instalments.

B None of it, because the deadline for payment is six months after the end of the month of death.

C £350,000, because HMCTS will not issue the grant until all the IHT has been paid.

D Only the IHT on the chattels and bank account if they elect to pay IHT on the house and shares by instalments.

E £175,000 if they elect to pay the IHT on the house by instalments.

Answer

Option E is correct. The house is instalment option property. IHT on instalment option property does not have to be paid before the grant if the PRs elect to pay by instalments. IHT on instalment option property can be paid six months after the end of the month of death. However, the IHT on the other property (the chattels, a bank account and small holdings of shares in quoted companies) must be paid before the grant because this property does not attract the instalment option. The non-instalment option property accounts for half the value of the estate and therefore, half the IHT bill.

Option A is wrong. The instalment option is available only for the land (the house). It does not apply to the other assets. IHT on the non-instalment option property must be paid before the grant.

Option B is wrong. IHT on the non-instalment option property must be paid before the grant.

Option C is wrong because, as explained above, IHT on instalment option property can be paid by 10 annual instalments.

Option D is wrong. The quoted shares do not attract the instalment option because they did not give the man a controlling interest in the companies.

Question 3

A woman died four months ago. In her valid will, she left a legacy of £30,000 to a charity and the residue of her estate to her husband. She also appointed the husband to be her executor. Before the woman died, she and her husband were divorced. The woman's husband and her adult son survived her. The woman's estate comprises public company shares and money in building societies. It is worth £300,000. She made no lifetime gifts and was not a beneficiary under a trust.

A newly qualified solicitor has put together the following documents to send to HMCTS in order to obtain the grant:

- The woman's will
- A PA1P
- An IHT400
- The amount required for the probate court fee.

Are these the right items to send?

A No, because the application for the grant should be on form PA1A.

B No, because it is an excepted estate and no IHT form is required.

C No, because the will was revoked by the woman's divorce and she died intestate.

D Yes, because an IHT 400 is required in all cases.

E Yes, because the husband will be applying for a grant of probate.

Answer

Option B is correct. The divorce means that the husband is treated as though he predeceased. Therefore, his appointment as executor and the gift of residue to him cannot take effect. Residue will pass on intestacy to the woman's son. The legacy to the charity is still valid. The son should take a grant of letters of administration with the will annexed. The son is entitled to this grant as the person 'entitled to ... the undisposed of residue' under NCPR, Rule 20, category (c).

Option A is wrong. Form PA1A is not appropriate here. It is used where the deceased left no will and died totally intestate.

Option C is wrong because (unlike marriage) divorce does not revoke a will. Divorce has the effect of nullifying appointments of the former spouse as executor and gifts to the former spouse. The rest of the will stands.

Option D is wrong because no IHT400 is required. The woman's estate appears to satisfy the requirements for an excepted estate.

Option E is wrong because the divorce has nullified the husband's appointment as executor. As there is a will but no executor, the appropriate grant is one of letters of administration with the will annexed.

9 Administration: Dealing with the Estate

SQE1 syllabus

This chapter will enable you to achieve the SQE1 assessment specification in relation to functioning legal knowledge concerned with wills and the administration of estates.

- The validity of a will and interpretation of the contents of a will. The distribution of testate, intestate and partially intestate estates.
- The law and practice of inheritance tax in the context of lifetime gifts and transfers on death.
- The planning, management and progression of the administration of an estate including claims made under the Inheritance (Provision for Family and Dependants) Act 1975.
- The law and practice relating to personal representatives and trustees in the administration of estates and consequent trusts. The rights, powers and remedies of beneficiaries of wills and consequent trusts.
- Duties of personal representatives.
- Liabilities of personal representatives and their protection.
- The sale of assets to raise funds to pay funeral expenses, tax, debts and legacies.
- Distribution of the estate.
- Burden and incidence of inheritance tax.
- The personal representatives' liability to income tax and capital gains tax.
- The beneficiaries liability to capital gains tax on inherited assets.

In the SQE1 assessment the process available to personal representatives to protect themselves from liability to unknown beneficiaries/creditors may be referred to by way of the statutory authority, namely s 27 Trustee Act 1925; also, the process available to personal representatives to protect themselves from liability to missing beneficiaries/creditors may be referred to as a *Benjamin* order. Otherwise, in this chapter references to cases and statutory authorities are provided for illustrative purposes only.

Learning outcomes

By the end of this chapter you will be able to apply relevant core legal principles and rules appropriately and effectively, at the level of a competent newly qualified solicitor in practice, to realistic client-based and ethical problems and situations in the following areas:

- key steps required to administer an estate;
- the rules on the incidence of debts and pecuniary legacies;
- the methods by which personal representatives may seek to protect themselves from personal liability; and
- the tax implications of the sale and distribution of assets.

9.1 Introduction

Once the personal representatives (PRs) have obtained the grant, they are able to start the administration of the estate. The work involved in administering an estate is essentially the same whether the deceased left a will or died intestate. However, in the latter case, the beneficiaries will obviously have to be ascertained by application of the intestacy rules (see **Chapter 4**).

Broadly speaking, the administration of the estate will require the PRs to:

- collect the deceased's assets;
- pay the deceased's funeral and testamentary expenses and debts;
- distribute the legacies; and
- complete the administration and distribute the residuary estate.

This chapter looks at:

- the administration period;
- the duties of the PRs;
- protection against liability;
- administrative powers of PRs;
- collecting the assets;
- paying funeral and testamentary expenses and debts;
- paying the legacies;
- completing the administration;
- distributing the residuary estate; and
- estate accounts.

9.2 The administration period

The 'administration period' commences at the moment immediately following the death and ends when the PRs are in a position to vest the residue of the estate in the beneficiaries, or the trustees if a trust arises under the will or the intestacy rules.

It should be noted, however, that a PR holds office for life. If further assets or liabilities are discovered after the residue has been transferred, the PRs are still required to deal with them.

9.3 Duties of the PRs

The primary duty imposed on PRs is found in s 25 Administration of Estates Act 1925 (AEA 1925). The PRs must 'collect and get in the real and personal estate of the deceased and administer it according to the law'.

The duties to be undertaken by a PR are onerous. A PR who accepts office is personally liable for loss to the estate resulting from any breach of duty they commit as PR (although they are not generally liable for breaches committed by a co-PR). Such a breach of duty is known as *devastavit* (meaning, 'he wasted') (see **10.2.3**). The test is whether there has been a loss caused by a breach of duty, not whether the PR is culpable.

There are several types of breach of duty, including:

(a) failing to protect the value of assets;

(b) failing to pay the people entitled to assets.

Section 61 Trustee Act 1925 gives the court power at its discretion to relieve a PR from liability for breach of duty if satisfied that the PR 'has acted honestly and reasonably and ought fairly to be excused for the breach' (see **10.2.3**). Alternatively, an executor may be able to rely on a clause in the will providing protection from liability for mistakes made in good faith.

9.4 Protection against liability

PRs are responsible for administering the estate correctly. Consequently, if the PRs fail to pay someone who is entitled either as a creditor or as a beneficiary, they will be personally liable to that person.

PRs may face three issues:

(a) There may be creditors of whom they are unaware or unknown relatives (eg children born outside marriage whose existence has been kept secret).

(b) They may not know the whereabouts of some beneficiaries who may have lost contact with the deceased's family.

(c) There could be a successful claim against the estate under the Inheritance (Provision for Family and Dependants) Act 1975 (see **Chapter 7**).

9.4.1 Unknown beneficiaries and creditors

PRs can protect themselves against unknown claims by advertising for claimants in compliance with the requirements of the s 27 Trustee Act 1925. Provided the PRs wait for the time period specified in the statute (at least two months) before distributing the estate, the PRs will be protected from liability if an unknown claimant later appears. However, the claimant will have the right to claim back assets from the beneficiaries who received them.

In view of the minimum notice period of two months, PRs should advertise as early as possible in the administration. If they are executors, they may advertise at any time after the death; if they are administrators, they have power to advertise at any time after obtaining the grant of representation.

The PRs must give notice of the intended distribution of the estate, requiring any person interested to send in particulars of their claim, whether as a creditor or as a beneficiary, by:

(a) advertisement in the *London Gazette*;

(b) advertisement in a newspaper circulating in the district in which land owned by the deceased is situated; and

(c) 'such other like notices, including notices elsewhere than in England and Wales, as would, in any special case, have been directed by a court of competent jurisdiction in an action for administration'.

If the PRs are in any doubt as to what notices should be given, they should apply to the court for directions.

Each notice must require any person interested to send in particulars of their claim within the time specified in the notice, which must not be less than two months from the date of the notice.

The PRs should also make searches which the prudent purchaser of land would make in the Land Registry, the Land Charges Register and the Local Land Charges Registry, as appropriate. The purpose of these searches is to reveal the existence of any liability in relation to the deceased's ownership of an interest in land, for example a second mortgage.

When the time limit in the notice has expired, the PRs may distribute the deceased's estate, taking into account only those claims of which they have actual knowledge, or which they discover as a result of the advertisements. The PRs are not personally liable for any other claim, but a claimant may pursue the claim by following the assets into the hands of the beneficiaries who have received them from the PRs.

9.4.2 Missing beneficiaries and creditors

Section 27 Trustee Act 1925 does not give any protection to PRs who know that there is a person with a claim but cannot find them.

Where PRs cannot trace a known beneficiary, they will need to consider one of the following:

(a) Keeping back assets in case the claimant appears. This option is usually unpopular with the other beneficiaries.

(b) Taking an indemnity from the beneficiaries that they will meet any claims if the claimant reappears. This represents a risk for the PRs as the beneficiaries may lack the means to satisfy the claim when the claimant appears.

(c) Taking out insurance to provide funds. This can be expensive and, as the claimant may be entitled to interest on the amount of their entitlement for the period up to payment, it is difficult to know what sum to insure. Insurance does not absolve the PR from personal liability, it simply means that there will be insurance money available to pay the claim. In the event of a shortfall, the PRs are liable to pay the difference.

(d) Applying to the court for an order authorising the PRs to distribute the estate on the basis that the claimant is dead. This is referred to as a *Benjamin* order after the case in which it was first ordered (*Re Benjamin* [1902] 1 Ch 723). Before making an order, the court will require evidence that the fullest possible enquiries have been made to trace the missing person. A *Benjamin* order protects the PRs from liability, although the claimant retains the right to recover the assets from the beneficiaries. Applying to court is an expensive process, but it is the only solution that offers the PR full protection.

9.4.3 Inheritance (Provision for Family and Dependants) Act 1975

The PRs will be personally liable if the assets have been distributed and an applicant under the Inheritance (Provision for Family and Dependants) Act 1975 then successfully obtains an order for 'reasonable financial provision' from the estate (see **Chapter 7**). The PRs can protect themselves against such liability by waiting more than six months following the date of the grant of representation before distributing the assets. If earlier distribution is required, PRs should ensure they retain sufficient assets to satisfy an order should an applicant be successful within six months of the grant.

9.5 Administrative powers of PRs

The PRs have a wide range of powers which they may exercise in carrying out the administration of an estate. These powers are largely conferred on them by statute. The AEA 1925 gives some powers specifically to PRs. The Trustee Act 1925 and the Trustee Act 2000 confer powers on trustees for use in administering a trust. Since 'trustee' in the legislation includes a 'personal representative', PRs have these powers as well (see **Chapter 5**).

9.6 Collecting the assets

Assets which pass under the will or intestacy rules automatically devolve on (ie ownership passes to) the PRs. Real property devolves by virtue of s 1 AEA 1925 and personal property by common law. For executors devolution happens immediately on the death, for administrators when the grant of representation is issued. The PRs hold the assets for the purpose of the administration.

Devolution gives the PRs ownership of the assets in the estate, but their duty is to collect them in as soon as is practicable. Although the PRs will be able to take possession of some assets immediately (cash found at the deceased's house, for example), in most cases in order to collect the property, the PRs will need to produce their grant of representation to whoever is holding the asset, for example to the deceased's bank or building society. An office copy grant will usually be accepted as evidence of title.

Having collected in the assets the PRs must preserve them pending the completion of the administration. In preserving the assets, essentially PRs have the same powers as trustees in terms of management and investment and are subject to the same duty of reasonable care and skill under s 1 Trustee Act 2000.

Assets which pass independently of the will and the intestacy rules (see **Chapter 1**) do not devolve on the PRs. The PRs have no obligation, or indeed power, to deal with these assets. So, for example, the deceased's interest in a property held as joint tenant will pass to the other joint owner by right of survivorship.

9.7 Paying funeral and testamentary expenses and debts

9.7.1 Preliminary considerations

9.7.1.1 Immediate sources of money

As soon as monies can be collected from the deceased's bank or building society, or realised through insurance policies etc, the PRs should begin to pay the deceased's outstanding debts and the funeral account. Administration expenses, for example estate agents' and valuers' fees, will arise during the course of administration of the estate and will have to be settled from time to time while the administration is proceeding.

9.7.1.2 Repayment of loan to pay inheritance tax

It may have been necessary for the PRs to take out a loan from the deceased's bank to pay inheritance tax to obtain the grant. If an undertaking has been given to the bank in connection with the loan, it will probably be a 'first proceeds' undertaking. This means that the PRs must use money first realised by them during the administration to repay the bank. Failure to do so will be a breach of the terms of the undertaking.

9.7.1.3 Sale of assets

Any assets in the estate can be used for the payment of debts and expenses (s 32(1) AEA 1925). However, the PRs must take considerable care when deciding which particular assets they will sell in order to raise money. They should consider the following points.

Provisions of the will

The will may direct from which part of the deceased's estate the debts, funeral account, testamentary and administration expenses should be paid; usually they will be paid from the residue. In the absence of such direction, the PRs must follow the statutory rules for the incidence of liabilities (see **9.7.3**). In any event, it will be generally incorrect for PRs to sell property given specifically by will unless all other assets in the estate have been exhausted in payment of the debts, etc.

The beneficiaries' wishes

Where possible, the wishes of the beneficiaries of the residuary estate should be respected by the PRs. Although the PRs have power to sell any assets in the residuary estate, it is clearly appropriate that the residuary beneficiaries should be consulted before any sale takes place. Generally, beneficiaries have clear views as to which assets they desire to be retained for transfer to them; other assets may be sold by the PRs to raise the necessary money, possibly following receipt of professional advice as to particular sales.

Tax consequences

Before selling assets, the PRs should consider the amount of any capital gains (or losses) likely to arise as a result of the sale, and the availability of any exemptions, etc (see **9.9.5.3**). Full use should be made of the annual exemption for capital gains tax. If assets are to be sold at a loss (compared to their value at the date of death), loss reliefs for capital gains tax and inheritance tax purposes (see **9.9.1.2**) may be available for the PRs.

9.7.2 Payments to be made

9.7.2.1 The deceased's debts and liabilities

The PRs must settle any outstanding debts owed by the deceased at the time of death, such as outstanding utility bills or payments of income tax. The PRs must pay the debts and liabilities with due diligence and will be liable for any loss if they fail to do so, eg because the debt carries interest.

9.7.2.2 Funeral expenses

The PRs are required to pay reasonable expenses of a funeral conducted in a manner suitable to the deceased's position and circumstances, but are only liable in so far as they have available assets of the deceased to make the payment. The reasonableness of the funeral cost is a question of fact to be determined in the circumstances of the case.

9.7.2.3 Testamentary expenses

The phrase 'testamentary and administration expenses' is not defined in the AEA 1925, but it is generally considered to mean expenses which are incidental to the proper performance of the duties of a PR. Testamentary expenses will include:

(a) the costs of obtaining the grant;

(b) the costs of collecting in and preserving the deceased's assets;

(c) the costs of administering the deceased's estate, for example solicitors' fees for acting for the PRs, valuers' fees incurred by PRs in valuing the deceased's stocks and shares or other property; and

(d) any inheritance tax payable on death on the deceased's property in the UK which vests in the PRs (s 211 Inheritance Tax Act 1984). (The inheritance tax payable on property falling outside this definition, such as property passing by survivorship, is borne by the beneficiary. The PRs can claim reimbursement of any tax they have paid from the person in whom the property is vested, although there may be practical difficulties in securing payment unless the beneficiary is also entitled to other assets from the estate.)

9.7.3 Administration of assets: solvent estates

The rules applying to the payment of funeral and testamentary expenses and debts depend on whether the estate is solvent or insolvent. The insolvent estate is considered at **9.7.4**.

A solvent estate is one in which there are sufficient assets to pay all the expenses, debts and liabilities in full (irrespective of whether there remains anything with which to pay the legacies). In a solvent estate all the debts will be paid, but s 35 and s 34(3) AEA 1925 govern the order in which assets are to be used to pay the debts. This is important for the beneficiaries. They have an entitlement under the will, but they may see that entitlement reduced or dwindle to nothing because the assets which form the subject matter of that entitlement is taken to pay the debts.

9.7.3.1 Secured debts

Section 35 AEA 1925 deals with secured debts, ie debts owing by the deceased which are charged on particular items of property. A common example is a loan secured by legal mortgage on the deceased's house. The effect of this rule is that a beneficiary taking the asset takes it subject to the debt and will be responsible for paying the debt.

Section 35 applies subject to any contrary intention shown in the will, deed or other document. Intention is not signified by a general direction to pay debts out of the residue. Such a direction would be construed as a direction to pay those debts other than the secured debts. To constitute a contrary intention for the purpose of s 35 there must be an express reference to the mortgage. So, a gift of 'my cottage to my daughter free of mortgage' will suffice, as will a direction that the mortgage be paid from the residue.

9.7.3.2 Unsecured debts and expenses

Section 34(3) AEA 1925 provides that the assets must be applied in the order set out in Part II of Schedule 1 to pay debts and expenses. This is the so-called 'statutory order' which the PRs must follow when deciding which part of the deceased's estate should be used for the purposes of payment of the funeral and testamentary expenses and unsecured debts:

1. **Property undisposed of by will subject to retention of a fund to meet pecuniary legacies.** (There will be some cases where the terms of the will simply fail to dispose of the entire estate or where the testator has tried to dispose of it in the will but failed, eg a lapsed share of residue. The property which is undisposed of will be applied first.)

2. **Property included in a residuary gift subject to retention of a fund to pay pecuniary legacies not already provided for.** (Hence, in most estates the residue will bear the burden of the debts and expenses.)
3. **Property specifically given for the payment of debts.** (Property is given for the payment of debts where the testator directs in the will that a particular asset is to be used for this purpose, but leaves no direction as to what is to happen to any money left over, eg 'my debts are to be paid from the proceeds of sale of my shares in X Co'.)
4. **Property charged with the payment of debts.** (Property is charged with the payment of debts where the testator directs in the will that the asset is to be used for this purpose but provides that any money left over is to go to a beneficiary, eg 'my debts are to be paid from the proceeds of sale of my shares in X Co and the balance paid to John'.)
5. **The fund, if any, retained to meet pecuniary legacies.**
6. **Property specifically devised or bequeathed, rateably according to value.**
7. **Property appointed by will under a general power rateably according to value.**

It will be seen that, broadly, assets forming part of the residue are to be used before using property given to specific legatees.

Section 34(3) applies subject to a contrary intention shown in the will. So, the testator can vary the order by making express provision in the will which makes it clear that the testator intends to exonerate property which would otherwise be taken in priority. The will may, for example, provide for a gift to be 'subject to the payment of tax' with the result that the inheritance tax attributable to the subject matter of the gift is payable from the asset itself. If the gift was silent or expressed to be 'free of tax', the inheritance tax attributable to the subject matter of the gift is payable as a testamentary expense. In practice it is common for a will to include a stipulation that debts and expenses should be paid from the residuary estate.

9.7.4 Administration of assets: insolvent estates

An estate is insolvent if the assets are insufficient to discharge in full the funeral, testamentary and administration expenses, debts and liabilities. In an insolvent estate the assets are applied to pay the debts until they have been used up. In such cases, the creditors will not be paid in full (or at all) and the beneficiaries under the will or the intestacy provisions will receive nothing from the estate.

In the case of an insolvent estate which is being administered by the deceased's PRs out of court (this being the most common method of administration), the order of distribution in the Administration of Insolvent Estates of Deceased Persons Order 1986 (SI 1986/1999) should be followed. Broadly, this ranks debts and expenses in order of priority for payment.

Secured creditors, for example those holding a mortgage or charge over the deceased's property, are in a better position than unsecured creditors in that they may (inter alia) realise the security, ie sell the property by exercising a power of sale as mortgagee or chargee.

Unsecured creditors will have to look to any remaining assets for payment. Funeral and testamentary expenses are paid in priority to ordinary unsecured debts and liabilities of the deceased. By definition, in an insolvent estate there will be insufficient funds to pay all the unsecured debts, and these will therefore abate equally.

Example

Under the terms of Rashid's will his entire estate passes to his nephew. Rashid's estate comprises £10,000 in a bank account, personal effects worth £2,000 and his house which is valued at £200,000 and subject to a mortgage in favour of a Building Society of £175,000. Rashid had a credit card debt of £15,000 and the cost of Rashid's funeral was £5,000. At the time of his death Rashid still owed £25,000 to a builder in respect of some work carried out at his house.

There are insufficient assets in Rashid's estate to pay his debts and expenses.

The mortgage on the house is a secured debt and so will be considered first. The Building Society is entitled to be paid the £175,000 owed to them from the proceeds of sale of the house.

The assets then available to the PRs are the £25,000 remaining from the house after the Building Society has been paid, £10,000 in the bank account and the personal effects worth £2,000. A total of £37,000.

Funeral, testamentary and administration expenses are dealt with in priority to ordinary unsecured creditors. So, next the PRs must pay the funeral expenses of £5,000. This leaves £32,000.

Both the credit card bill and the builder's bill are ordinary unsecured debts. Together they total £40,000 and the remaining assets total £32,000. The ordinary debts will therefore abate equally with the result that the personal representatives will pay the credit card provider £12,000 and the builder £20,000.

In doubtful cases, the PRs should administer the estate as if it is insolvent. Failure to administer an insolvent estate in accordance with the statutory order is a breach of duty by the PRs.

9.8 Paying the legacies

Once the funeral, testamentary and administration expenses and debts have been paid, or at least adequately provided for by setting aside sufficient assets for the purpose, the PRs should consider discharging the gifts arising on the death, other than the gifts of the residuary estate.

9.8.1 Specific legacies

Unless an estate has significant debts, it is unusual for property given by specific bequest or devise to be needed for payment of the deceased's funeral and testamentary expenses and debts (see **9.7.3**). Once the PRs are satisfied that the property will not be so required, they should consider transferring it to the beneficiary, or to trustees if a trust arises, for example if the property is given to a beneficiary contingently on attaining a stated age and the beneficiary has not yet reached that age.

The method of transferring the property to the beneficiary or trustee will depend on its particular nature. For example, the legal estate in a house or flat should be vested in a beneficiary by a document known as an assent (it is the beneficiary's responsibility to send the assent to the Land Registry for registration). If the specific legacy is of company shares, a stock transfer form should be used.

In the case of specific gifts only, the vesting of the asset in the beneficiary is retrospective to the date of death, so that any income produced by the property, for example dividends on a specific gift of company shares, belongs to the beneficiary. The beneficiary is not entitled to the income as it arises but must wait until the PRs vest the property in them. As the beneficiary is entitled to the income, they will be liable to be assessed for any income tax due on that income since the death (see **9.9.5.2**).

Any costs of transferring the property to a specific legatee, and the cost of any necessary insurance cover taken to safeguard the property are the responsibility of the legatee who should reimburse the PRs for the expenses incurred (subject to any contrary direction in a will indicating that such expenses should be paid from residue). If the deceased's title to the asset is disputed by a third party, the specific legatee will be responsible for the cost of litigation to establish ownership.

9.8.2 Pecuniary legacies – provision for payment in the will

Often a testator has expressly dealt with the payment of pecuniary legacies in the will itself. Typically, the gift of the residuary estate will be 'subject to' or 'after payment of' the pecuniary legacies. In both cases the legacies should be paid from the fund of residue before the division of the balance between the residuary beneficiaries.

9.8.3 Pecuniary legacies – no provision by will for payment

If the will does not contain an express provision, the PRs will have to decide which assets are to be used to pay the pecuniary legacies. The law in this area is far from clear cut, but in essence pecuniary legacies are paid from the residuary estate, with personalty being used in preference to realty.

Example

A will leaves a legacy of £5,000 to Desmond. There is no direction as to payment of the legacy. Residue consisting of personalty and realty is given by the will to 'Errol if he shall survive me by 28 days'. Errol does survive the testator by more than 28 days, and residue is, therefore, fully disposed of. The PRs should pay the £5,000 legacy from the personalty contained in the residue, with the proceeds of the realty being used afterwards if necessary.

If a partial intestacy arises, for example where part of a gift of residue fails because one of the beneficiaries dies before the testator, it is often unclear as a matter of law which is the appropriate part of the estate for the payment of the pecuniary legacies. The most likely outcome is that the legacies will be paid from the property which is undisposed of, with ready money being used first.

9.8.4 Time for payment of pecuniary legacies

The general rule is that a pecuniary legacy is payable at the end of 'the executor's year', ie one year after the testator's death. PRs are not bound to distribute the estate to the beneficiaries before the expiration of one year from the death (s 44 AEA 1925). It is often difficult to make payment within the year and, if payment is delayed beyond this date, the legatee will be entitled to interest by way of compensation. The rate of interest will either be the rate prescribed by the testator's will, or, in default of such provision, the rate payable on money paid into court. If the testator stipulates that the legacy is to be paid 'immediately following my death', or that it is payable at some future date, or on the happening of a particular contingency, then interest is payable from either the day following the date of death, the future date or the date the contingency occurs, as may be appropriate.

There are four occasions when, as an exception to the normal rule, interest is payable on a pecuniary legacy from the date of the death. These occur when legacies are:

(a) payable in satisfaction of a debt owed by the testator to a creditor;

(b) charged on land owned by the testator;

(c) payable to the testator's minor child (historically this was so that provision was made for maintenance of the child, and interest is not payable under this provision if other funds exist for the child's maintenance); or

(d) payable to any minor (not necessarily the child of the testator) where the intention is to provide for the maintenance of that minor.

9.9 Completing the administration

Once the PRs have paid the deceased's funeral, testamentary expenses and debts and any legacies given by the will, they can consider distribution of the residuary estate in accordance with the will or the intestacy rules. Before drawing up the estate accounts and making the final distribution of residue, the PRs must deal with all outstanding matters. Such matters relate mostly to inheritance tax liability, but there will also be income tax and capital gains tax to consider.

9.9.1 Adjusting the inheritance tax assessment

9.9.1.1 The need for adjustment

An adjustment to the amount of inheritance tax payable on the instalment and non-instalment option property in the estate may be necessary for a number of reasons, including:

(a) discovery of additional assets or liabilities since the IHT account was submitted;

(b) discovery of lifetime transfers made by the deceased within the seven years before death;

(c) agreement of provisionally estimated values, for example with the shares valuation division of HMRC (in the case of shares in private companies) or the district valuer (in the case of land). Such valuations may require long negotiations and can often delay reaching a final settlement of inheritance tax liabilities;

(d) agreement between the PRs and HMRC of a tax liability or repayment, in relation to the deceased's income and capital gains before the death;

(e) sales made by the PRs after the deceased's death which have given rise to a claim for inheritance tax 'loss relief'.

9.9.1.2 Inheritance tax loss relief

The PRs may have to sell assets because they need cash to meet debts, tax liabilities or legacies. The value of some assets, such as quoted shares and land, fluctuates depending on market conditions, and PRs may find that they sell these assets for less than their value at the date of death. Loss on sale relief can reduce the inheritance tax liability of the estate in such cases.

Where 'qualifying investments' are sold within 12 months of death for less than their market value at the date of death (ie 'probate value') then the sale price can be substituted for the market value at death and the inheritance tax liability adjusted accordingly. 'Qualifying investments' are shares or securities which are quoted on a recognised stock exchange at the date of death and also holdings in authorised unit trusts. The relief must be claimed; it is not automatic. It is normally available only when the PRs make the sale and not where a beneficiary to whom assets have been transferred does so.

9.9.2 PRs' continuing inheritance tax liability

9.9.2.1 Inheritance tax by instalments

The PRs may have opted to pay inheritance tax by instalments on the property in the deceased's estate attracting the instalment option (see **6.9.1.2**). By the time they are ready to transfer the assets to those entitled, it is likely that only one or two instalments will have been paid. The PRs continue to be liable for the remaining instalments. It would be risky for the PRs to transfer all the assets to the beneficiaries in reliance on a promise that the beneficiaries will pay the tax. If the beneficiaries become insolvent or disappear, the PRs will be liable for the unpaid tax but will have no assets from the estate to meet the liability. The PRs should consider retaining sufficient assets in the estate to cover the remaining tax.

Harris v Commissioners for HMRC [2018] UKFTT 204 (TC)

In this case the administrator distributed all the assets to the sole beneficiary on the basis that the beneficiary would pay all costs and taxes due. The beneficiary then returned to his home in Barbados. Thereafter the administrator was unable to make any further contact with the beneficiary. The Tribunal said that the law was absolutely clear: the administrator remained personally liable for unpaid inheritance tax of a little over £341,000.

9.9.2.2 Inheritance tax on lifetime transfers

If the deceased dies within seven years of making either a potentially exempt transfer (PET), or a lifetime chargeable transfer (LCT), inheritance tax (if a PET) or more inheritance tax (if an LCT) may become payable (see **6.5** and **6.6**). Although the general rule is that the donees of lifetime transfers are primarily liable for the tax, the PRs of the donor's estate may become liable if the tax remains unpaid by the donees 12 months after the end of the month in which the donor died. However, the PRs' liability is limited to the extent of the deceased's assets which they have received or would have received in the administration of the estate, but for their neglect or default.

In addition, if the deceased gave away property during his lifetime but reserved a benefit in that property, such property is treated as part of his estate on death (see **6.4.1.2**). The donee of the gift is primarily liable to pay the tax attributable, but if the tax remains unpaid 12 months after the end of the month of death, the PRs become liable. Again, the PRs should consider how they can protect themselves in case this liability materialises.

9.9.3 Corrective account

When all variations in the extent or value of the deceased's assets and liabilities are known, and all reliefs to which the estate is entitled have been quantified, the PRs must report all outstanding matters to HMRC. This report is made by way of a corrective account.

9.9.4 Inheritance tax clearance

PRs will normally want to obtain confirmation from HMRC that there is no further claim to inheritance tax. If HMRC is satisfied that inheritance tax attributable to a chargeable transfer has, or will be, paid, it can, and if the transfer is one made on death must, confirm that this is the case. PRs can apply (using form IHT30) for such confirmation to be provided in the form of a clearance certificate. The effect is to discharge all persons, in particular the PRs, from further liability to inheritance tax (unless there is fraud or non-disclosure of material facts).

9.9.5 Income tax and capital gains tax

9.9.5.1 The deceased's liability

Immediately following the death, the PRs must make a return to HMRC of the income and capital gains of the deceased for the period starting on 6 April before the death and ending with the date of death. Even though the deceased died part way through the income tax year, the PRs, on the deceased's behalf, may claim the same reliefs and allowances as the deceased could have claimed had they lived throughout the whole year. Any liability to tax is a debt of the deceased which must be paid by the PRs during the administration (see **9.7.2.1**). The debt will be deductible when calculating the amount of inheritance tax. Alternatively, if a refund of tax is obtained, this will represent an asset, so increasing the size of the estate for inheritance tax purposes.

9.9.5.2 Income tax

PRs are subject to income tax in their capacity as PRs on any income paid to the estate during the administration. There may be income producing assets already in the estate, such as a property let out to tenants who will continue to pay rent to the estate. Income may also be generated by the actions of the PRs during the administration. For example, the PRs would be expected to put any cash into a savings account where it can earn interest.

The rates at which PRs pay income tax depends on the type of income they receive. PRs do not pay income tax at any higher rate(s) but nor do they benefit from any of the allowances available to individuals.

PRs will therefore pay tax at the following rates on all income received:

dividends	8.75%
other income	20%

The Welsh Government has devolved powers in relation to a portion of the rate of income tax on non-savings, non-dividend income (Welsh income tax). To date those powers have been so exercised that the overall rates of Welsh income tax are the same as those applicable in England and so are as above.

Where the income of the estate in a tax year does not exceed £500, the PRs pay no income tax. If the income exceeds £500, income tax is payable on the whole amount. Beneficiaries do not pay tax on income distributed to them that is within the £500 limit.

In calculating any income tax liability on the income of the administration period, the PRs may be able to claim relief for interest paid on a bank loan to pay inheritance tax. If the PRs use this loan to pay the inheritance tax on the deceased's personal property in the UK which devolves on them in order to obtain the grant, income tax relief is generally available to them.

Example

PRs' only income is gross interest of £4,000 for a tax year in the administration period (none of the income is from dividends). The PRs pay £1,000 interest to the bank on a loan to pay inheritance tax to obtain their grant.

Gross income	£4,000
Less: interest paid	£1,000
Taxable income	£3,000
Income tax payable £3,000 x 20% =	£600
Net income for the beneficiaries	£2,400

Once the PRs' tax position has been settled, the remaining net income will be paid to the beneficiary. The payment forms part of the beneficiary's income and the gross amount should therefore be included in their return of income for the income tax year to which it relates. The beneficiary receives credit for the tax already paid by the PRs. Whether there is any more tax to pay, or, indeed, whether a refund can be claimed, will depend on the beneficiary's own income tax position.

9.9.5.3 Capital gains tax (CGT)

CGT is charged on the gains made on the disposal of a chargeable asset. CGT effectively taxes the increase or gain in the value of an asset during the individual's period of ownership.

CGT is basically assessed on the difference between the purchase and sale price, or market value of the asset if it is given away. The individual is also allowed to deduct certain expenses and fees incidental to the sale or purchase, for example conveyancing fees. The individual is taxed on the total of all the gains made during the year. There is an exemption for the first part of the gains made by an individual each year – £3,000 for the tax year 2025/26. This is called the annual exemption.

On death, there is no disposal for CGT purposes, so that no liability to CGT arises. The PRs acquire all the deceased's assets at their probate value at death. This has the effect of wiping out gains which accrued during the deceased's lifetime so that these gains are not charged to tax. Although there is no disposal, the probate value becomes the PRs' 'base cost' of all the deceased's assets for future CGT purposes.

If the PRs dispose of chargeable assets during the administration of the deceased's estate to raise cash (eg to pay inheritance tax, or other outgoings or legacies), they are liable to CGT on any chargeable gains that they make. The rate at which individuals pay CGT varies according to whether they are basic or higher rate income tax payers. However, for PRs the position is much simpler as they pay at a flat rate. For gains arising in 2025/26 the rate for PRs is 24%.

In addition to deducting their acquisition cost (probate value), the PRs may deduct from the disposal consideration the incidental costs of disposal (eg stockbroker's commission on sale of shares). In addition, they may deduct a proportion of the cost of valuing the deceased's estate for probate purposes.

The PRs may claim the annual exemption for disposals made in the tax year in which the deceased died and the following two tax years only (if the administration lasts this long). The exemption is the same as for an individual (ie £3,000 for 2025/26). Maximum advantage will be taken from this exemption if the PRs plan sales of assets carefully so that gains are realised in stages in each of the three tax years for which it is available.

Example

PRs realise they will need to raise £50,000 to pay administration expenses. They sell some investments for £50,000. The probate value of the investments was £37,000. There are no costs associated with the sale. The PRs have no unused losses.

	£
Disposal value	50,000
Less: acquisition (probate) value	37,000
Gain	13,000
Less: annual exemption	3,000
Chargeable gain	10,000

CGT payable £10,000 x 24% = £2,400

If the PRs sell assets for less than their value at death, an allowable loss for CGT will arise. This loss may be relieved by setting it against gains arising on other sales by the PRs in the same, or any future, tax year in the administration period. Any loss which is unrelieved at the end of the administration period cannot be transferred to the beneficiaries. In view of this limitation, the PRs should plan sales carefully to ensure they can obtain relief for all losses which they realise. If there is a possibility of losses being unused, the PRs should either plan sales of other assets, or consider transferring the assets worth less than their probate value to the beneficiaries (see below).

If, instead of selling assets, the PRs vest them in the beneficiaries (or trustees if a trust arises), no chargeable gain or allowable loss arises. The beneficiary or trustee is deemed to acquire the asset transferred at its probate value. This 'base cost' of the asset will be relevant to the CGT calculation on a future disposal by the beneficiary.

Example

A testator by will leaves his residuary estate to Parvez. Among the assets forming residue are 1,000 shares in XYZ plc. The testator had bought the shares for £1,000 ten years before he died. The probate value of the shares was £5,200. By the time the shares were transferred to Parvez the value had risen to £10,000. Five years later Parvez sells the shares for £19,200.

The sale of the shares is a disposal for CGT purposes. Parvez will be taxed on the chargeable gain. Parvez is deemed to have acquired the shares at the probate value.

	£
Disposal value	19,200
Less: acquisition (probate) value	5,200
Gain	14,000
Less: annual exemption	3,000
Chargeable gain	11,000

Key points on CGT and death:

(1) No CGT is payable on death itself.

(2) If PRs sell assets, they make a disposal. Their acquisition value is the market value at the date of death. They have an annual exemption equal to an individual's in the tax year of death and the two following tax years, so there will often be no tax liability on their disposals.

(3) The rate of tax payable by PRs is 24%.

(4) If PRs transfer assets to beneficiaries, they do not make a disposal. The beneficiary acquires the asset at market value at the date of death.

9.9.5.4 The administration period

For each income tax year (or part) during the administration period, the PRs must calculate their income tax and any CGT liability on assets disposed of for administration purposes. Provided the estate is not classified as a complex estate, they can make an informal payment without having to provide a tax return. If the estate is 'complex', they must make a return to HMRC of the income they receive on the deceased's assets, and any gains they make on disposals of chargeable assets for administration purposes. An estate is considered complex if either: (1) the value of the estate exceeds £2.5 million; or (2) tax due for the whole of the administration period exceeds £10,000; or (3) the value of assets sold in a tax year exceeds £500,000.

Provided the estate is not complex, income tax and CGT are normally paid in one lump sum at the end of the administration period. However, CGT on the disposal of UK residential land must be paid within 60 days of completion.

9.10 Transferring assets to residuary beneficiaries

9.10.1 Interim distributions

Once the outstanding tax, legal costs and other matters have been disposed of, PRs should consider transferring any remaining assets to the residuary beneficiaries. In doing so they must remember that payments may have been made already to the beneficiaries as interim distributions on account of their entitlement. If so, these will be taken into account when determining what and how much more should be transferred to those beneficiaries.

9.10.2 Adult beneficiaries

If the beneficiaries are adults and have a vested entitlement to property in the residuary estate, their entitlement can be transferred to them. If they have a contingent entitlement, the property cannot be transferred to them but will instead be transferred to trustees to hold on their behalf until the contingency is satisfied.

9.10.3 Minor beneficiaries

If any beneficiaries are under 18 years of age, whether the interest enjoyed is vested or contingent, the property will usually be held in trust for them until the age of majority is reached or the contingency is satisfied. If a minor beneficiary has a vested interest the PRs may be able to transfer their entitlement to them (if expressly authorised in the will), or to parents and guardians on behalf of the minor.

9.10.4 Transferring property

The manner in which the property is transferred to residuary beneficiaries, or to trustees on their behalf, will depend on the nature of the property remaining in the estate.

Personal property

The PRs indicate that they no longer require property for administration purposes when they pass title to it by means of an assent. Generally, no particular form of assent is required in the case of personalty so that often the property passes by delivery. The beneficiary's title to the property derives from the will; the assent is merely the manner of giving effect to the gift by the PRs. Company shares are transferred by share (stock) transfer form. The PRs must produce their grant to the company as proof of title to the shares. They, as transferors, transfer the shares 'as PRs of X deceased' to the beneficiary (the transferee), who then applies to be registered as a member of the company in place of the deceased member.

Freehold or leasehold land

PRs vest the legal estate in land in the person entitled (whether beneficially or as trustee) by means of an assent, which will then become a document of title to the legal estate. If PRs are to continue to hold property in their changed capacity as trustees under trusts declared by the will, or arising under the intestacy law, an assent will again be appropriate. The PRs should formally vest the legal estate in themselves as trustees to hold for the beneficiaries.

The assent must be in writing, it must be signed by the PRs, and it must name the person in whose favour it is made. It then operates to vest the legal estate in the named person. A deed is not necessary to pass the legal estate, but PRs may choose to use a deed, for example if they require the beneficiary to give them the benefit of an indemnity covenant.

9.11 Estate accounts

The final task of the PRs is usually to produce estate accounts for the residuary beneficiaries. The purpose of the accounts is to show all the assets of the estate, the payment of the debts, administration expenses and legacies, and the balance remaining for the residuary beneficiaries. The balance will normally be represented by a combination of assets transferred to the beneficiaries and some cash. The residuary beneficiaries sign the accounts to indicate that they approve them. In the absence of fraud or failure to disclose assets, their signatures will also release the PRs from further liability to account to the beneficiaries.

There is no prescribed form for estate accounts. Any presentation adopted should be clear and concise so that the accounts are easily understood by the residuary beneficiaries. If interim distribution payments were made to the residuary beneficiaries during the administration period, these must be taken into account and shown in the estate accounts.

Normally accounts show capital assets, and income produced by those assets during the administration period, in separate capital and income accounts. In small estates this may not be necessary, so that one account showing both capital and income will be sufficient. However, it is always necessary to prepare separate accounts if the will (or the intestacy rules) creates a life or minority interest, since the different interests of the beneficiaries in the capital and income need to be distinguished throughout the period of the trust, and when it ends.

Summary

- PRs are under a statutory duty to administer the estate correctly.
- PRs are personally liable for any errors and so must be careful to protect themselves against beneficiaries and creditors who are unknown or missing and claimants under the Inheritance (Provision for Family and Dependants) Act 1975.
- PRs have various statutory powers in dealing with the estate. These powers may be extended by the will.
- PRs must collect in the deceased's assets.
- PRs must pay the funeral and testamentary expenses and debts as directed by the will, or as prescribed by statute.
- After the payment of debts and expenses, the PRs must pay the legacies.
- PRs are liable to income tax on income of the administration period at basic and dividend ordinary rate.
- PRs are liable to capital gains tax on the sale of an asset.
- If the PRs transfer an asset to a beneficiary, there is no disposal for capital gains tax purposes; the beneficiary acquires the asset at the probate value.
- At the end of the administration, PRs prepare estate accounts for approval by the residuary beneficiaries.

Sample questions

Question 1

A man died six months ago. He owned assets in his sole name worth £1,500,000, including a cottage (worth £300,000), which was subject to a £50,000 mortgage. The man had one other debt (£10,000 owed to his credit card provider). In his valid will, the man left his cottage to his niece and the residue of his estate to his nephew. Both gifts are effective. The will was silent on the burden of inheritance tax ('IHT') and all debts, including the mortgage secured on the cottage.

Which of the following best describes the position in relation to the burden of the IHT and all the debts?

A The residue will bear the burden of all the debts, including the mortgage, and the IHT attributable to the cottage.

B The residue will bear the burden of all the debts, including the mortgage, but not the IHT attributable to the cottage.

C The residue will bear the burden of the credit card debt but not the mortgage and not the IHT attributable to the cottage.

D The residue will bear the burden of the IHT on the cottage, and the credit card debt but not the mortgage.

E The residue will bear the burden of the IHT on the cottage but not on any of the debts.

Answer

Option D is correct. The will is silent on the payment of debts and testamentary expenses. The mortgage is a secured debt and so the beneficiary who is given charged property bears the burden of the debt (s 35 Administration of Estates Act 1925). All other debts and testamentary expenses (including the IHT payable on property in the UK which vests in the PRs) are borne by the residue. The residue therefore bears the burden of the credit card debt and the IHT.

Question 2

A man died six months ago. In his valid will, he left a legacy of £5,000 to a school friend and the rest of his estate to his son. Nobody knows the current whereabouts of the school friend or whether he is still alive. The man left nothing to his partner with whom he had been living for three years before his death. They were not married and had not formed a civil partnership. The partner is threatening to make a claim under the Inheritance (Provision for Family and Dependants) Act 1975. The personal representatives ('PRs') obtained the grant of representation three months ago and immediately placed advertisements complying with s 27 Trustee Act 1925 in the *London Gazette* and in a local newspaper. Having received no response, they distributed the whole estate to the deceased's son last week.

Which of the following best describes the PRs' protection from personal liability on claims by creditors, claimants and beneficiaries?

A The PRs are protected against all possible claims.

B The PRs are protected against possible claims by unknown creditors but not against possible claims by the school friend and the partner.

C The PRs are protected against possible claims by the school friend and the partner but not against claims by unknown creditors.

D The PRs are protected against possible claims by unknown creditors and the school friend, but not against possible claims by the partner.

E The PRs are protected against possible claims by unknown creditors and the partner, but not against possible claims by the school friend.

Answer

Option B is correct. The PRs have followed the requirements of s 27 Trustee Act 1925, including waiting more than two months from the placing of the advertisements before distributing the estate. This protects the PRs against claims by unknown creditors/beneficiaries. Section 27 does not protect against claims by creditors/beneficiaries who are known about but cannot be traced, such as the school friend. To secure protection the PRs should have taken additional steps regarding the school friend, such as obtaining a *Benjamin* order. The PRs are not protected against possible claims under the Inheritance (Provision for Family and Dependants) Act 1975 because they distributed within six months from the grant (the time limit for making claims under the Act).

Question 3

A person died with an estate including shares worth £213,000 at the date of death and a painting worth £480,000 at the date of death. During the period from death to the end of the tax year the only relevant events were that the personal representatives ('PRs') sold the shares for £225,000 and transferred the painting to the beneficiary entitled to it at a time when it had risen in value to £510,000. In this period the Capital Gains Tax ('CGT') rate was 24% and the annual exemption was £3,000. Assume that there were no disposal costs associated with these events.

What is the amount of CGT that the PRs must pay on the estate for the tax year in which the person died?

A £2,160.

B £9,360.

C £10,080.

D £2,880.

E £6,480.

Answer

Option A is correct because the sale of the shares makes a chargeable gain of £12,000. After deducting the annual exemption of £3,000 the £9,000 gain is taxed at 24%. £9,000 x 24% = £2,160. The transfer of the painting to the beneficiary is not a disposal for CGT purposes and so no CGT is payable. The beneficiary acquires the painting at its probate value.

Option B is wrong as it includes the increase in value for the transfer.

Option C is wrong as it includes the increase in value for the transfer and also does not deduct the annual exemption.

Option D is wrong as while it correctly only includes the gain on the sale it does not deduct the annual exemption.

Option E is wrong as it does not tax the gain on the sale, but taxes the increase in value of the transfer instead.

10 Administration: Rights of Beneficiaries and Liabilities of Personal Representatives

SQE1 syllabus

This chapter will enable you to achieve the SQE1 assessment specification in relation to functioning legal knowledge concerned with wills and the administration of estates.

- The law and practice relating to personal representative and trustees in the administration of estates and consequent trusts. The rights, powers and remedies of beneficiaries of wills and consequent trusts.
- Duties of personal representatives in the administration of estates.
- Liabilities of personal representatives and their protection in the administration of estates.

Note that for SQE1, candidates are not usually required to recall specific case names or cite statutory or regulatory authorities. Cases are provided for illustrative purposes only.

Learning outcomes

By the end of this chapter you will be able to apply relevant core legal principles and rules appropriately and effectively, at the level of a competent newly qualified solicitor in practice, to realistic client-based and ethical problems and situations in the following areas:

- challenges relating to the personal representatives' ('PRs') application for a grant of representation;
- beneficiaries' rights in the administration of an estate;
- actions beneficiaries and creditors can bring against PRs and possible defences; and
- distinctions between PRs and trustees and the types of actions that can be brought against the latter.

10.1 Introduction

The main duties of PRs are to obtain a grant of representation, to collect and manage the assets of the estate, to ascertain and pay the deceased's debts and liabilities, and to distribute the remaining cash and assets in accordance with the will or the intestacy rules.

The administration of most estates is not contentious. However, litigation against PRs is on the increase. Beneficiaries and creditors who are dissatisfied with the administration of the estate may want to take action against the PRs. The other side of the coin, of course, is that PRs often seek legal advice on their liability. Wills and the intestacy rules can give rise to ongoing trusts. Often the same people are appointed to be the PRs and the trustees of the trust. While the offices of PR and trustee are similar, there are differences. Therefore, it can be important to know when the PRs become trustees.

This chapter therefore looks at:

- the rights of beneficiaries;
- the rights of creditors; and
- the transition from PRs to trustees.

10.2 The rights of beneficiaries

10.2.1 Action regarding the grant

(a) Preventing the issue of a grant

Following a person's death, there may be a dispute over the validity of the deceased's will or some other reason why family members wish to prevent the issue of a grant. If they have just cause, they should lodge a caveat at HMCTS. Once a caveat has been entered, no grant can be issued until the caveat is removed or ceases to be effective.

Caveats might be considered, for example, where a beneficiary believes the executor named in the will lacks the mental capacity to act, or where the validity of the will is questioned as in the following examples:

Example

The will appoints Eric as executor, gives a legacy to Ann and the residue to Ben.

Eric wants to act as executor but Ann challenges his capability. Ann should enter a caveat before a grant of representation is issued so that the court can decide who should act as PR.

Example

On Dinar's death a homemade will is found appointing Eisaz as executor and sole beneficiary. Fahima would be entitled to Dinar's estate under the intestacy rules and Fahima believes the will is invalid. She should enter a caveat to prevent any grant of representation issuing until the court has decided the validity or otherwise of the will.

An application for a caveat can be made online or using form PA8A. The person lodging or entering a caveat is called a 'caveator'. A caveat lasts for six months although its duration can be extended. An applicant for a grant may issue a 'warning' to the caveator, which requires the caveator to enter an appearance within 14 days setting out their interest. If the caveator fails to do so, the applicant for the grant can remove the caveat.

(b) Compelling the issue of a grant

Potential beneficiaries will want the administration of the estate to proceed in a timely manner and may become frustrated if the PRs delay their application for the grant. In these circumstances, the beneficiaries might apply to HMCTS to issue a citation. A citation is a method of a forcing a party with a right to the grant to act.

Example

Only executors or persons specified under NCPR 1987, r 20 or r 22 can take a grant of representation. If the person initially entitled to take the grant refuses to do so and also refuses to renounce, the estate would remain unadministered and the beneficiaries would be left waiting indefinitely for their inheritance. In such circumstances, a citation provides a remedy.

There are several types of citation which may be issued at the request of a beneficiary ('the citor').

Citation to take probate

A citation to take probate may be used where an executor has lost his right to renounce probate by intermeddling in the estate (eg by selling the deceased's chattels) but has not applied for a grant of probate and shows no signs of so doing. Once cited, the executor must proceed with an application for a grant of probate. If the executor does not do so (without good reason) the citor can apply to the court for an order allowing the executor to be passed over and a grant of letters of administration with will annexed to issue to the person(s) entitled under NCPR 1987, r 20.

Citation to propound will

A citation to propound a will (authenticate the will by obtaining a grant of probate) is used where a person becomes aware that there may be a will that would diminish their entitlement under an earlier will or under an intestacy. That person can cite the executors named in the later will and any persons interested under that will to propound it. If the citees fail to enter an appearance or to proceed diligently to propound the will, the citor can apply to the court for an order for a grant as if the will were invalid.

Citation to accept or refuse a grant

A citation to accept or refuse a grant is the standard method of clearing off a person with a prior right to any type of grant who has not applied, and shows no intention of applying, for a grant. If the person cited does not take steps to take out the grant, a grant may be issued to the citor.

Example

Adam's will appoints Bert his executor and Clare the residuary beneficiary. Bert takes no steps towards administering the estate or proving the will. Clare may cite Bert to act and, if Bert does nothing, Clare may apply by virtue of NCPR 1987, r 20 for a grant of letters of administration with will annexed.

(c) Passing over

To compel an unwilling person to take a grant is likely to produce more problems than it solves. If a person is unwilling to act as executor in the administration of an estate, it is often preferable to apply to the Court under s 116 Senior Courts Act 1981 for an order passing over that person in favour of someone else. For example, in *Re Biggs* [1966] 1 All ER 358, an executor had intermeddled but then refused to have anything to do with the estate. The applicants obtained an order that he be passed over.

10.2.2 The right of beneficiaries to compel due administration

Unlike beneficiaries of trusts, beneficiaries of an unadministered estate do not have an equitable interest in the deceased's property until the PRs transfer or assent the property to them. Until that point, the legal and equitable interests are vested in the PRs.

Although, the beneficiaries of an unadministered estate do not have equitable interests, they do have the right to compel due administration of the estate. In the exercise of that right, the beneficiaries might want to see accounts or they may require information about the administration.

(a) Accounts and information

Throughout the administration, the PRs must keep accurate records of receipts and payments. Beneficiaries (or anyone else interested in the estate) can ask to inspect accounts. If the PRs refuse the request for accounts, or if they are unclear or inaccurate, anyone interested can apply to the court for an order compelling the PRs to provide an inventory and accounts (s 25 Administration of Estates Act 1925).

At the end of the administration, immediately prior to the final distribution of the estate, the PRs (or their legal adviser) will prepare estate accounts showing all the assets, income and payments made (see **9.11**). The estate accounts are sent to the residuary beneficiaries, who will be asked to sign a receipt approving the accounts and discharging the PRs from further liability.

The position for disclosure of documents or information (other than accounts) is similar to that for trusts (see the **Trusts** manual at **9.10**). There is no automatic entitlement to disclosure of the reasons for the PRs' decisions and deliberations on a discretionary matter. However, if PRs refuse disclosure, the beneficiaries can apply to the court. Documents which a PR is not required to disclose under trust law principles may still be subject to disclosure in a subject access request under the Data Protection Act 1998, or as part of the disclosure requirements in court proceedings.

(b) Administration proceedings

Administration proceedings can be brought by anyone interested in the estate (including beneficiaries, creditors and PRs). The proceedings fall into two categories, namely:

- Applications limited to a particular issue. This type of application may be non-contentious; for example, PRs may seek guidance from the court on the performance of a duty or the meaning of words used in a will.
- Applications for a general administration order. These applications are less common.

  Under a general administration order, the court supervises the PRs: they cannot exercise their powers without the court's permission. Such an order is regarded as a last resort (not least because of the cost involved). Another option would be for the court to appoint a judicial trustee to act as PR with another person or alone.

(c) Executor's year

A common complaint from beneficiaries is that there has been undue delay in paying them their entitlement. Section 44 of the Administration of Estates Act 1925 provides that 'a personal representative is not bound to distribute the estate of the deceased before the expiration of one year from the death'. Thus, personal representatives have at least one year – the so-called 'executor's year' – from the date of the deceased's death before they can be called on to distribute the estate. The term 'executor's year is actually a misnomer since it applies to administrators as well. The amount of time taken to administer an estate will inevitably vary according to the extent and complexity of the assets. It should be possible for PRs to complete the administration of a straightforward estate within a year.

10.2.3 Actions against the PRs for breach of duty

Rather than bring administration proceedings, beneficiaries may be able to sue PRs directly for breach of duty.

(a) Breach of fiduciary duty

Personal representatives are fiduciaries and are obliged to avoid placing themselves in a situation where there is a conflict between their duties and personal interest. They must account to the estate for any unauthorised profit (whether or not the estate has suffered loss). Where a PR purchases property from the estate, the transaction is voidable by the beneficiaries within a reasonable time. Profits may be authorised by a provision in the deceased's will, a court order or the consent of all the beneficiaries who must be aged 18 or more.

Example

PRs receive commission from a stockbroker as a result of instructing the stockbroker to sell some shares forming part of the estate.

Unless the deceased's will authorises the PRs to retain any commission or they obtain the consent of the court, or all the beneficiaries (who must be adults), the commission would be an unauthorised profit. The PRs would have to pay the commission to the estate.

There are further examples of breaches of fiduciary duty in the **Trusts** manual, **Chapter 11**.

(b) Devastavit

(i) The claim

Beneficiaries may bring a devastavit claim where a PR has caused loss to the estate by a breach of duty. 'Devastavit' means a wasting of assets. If the PRs are found to be liable they will have to pay the beneficiaries out of their own resources.

Claims may be based on:

- misuse of assets (for example, a PR takes assets for their own use);
- maladministration (for example, distributing the estate other than in accordance with the will or the intestacy rules, failing to collect and get in the deceased's real and personal estate, breaching any of their duties or acting outside the powers covered in **5.9**); or
- negligence (a PR carries out their duties without taking the care which would be reasonable in the circumstances).

Examples

*A widower dies intestate survived by four children from his marriage. His PRs divide his estate equally between the four children, not knowing that the intestate had a fifth child outside his marriage. The fifth child could sue the PRs for breach of their duty to distribute the estate correctly according to the intestacy rules (unless the PRs had advertised under s 27 Trustee Act 1925 – **9.4.1** and **(ii)** below). The PRs would be personally liable to pay the fifth child their entitlement.*

PRs fail to monitor volatile investments forming part of the deceased's estate. As a result, there has been a delay in selling them and their value has declined significantly. This is a case of maladministration and negligence. Had the PRs sold the investments earlier, they would have obtained a better price. The PRs would be personally liable for the loss.

The deceased owed rent of £20,000. The lease provides that late payments of rent bear interest. The PRs delay paying the rent despite having sufficient assets in the estate to do so and thereby accrue unnecessary interest. This is a case of maladministration and negligence. The PRs would be personally liable for the interest.

(ii) Defences

There are a number of defences to a claim for devastavit.

- **Section 61 Trustee Act 1925**

  The court has a discretion to totally or partially relieve a PR of personal liability if they acted honestly and reasonably and ought fairly to be excused for the *devastavit* and for omitting to obtain the directions of the court in the matter.

Re Gale [1941] Ch 209

The testator's will contained a direction that trustees should allow Dorothy to occupy a house and that they should pay her an annual sum 'during her widowhood'. The trustees carried out his wishes for a few years, but then discovered that Dorothy was not a widow and had never married. She had however called herself 'Mrs' and fostered the belief that she was married. The court declared that she should not have received the benefits of the annual sum and use of the house but it relieved the trustees from liability under s 61 because they had acted honestly and reasonably.

- **Exclusion clause in the will**

  The PRs may escape liability because the deceased's will contains a clause modifying their duties or excluding liability.

- **Acquiescence of beneficiaries**

  An adult beneficiary who, with full knowledge of the facts, consented to a PR's breach of duty cannot succeed in a claim against the PR.

- **Protection against unknown or missing claimants**

  Where the PRs have distributed the estate not knowing of the existence of a beneficiary, the PRs are personally liable if the omitted beneficiary later brings a claim. However, the PRs will be protected from liability if they placed advertisements and followed the procedures in s 27 Trustee Act 1925 (**see 9.4.1**). The omitted beneficiary would then be able to claim their entitlement from the beneficiaries who wrongly received the estate.

  Section 27 does not protect PRs against personal liability to beneficiaries who are known to have existed but cannot be found. The PRs should have obtained a *Benjamin* order, or insurance or an indemnity from beneficiaries (but an indemnity will not help if the beneficiaries do not have the money) (see **9.4.2**).

  Furthermore, s 27 does not protect PRs against personal liability to successful family provision claimants. To avoid personal liability, the PRs should wait at least six months from the date of the grant before distributing the estate (see **9.4.3**).

- **Limitation**

  The time limit for an unpaid or underpaid beneficiary to bring a claim to recover a share or interest in an estate is 12 years running from the date on which the right to receive the estate accrued. There is no time limit laid down in the Limitation Act 1980 to bring actions for fraudulent breaches of duty or where the PR has taken property from the estate for their own use.

Example

Seven years ago, Jack died intestate. He was survived by two half-brothers, Derek and Frank. Derek, took out a grant of letters of administration and divided Jack's estate between himself and Frank. Derek did not know that Jack had a full brother (Eric) who is entitled to the whole estate on intestacy in priority to Derek and Frank. Derek did not place advertisements under s 27 Trustee Act 1925.

Is Eric out of time to claim his entitlement?

The limitation period for Eric to claim his entitlement from Frank is 12 years.

There is no period of limitation for Eric to claim his entitlement from Derek because he is a PR who has wrongly taken property from the estate for his own use.

10.2.4 Following and tracing the assets

If a PR distributes assets to someone who is not entitled, the beneficiary (or creditor) may be able to follow the assets into the hands of the recipient. There are two potential remedies:

- First, the beneficiary may bring a proprietary claim to the assets (or their traceable proceeds) from the recipient unless they are a bona fide purchaser of the assets for value without notice. (See the **Trusts** manual, **Chapter 13**.)

Example

PRs misinterpret the provisions of a will. They wrongly give the deceased's shares in Proman Ltd to Fred instead of the true beneficiary, Harry. Fred has sold the shares and bought an apartment with the proceeds.

Harry could bring a personal action against the PRs if they have been negligent. Alternatively, he could claim Fred's apartment in a proprietary claim using equitable tracing principles.

- Secondly, the beneficiary can bring a personal claim for compensation against the *recipient* of assets wrongly paid by PRs, provided that all remedies against the PRs have been exhausted.

In Ministry of Health v Simpson [1951] AC 251, Caleb Diplock left his residuary estate to such 'charitable or benevolent' objects as his executors might select. The executors distributed over £200,000 among 139 charities. It transpired that the original gift in the will was void for uncertainty and the money should have passed on intestacy to Caleb's next of kin. The next of kin recovered £15,000 from the PRs (thereby exhausting their remedies against them) and sought the balance from the charities.

*The proprietary claim against some of the charities failed because they had spent the money on improving their buildings and it was held that it would be inequitable to enforce a proprietary claim against them (see the **Trusts** manual at **14.5.2**). However, the personal claim for a refund from the charities succeeded.*

The time limit for both claims is 12 years.

10.2.5 Removal of PRs

PRs cannot be forced to accept office; they can renounce their right to the grant (**8.7.4**; **8.8.5**; **8.9.4**). Once they have extracted the grant, the office is for life unless the court removes them. The court has a discretion to remove PRs under s 50 Administration of Justice Act 1985. This provision is used to remove or substitute a PR (including agreed retirements). Applications can be made by the PR or a beneficiary. The court has a discretion to replace existing PRs with others or simply terminate an appointment without replacement. However, the court must ensure that there is at least one PR remaining. The main factor guiding the exercise of the court's discretion is the welfare of the beneficiaries.

10.3 The rights of creditors

PRs take on all the deceased's debts and liabilities. Causes of action against the deceased continue against the deceased's PRs. Also, PRs must perform the deceased's contracts. However, they are liable only to the extent of the deceased's assets. The limitation period is generally six years.

However, the PRs may be *personally* liable to creditors for devastavit - for loss of assets caused by a breach of their duties. Personal liability means that the PRs would have to pay the creditor out of their own resources. Examples include: executors paying a legacy before advertising for creditors so that there was insufficient left to pay all the creditors; failure to collect and preserve the deceased's estate; spending an excessive amount on the deceased's funeral; paying the debts of an insolvent estate in the wrong order.

The procedure set out in s 27 Trustee Act 1925 should be followed to provide a defence against creditors of whose existence the PR was unaware at the time of distribution to the beneficiaries.

10.4 The transition from PRs to trustees

Where a testator creates a trust in their will, it is common to appoint the same people to act as PRs and trustees. There are many similarities between the offices; both are fiduciaries and the duties and powers contained in the Trustee Act 2000 apply to both. However, there are some stark differences; for example, trustees can retire whereas PRs cannot do so without obtaining a court order and the limitation periods are different.

The rights of beneficiaries under trusts together with the powers and duties of trustees is dealt with in the **Trusts** manual. Where the same people are appointed in both capacities a transition occurs. In relation to real estate, PRs mark the transition by executing an assent to themselves as trustees. As far as personalty is concerned, the PRs become trustees when they have finished the administration of the estate by paying the debts and distributing the assets.

Summary

- Anyone interested can lodge a caveat at HMCTS to prevent the issue of a grant. Interested parties can lodge a citation to compel PRs to take a grant or be passed over.
- Beneficiaries of an unadministered estate do not have equitable interests in the assets but they do have a right to compel due administration.
- PRs are fiduciaries.
- When PRs administer an estate they are under a statutory duty to administer it correctly.
- PRs are personally liable to beneficiaries and creditors for any errors and so they must be careful to protect themselves.
- Beneficiaries and creditors can follow assets to which they are entitled into the hands of the wrongful recipient. They also have a personal action against wrongly paid recipients.

- Unlike trustees, PRs cannot retire and cannot be removed without a court order.
- Where PRs are also trustees of a trust created by the will or intestacy rules, they become trustees following an assent or at the end of the administration. **Trusts** deals with the powers and duties of trustees and the rights of beneficiaries under trusts.

Sample questions

Question 1

A sole executor obtained a grant of probate six months ago but has taken no further steps in the administration of the estate because the executor has had an argument with the main beneficiary ('the beneficiary').

What action, if any, can the beneficiary take to remove the executor?

A The beneficiary should issue a citation.

B The beneficiary should apply to the court to replace the executor.

C The beneficiary can replace the executor by serving a notice on them to retire and appoint a substitute.

D The only possible recourse is to seek a general administration order.

E Once a PR has obtained the grant, the executor cannot be removed.

Answer

Option B is correct. Under s 50 Administration of Justice Act 1985, the court has a discretion to replace a PR. It will exercise its discretion if it is necessary for the welfare of the beneficiaries.

Option A is wrong. A citation is not appropriate in this case because the executor has already obtained a grant.

Option C is wrong. Unlike trustees, it is not possible for beneficiaries to secure the removal of PRs by serving notice on them.

Option D is wrong. A general administration order does not remove the PR. The PR still carries out the administration but must seek the court's consent for every act. Furthermore, it would not be the beneficiary's ONLY recourse.

Option E is wrong. A PR can be removed/replaced by a court order.

Question 2

Personal representatives ('PRs') wrongly paid £30,000 to the deceased's son when this sum should have been paid to the deceased's civil partner. The son has spent the £30,000 paying off his overdraft.

Which of the following best describes the action the civil partner could take to recover the £30,000?

A The civil partner could sue the PRs for breach of trust or pursue a personal action against the son.

B The civil partner could sue the PRs for breach of fiduciary duty or pursue a personal action against the son.

C The civil partner could sue the PRs in a devastavit action and pursue a personal action against the son to recover any balance not obtained from the PRs.

D The civil partner could sue the PRs in a devastavit action and pursue a proprietary claim against the son.

E The civil partner could sue the PRs and the son in a devastavit action.

Answer

Option C is correct. The PRs have been guilty of maladministration which can be the subject of a devastavit claim. In *Ministry of Health v Simpson* [1951] it was held that the correct beneficiary can recover compensation from the recipient who was wrongly paid. The compensation will be equal to the amount which the beneficiary cannot recover from the PRs.

Option A is wrong. The correct description of the action against PRs is devastavit.

Option B is wrong. The correct description of the action against PRs is devastavit. It was not a breach of fiduciary duty because the PRs did not make an unauthorised profit for themselves.

Option D is wrong because a proprietary action will not succeed where the defendant has dissipated the money, as is the case here.

Option E is wrong. Devastavit is a wasting of assets by the PRs, not by third parties.

Question 3

Personal representatives ('PRs') advertised for claimants and waited two months before distributing the estate to the beneficiaries. They had forgotten about a £3,000 debt which the deceased owed to a builder.

Can the builder recover the £3,000?

A No, because all the estate has been distributed.

B No, because the PRs are protected due to the adverts.

C No, because PRs are not liable to pay the deceased's debts.

D Yes, because although the PRs are protected, the builder can recover the sum from the beneficiaries.

E Yes, because the PRs are personally liable for devastavit.

Answer

Option E is correct. By neglecting to pay the debt, the PRs are guilty of maladministration (or a breach of duty to pay all the debts) and the creditor can bring a claim for devastavit.

Option A is wrong. In this situation, the PRs are personally liable for breach of duty and will have to pay the creditor out of their own resources.

Option B is wrong. Under s 27 Trustee Act 1925, the fact that the PRs advertised and waited two months before distributing the estate only protects them against claims of which they were unaware. In this case, they were aware of the builder's claim but overlooked it.

Option C is wrong because PRs are liable to pay the deceased's debts from the assets in the estate.

Option D is wrong. The PRs are not protected from liability (as explained above) and the builder should exhaust their claim against the PRs before seeking a personal remedy against the beneficiaries (*Ministry of Health v Simpson*).

Index

J

K

L

T

U

V